LINDA KUSH

THE RICE PADDY NAVY

U.S. SAILORS UNDERCOVER IN CHINA

ESPIONAGE AND SABOTAGE
BEHIND JAPANESE LINES DURING WORLD WAR II

To Spencer Morrow

First published in Great Britain in 2012 by Osprey Publishing,
Midland House, West Way, Botley, Oxford OX2 0PH, United Kingdom.
Osprey Publishing Inc., 44-02 23rd Street, Suite 219, Long Island City, New York, NY 11101, USA.
Email: info@ospreypublishing.com
OSPREY PUBLISHING IS PART OF THE OSPREY GROUP

A CIP catalogue record for this book is available from the British Library.

ISBN: 978 1 84908 811 4
PDF e-book ISBN: 978 1 84908 752 0
E-pub ISBN: 978 1 78200 312 0

Page layout by Ken Vail Graphic Design (kvgd.com)
Index by Zoe Ross
Typeset in Conduit ITC and Minion pro
Originated by PDQ Media, Bungay, UK
Printed in HongKong throught Worldprint Ltd

12 13 14 15 16   10 9 8 7 6 5 4 3 2 1

Osprey Publishing is supporting the Woodland Trust, the UK's leading woodland conservation charity,
by funding the dedication of trees. To celebrate the Queen's Diamond Jubilee we are proud to support
the Woodland Trust's Jubilee Woods Project.

JUBILEEWOODS.ORG.UK

www.ospreypublishing.com

Front cover image: detail from *Boats on the river near the city of Chongqing* © Vinton, S.R./National
Geographic Society/Corbis

Back cover image © Neil and Randy Smith

Contents

Setting the Stage for the Rice Paddy Navy

CHAPTER 1

The U.S. Navy Mission in China

"WHAT THE HELL IS THE NAVY DOING HERE?"

Those were the first words U.S. Navy Radioman First Class Richard Rutan heard in June 1944 as he stepped down from a C-47 airplane surrounded by a crowd of curious U.S. Army Air Force men on a desolate airstrip in central China. His blue jacket with the word "NAVY" across the back in three-inch letters clearly identified him as a sailor six hundred miles from the sea.

The way the man had framed the question was oddly appropriate. Rutan was a member of the Sino–American Cooperative Organization, or SACO, a secret joint venture between Nationalist China and the U.S. Navy formed to gather intelligence for the navy while fighting the Japanese, who had occupied parts of China since 1937. SACO's insignia was a string of punctuation marks that looked like cuss words in a comic strip. Translation: "What the hell?"

The men who met the plane had good reason to be excited. It was the first ever to land on the new airstrip they had just built. But it must have been something of a letdown to find just one passenger, and a navy boy at that, with a load of equipment the likes of which they'd never seen before.

Rutan was nervous. Two days earlier he had been monitoring Japanese radio signals with a dozen SACO radio operators in Guilin in southern China when his superior officer, Lieutenant Junior Grade Harned Hoose, tapped him for this mission. The flight had felt surreal as he sat alone in a big transport plane with only the pilot, who looked barely out of his teens and cracked jokes about having to parachute in. When they landed, Rutan knew he was in a place called Liulang, but he might as well have been on the moon. He had no idea where this place was, and at age twenty-three, he had never before felt so utterly alone. He was the only navy man for hundreds of miles, with no parent, supervisor, or mess buddy to guide him.

His verbal orders were to find the major in charge of the base, identify himself, and request a private workspace. He then had to assemble a concealed radio station with no assistance. And he had to do everything in total secrecy. Not even the major was to know anything about his mission.

The task seemed impossible. First of all, no army major was going to give him private quarters without some explanation, and second, he had never assembled a radio station before. All he had to fall back on were some radio theory courses he had taken at the University of Wisconsin two years earlier.

The first part turned out to be easy. The major unceremoniously handed him keys to a brand-new building. Rutan had it all to himself.

The second part proved more intimidating. In order to maintain secrecy, he couldn't ask for help. But as he worked to assemble the radio station, the pieces began to fit in place. After two days of tinkering, the receiver crackled for the first time, and Rutan intercepted his first bit of Japanese code to relay to SACO headquarters.

His experience was not unusual for the outfit nicknamed the "Rice Paddy Navy." Working in small groups or even solo all over China, twenty-five hundred members of the U.S. Navy gathered weather data, watched the coast for Japanese shipping, spied on Japanese communication, sabotaged transportation, and trained thousands of Chinese soldiers. All in secrecy.

SACO WAS BORN OUT OF COFFEE CONVERSATION among navy officers in Washington, D.C., that began in the fall of 1939, just after Germany invaded Poland and the threat of war hung heavy over Washington. Against this ominous backdrop, with news from the Far East taking a back seat to Europe, several officers who had served in China over the previous two decades would get together during coffee breaks. They swapped memories and discussed the turbulent situation in China through the unique perspective of those who had been there. It was a time to keep up with day-to-day news about the Sino–Japanese war and how China was holding up under Japanese occupation.

The host was Commander Milton "Mary" Miles, who had served on Yangtze River patrol boats for five years right after graduation from the U.S. Naval Academy in Annapolis in 1922 and returned to China for a second three-year tour with the Asiatic Fleet in 1934. His feminine nickname was a remnant of his plebe year at the U.S. Naval Academy, a takeoff on the silent screen actress Mary Miles Minter.

As secretary of the navy's Interior Control Board, Miles wrote specifications for ships and weapons. The strong coffee he brewed in his office became a magnet for old and new friends with connections to the Far East.

Another member of the circle also had an unusual nickname. Captain Willis A. "Ching" Lee's moniker acknowledged his Chinese-sounding surname and his fondness for China.[1] He had served on the gunboat *Helena* in the Asiatic Station before World War I and later commanded the destroyer the *William B. Preston* in the early 1920s, cruising coastal China and the Yangtze River.

In his youth, Lee had been a world-class competitive marksman, winning seven medals—five gold, a silver, and a bronze—in the 1920 Olympics. His navy career alternated between sea duty and weapons-related administrative posts. During the time this group of officers was meeting, he also was a member of the Interior Control Board. He served with the Division of Fleet Training, first as assistant director, and then as director beginning in January 1941. He was promoted to rear admiral during the course of the get-togethers.

A Chinese friend of Miles dropped in often. Major Xiao Bo, China's military attaché in Washington, had first met Miles's wife Billy when she gave a talk in Washington about a trip the family had taken over the Burma Road. A mutual acquaintance later introduced Xiao to Miles at the ICB while Xiao was in the building on business. Miles, Xiao, and their wives became good friends, exchanging frequent dinner invitations. While their wives dozed in the living room, Miles and Xiao would talk late into the night at the dining room table about ways the United States could help China fight the Japanese occupation.

4

Despite their frequent gatherings and long conversations, however, Miles was unaware that Xiao was also an agent for General Dai Li, the head of Nationalist China's Military Bureau of Investigation Services.

Like Miles's dinner conversations, his kaffeeklatsches touched on a wide range of topics about America's military potential in the Far East. With Lee's professional and personal interest in weaponry, he observed that the U.S. military knew little about Japan's armaments and technical capabilities. In contrast, the United States had detailed information about the German and Italian war machines. He thought something should be done to fill that serious intelligence gap.

Miles was working on specifications for mines at the ICB and had the idea that a new one weighing in at only thirty-five pounds could be very effective in China to disrupt Japanese river traffic.

By the summer of 1941, "Ching" Lee was promoted to rear admiral. He advised the ICB that it would be a good idea to send a navy representative to China to work with Chinese intelligence to find out what kind of firepower the Japanese had and how much they knew about American capabilities.

The navy did not act on his advice right away, but the need for such an agent became urgent on December 7, 1941.

Japan's bombing of Pearl Harbor suddenly thrust China into the forefront of naval intelligence. Japan was no longer just a threatening, growling beast; it was a mortal enemy. The day President Franklin D. Roosevelt announced that the United States was in a state of war with Japan, that country had already been at war with China for four years and occupied major regions of its homeland.

It was clear, then, that to wage an effective war against Japan, the United States would need to understand what was going on inside China.

In the immediate aftermath of the attack, top navy brass gathered to plot out what they should do first. They needed someone on the ground in China immediately, and Lee recommended Miles. Even if Miles may have lacked certain intelligence experience, he genuinely respected the Chinese people, spoke Chinese coastal dialects, and understood the culture in a way that few Americans did. He also was a proven self-starter and project manager.

At 2:00 a.m. on December 8, 1941, the telephone jolted Mary and Billy Miles from their sleep. It was Rear Admiral Lee. He told Miles to get ready to go to China.

A few days later, Miles was summoned to the office of Admiral Ernest King, fleet admiral of the U.S. Navy and a member of the Joint Chiefs of Staff. There, Miles received verbal orders for his mission to China. He recalled King's words as something like this:

"Admiral Lee recommends you as the only officer around here with sufficient knowledge of China for this assignment. We're going to have some tough sledding out there. You are to go to China and make the coast safe for Allied landings in three or four years. Meanwhile, do whatever you can to hamper the Japs."[2]

Though the charge to harass the enemy while in China almost sounded like an afterthought, it was to prove portentous months later when Miles received an offer from a Chinese general that he could not refuse.

IN JANUARY 1942, Miles found himself in a Washington hotel room with Admiral King, Rear Admiral Lee, and the recently promoted Chinese Colonel Xiao, all in plain clothes. The venue and attire were chosen for secrecy. They couldn't risk a word of office gossip about the plan they were hatching.

Miles was to go to China as soon as possible and work with Xiao's contacts to accomplish several things for the navy.

First, there was the matter of the weather. The Japanese were already using weather patterns to their advantage. They had concealed their planes behind a bank of clouds just before the Pearl Harbor attack. With weather stations from northern Manchuria to Indonesia, they had the tools to track Pacific storms.

In contrast, the United States had no weather monitoring west of Hawaii, which meant it had absolutely no means of forecasting weather further out in the Pacific. The same prevailing winds that blow Mongolian dust storms from west to east across China and Korea sweep weather patterns from Asia into the Pacific. Thus, today's storms in China mean heavy seas in the Pacific tomorrow.

The navy could not afford to let Japan's superior position go unanswered. It needed to gather weather data on the ground from points throughout China to even the score.

China also held a potential gold mine of intelligence. With Japan's freighters and naval vessels moving freely along China's coast, a few strategically placed coast watchers could help build a picture of the enemy's material and military resources and produce rich targets for U.S. bomb attacks. Japan's occupation of China also meant there were radio communications and troop movements to be monitored.

Finally, looking ahead several years, the United States would almost certainly have to invade China to dislodge the Japanese. The military would need maps, a clear picture of civilian conditions and loyalties, and as much cooperation from the Chinese military as it could muster.

This was a tall order for one man, regardless of how well he knew China. But once Miles had a clear plan, the navy would send whatever personnel and materials he would require. And he would have inside help. He was to report to Chinese General Dai Li, the head of China's Military Bureau of Investigation and Statistics and Generalissimo Chiang Kai-shek's closest confidante. As the head of the nationalist government, Chiang Kai-shek was the nearest thing China had to a central leader at that time. He had reached out to help the United States in this way to defeat their common enemy.

As Dai's personal representative, Xiao assured the naval officers that his country was eager to work with the United States and that Dai would be very cooperative. He held enormous power in China to assist and protect the U.S. mission.

"Give us a try for a few months and see what we can do," said Xiao.

OVER THE NEXT FEW MONTHS, all activity in Washington increased in intensity, going "from rush to frantic," in Miles's words.[3] Miles worked as quickly as he could to make his preparations for his assignment.

The navy appointed Captain Jeffrey Metzel to coordinate supplies and communication for the mission from Washington. Having a partner in the operation at home relieved many of Miles's worries about logistics.

Though Miles's verbal orders had come from the highest authority of the navy, he would still need written orders in hand to carry them out. With few seats on overseas flights available, he would have to be able to prove that he was entitled to one. He and an assistant banged out a sample draft of orders and handed it over to the Bureau of Navigation, whose staff came up with an official document. The bureau cast him as a military attaché for the U.S. ambassador to China, Clarence Gauss. Miles would report to Gauss in Chongqing and then carry out his secret verbal orders from King on his own.

Miles's next priority was to find out about the man he would be working with.

At the State Department, the dossier he read about General Dai Li made his hair stand on end. This couldn't possibly be the cooperative friend Xiao had promised. The man was known as "the Himmler of China." He categorically hated all foreigners. As head of China's Military Bureau of Investigation and Statistics, Dai had as many as three hundred thousand agents throughout East Asia. He ruthlessly protected Chiang Kai-shek's political, military, and governing interests, executing and imprisoning Chiang's enemies. He headed a Gestapo-like organization known as the Blue Shirts. And, according to documents in the file, he had even ordered the execution of his own mother—twice.

That fantastic claim gave Miles pause, and suddenly, he doubted everything in the file. For better or for worse, Dai was to be his partner in this mission, by orders of Admiral King. So Miles decided to wait for a meeting with Dai face to face before passing judgment.

But first he had to get to China, and that posed challenges of its own. The outbreak of war had put an end to all commercial flights to the Far East. Japan occupied most of China's coast, rendering military flights from the Pacific side impossible. And traveling east was not much better. It was a much longer trek, and with fighting between the British and the Germans in North Africa, military flights were few and crowded. But it was the only option.

The navy's transportation department plotted a course for Miles that would take him on a Sikorsky Pan Am Clipper, the airline's storied flying boat, from New York to Natal, Brazil, and then on to Lagos in western Nigeria. There, he would take an Army transport plane to Cairo. From Cairo to Chongqing, though, the navy could only wish him luck.

The staff at the transportation department warned Miles that he could only carry sixty-two pounds of luggage, and that posed a bit of a problem because Miles had planned a mission of his own. He had a little surprise for Japanese ships plying the rivers and coastal waters of China.

That little surprise was the magnetic influence mine he had discovered through his work at the ICB. Developed by the British, its simplicity made it the ideal weapon in a country where four years of war had reduced arms manufacturing from difficult to primitive. The mine was lightweight and could be made easily with simple materials: wire, soft iron, and TNT, which Xiao had assured him

China could provide. Miles had pulled strings to obtain a sample, which he was determined to carry with him—minus the explosive, of course.

He packed the mine into a long handbag and nestled what uniforms he could fit around it. With this single piece of luggage, Miles, along with about fifty army personnel and a journalist, boarded the flying boat at LaGuardia Marine Terminal in New York on April 5, 1942.

Reaching Brazil took eight days. The plane landed at sea to refuel and could only fly during daylight hours because the same crew was at the helm for the entire trip. Miles flew on to Lagos and then Cairo during a journey riddled with misadventures such as midair engine failure and inexplicable flight cancellations. But in Cairo, he at last caught a lucky break. He met an American traveling with the Royal Canadian Air Force who offered to fly him to Karachi, then on the west coast of India.

In India, Miles found the country in an uproar for fear that the Japanese, who had just taken Burma, would soon be crossing Indian borders.

With travel between India and China reduced to a trickle, Miles decided to make a brief tour of major Indian cities to determine where he might set up a supply depot for his mission. After visits to Mumbai, Colombo in Sri Lanka, and New Delhi, he proceeded to Kolkata, where he hoped to find a flight to Chongqing.

He was stranded there for several days, during which he ran into Ambassador Gauss and his naval attaché, Marine Corps Colonel James McHugh, one of Miles's classmates from Annapolis, in the Great Eastern Hotel. They were returning to Chongqing after a visit to New Delhi on State Department business. The three chatted a few times in the corridors of the hotel, and McHugh was unfailingly gracious. But Gauss was another story. He gruffly demanded to know what Miles intended to do in China, but Miles demurred, offering to discuss it later in Chongqing.

During his journey, Miles had found messages from his superiors waiting for him at U.S. Navy offices asking, "Where is Miles?" They weren't the only ones keeping tabs on him. General Dai Li in China was following his movements through his agents in India, and what he learned made him nervous.

Miles had unwittingly hit several of General Dai's hot buttons during his unscheduled India stopover.

As a consummate master spy ever on the lookout for intrigues, Dai feared that Miles had dawdled in India to confer with British officials there about his mission in China. Chiang Kai-shek's government had recently quarreled with the British, reinforcing Dai's lifelong prejudices against them.

DAI'S RESENTMENT AND MISTRUST toward Great Britain had its roots in the superior, colonial attitude he encountered in some British citizens working in China and Hong Kong, and incidents that took place during the late 1930s did nothing to soften his attitude.

After the Sino–Japanese war began in 1937, Chiang Kai-shek was desperate for foreign support, and with Britain's colonies so close to the hostilities, he had hoped that country would step up. But as Japan advanced deeper and deeper into Chinese territory, the British continued to avoid becoming enmeshed in the conflict and risk going to war with Japan. When the United Kingdom signed an agreement with Japan in July 1939 known as the Craigie–Arita Formula, Chiang and Dai were filled with rage.

The formula acknowledged that the Japanese occupied parts of China and therefore had to maintain law and order in those areas, even if by force. The British agreed not to interfere with Japan's security measures, but at the same time, the formula did not recognize legality of the occupation itself.

The document was far from ideal, but it was the best British Ambassador to Japan Sir Robert Craigie could do short of going to war with Japan following a chain of events known as the Tianjin Incident. The port city of Tianjin was an established British concession, and the Japanese occupied surrounding territory after July 1937. In April 1939, a Japanese bank executive was assassinated in Tianjin. The British police captured four Chinese conspirators in the killing and turned them over to Japanese authorities on the agreement that they would not be tortured and would be returned to the British within five days. Japan released them to British custody, but the British later refused to return them upon learning that two had confessed to Japanese interrogators under torture.

The ensuing disagreement escalated to a full-blown diplomatic crisis in the summer of 1939. Japan blockaded Tianjin, and Japanese soldiers publicly strip-searched British citizens going in and out of the city. The Japanese government demanded that Britain turn over all of China's silver reserves in British banks.

Craigie maintained that the Craigie–Arita Formula merely stated the facts on the ground in China and was not a concession. The document was the first step to cooling down the crisis and ending the blockade. But to Chiang, it was an act of betrayal.

The other event in 1939 that entrenched Dai Li's anti-British stance was more personal. He had been arrested by British police in Hong Kong that year and spent a humiliating night in jail, but the charges against him were never explained. Chiang had secured his release and forced an apology, but the damage was done.

Despite the resentment, the relationship between the two countries warmed after Germany, Japan, and Italy formed an alliance, signing the Tripartite Pact in Berlin on September 27, 1940. It placed Great Britain, already at war with Germany and Italy, just one step away from war with Japan.

China and Britain formed a joint venture in which elite British army officers were to train crack Chinese troops in guerrilla tactics and sabotage. But the outfit, the Chinese Commando Group, was riddled with internal political conflict on the British side. To avoid direct engagement with the Japanese, the British recruited Scandinavians, who were to operate under the control of the Chinese army under Dai Li's direction and Britain's payroll. Dai, however, could not stomach the idea, owing to his contempt for the British, and instead appointed a deputy to do the job for him. The Chinese had intended that the command structure would place them in ultimate control, but the Scandinavian operatives were technically mercenaries in the employ of the British.

Great Britain's declaration of war against Japan on December 8, 1941, freed it to act directly. John Keswick, a British business executive whose family owned the Hong Kong firm Jardine Matheson, blew into China and announced that he was taking over the Chinese Commando Group. Keswick was an agent of the Special Operations Executive, the British intelligence agency upon which William Donovan was to model the U.S. Office of Strategic Services. Keswick explained that the SOE had been the behind-the-scenes sponsor of the Commando Group all along and that he was now appointed by his government to lead it. Chiang was shocked, but upon learning that Keswick was friends with Madame Chiang and her brother T. V. Soong, he accepted the businessman's authority, and Dai acquiesced to his superior.

Keswick was the quintessential example of an Englishman Dai did not trust. In Dai's view, he was a disrespectful imperialist working merely for his own interests, and his assistants were of the same ilk. Unfortunately, Keswick confirmed Dai's worst fears, acting behind Chiang's back, setting up radio stations without authorization, holding clandestine meetings with Chiang's communist enemies, and unleashing secret agents throughout China.

The Commando Group was supposed to be mutually run by China and Britain, but Keswick made it clear that he wanted only indirect help from the Chinese army. When the Chinese were included in mission plans, it was always in a secondary capacity, with British troops to sweep in at the end, claiming the victory and the credit. To Chiang, this implied that the British thought Chinese fighters were inferior. But the resounding defeat of the British at the fall of Singapore on February 15, 1942, seemed to prove the opposite. A Chinese army officer who witnessed the catastrophe reported to Dai that the British had been unwilling to fight.

In a matter of months, the Chinese had turned sour on the British partnership. As a final blow, Dai received a report that one of the Scandinavians had said the Chinese Commando Group's true mission was not to support China, but to take back Hong Kong, which had fallen to Japan on Christmas Day 1941. To Dai, that confirmed that Keswick was only interested in preserving Jardine Matheson.

In a messy business, Chiang Kai-shek kicked Keswick and the Chinese Commando Group out of the country in early April, a few days before Miles boarded the plane for Brazil. Dai told his officers that, although the British were leaving, better friends would soon replace them because the Americans were on the way that very moment.

Yet under a cloud of disappointment and bitterness, Dai Li misinterpreted Miles's innocent movements in India, potentially hampering his mission before it had begun. Furthermore, Dai took a dim view of reports that Miles had spoken regularly with the two American diplomats.

Dai simply didn't like Ambassador Gauss. He found the ambassador to be the kind of preachy, officious American that got on his nerves. The straightforward, aw-shucks American personality in the Jimmy Stewart vein was much more to his taste. As for Colonel McHugh, he was on intimate terms with the British intelligence community in Chongqing and had even lived at the British embassy for a period, adding to suspicions Dai already harbored about Miles's loyalties.

IGNORANT THAT DAI HAD BEEN WATCHING HIM, Miles flew out of Kolkata on the same plane as Gauss and McHugh and landed in Chongqing on May 4, 1942. McHugh invited Miles to stay with him, but Miles turned him down, unsure what General Dai Li might have arranged. He planned to meet with Dai and get settled before officially reporting to Gauss's office later.

At the airport, a uniformed Chinese official approached Miles, read his travel orders, and checked the contents of his bag, making no comment about the mine.

"Do you know Colonel Xiao?" the official asked. Instead of looking at Miles, he looked down, directing Miles's eyes to his feet. He wrote the name "Dai Li" in the dust with his toe and quickly erased it.

"Yes, I know Colonel Xiao," Miles replied.

The man then disappeared without a word.

Through this bizarre exchange, the official, an MBIS agent working for Dai Li, confirmed Miles's identity and simultaneously revealed his own connection with the general. Miles, however, had no idea who this man was, except that he must work for Dai. Baffled, Miles stood there for a few minutes expecting someone else, perhaps Dai himself, to appear, but no one approached him. Not knowing where to go, he accepted a lift to a hotel from Al Lusey of the Office of Coordination of Information (soon to become the Office of Special Services), who was there to meet Gauss and McHugh.

Miles's next move was to make no move at all. He was chomping at the bit to begin his work, and military manners compelled him to pay his respects to Ambassador Gauss without delay, but instead, he checked into the hotel expecting that Dai Li would contact him. For the rest of the day, he walked around the neighborhood buying noodles from street vendors, chatting with locals as best he could in Mandarin, and puzzling over his peculiar reception at the airport.

All the while, General Dai's agents were watching, and Miles innocently proved that Colonel Xiao's characterization of him had been accurate. His behavior to the vendors and hotel staff, his rejection of the hotel's American menu in favor of the noodle stands, and his choice to strike out on his own rather than cling to the embassy demonstrated his independence and his respect for the Chinese.

But Miles knew nothing of the world of spies and couldn't understand why Dai Li had not reached out to him. The general was certainly aware that Miles had arrived in Chongqing, and he had even made a point to let Miles know it through the bizarre airport incident.

Finding no message from Dai the next morning, Miles decided to visit his old classmate for advice. McHugh had been in Chongqing for a few years, spoke several Chinese dialects fluently, and knew the American and Chinese intelligence communities well.

Miles went out intending to catch a rickshaw to McHugh's house, but a brown Chevrolet pulled up to the curb, and the door opened to receive him. After a mere twenty-four hours in Chongqing, Miles had come to expect surprises. So he unceremoniously climbed in, directed the driver to McHugh's house, and asked him to wait. McHugh and Miles spoke briefly and agreed to meet later that day for a tour of Chongqing. The mysterious car was still there when Miles emerged, and the driver took him back to the hotel.

By the time Colonel McHugh picked him up that afternoon, Miles had resolved to pay a courtesy call on Nationalist Chinese intelligence officer Admiral Yang. But his motive was not one of decorum. He reasoned that Yang must be acquainted with Dai, whom he was determined either to meet personally or at least to contact through channels.

After exchanging pleasantries with the admiral and McHugh, Miles said he would like to call on General Dai Li to deliver a couple of gifts. Yang offered to bring his car around and take the two Americans to the general immediately. Minutes later, Miles was astonished to be riding in the same brown Chevrolet that had picked him up that morning, with the same driver at the wheel.

The three rode through Chongqing to a nondescript neighborhood. Yang escorted Miles and McHugh to a narrow door just off an ordinary street and left them inside with one of Dai Li's aides. The man led the pair through a maze of corridors, doorways, staircases, and chambers, until they finally stopped in a drawing room.

Miles had little time to reflect on the day's spy-novel-worthy events before General Dai Li entered the room and greeted them with a penetrating gaze and a broad, gold-toothed smile.

CHAPTER 2

A Handshake Creates the Sino–American Cooperative Organization

FOR THE NEXT HOUR over tea, cakes, and dumplings, Dai Li, Milton Miles, and James McHugh each played a role in a three-way scene foreshadowing the complicated relationships that were to develop between the United States and China and among squabbling factions within the U.S. military bureaucracy over the next three years.

Miles first offered the gifts for Dai that had been the pretense of the meeting: a camera from Colonel Xiao and a fine snubnose .38 automatic pistol from himself, identical to the one he wore on his own belt. Dai immediately put it on, clearly pleased. The elegant, easily concealed weapon was the perfect gift for the gadget-loving general whose personal security was constantly under threat. It remained clipped to Dai's waist from that day until the day he died.

If the pistol had softened him, Dai still had to determine whether Miles was the reliable friend Xiao had known in Washington or a double-dealing British agent. Though Miles knew a smattering of coastal Chinese dialects and some Mandarin, he did not understand Dai's obscure dialect, and thus, they communicated through an interpreter. The conversation seesawed from polite chat to interrogation as the general asked about Miles's children and his movements in India, which had so shaken Dai.

Just as on the previous day, Miles's ignorance of the cloak-and-dagger world worked in his favor. Though he detected tension in Dai's queries, he gave an utterly candid account of his fact-finding trips. He had seen promising facilities for a supply staging ground in Kolkata, and a navy captain in Colombo had proven helpful with technical information about radio transmitters.

As the conversation advanced, Dai Li's defenses relaxed, and Miles searched for signs of the sinister character described in the State Department file. Instead, the man before him seemed reserved but polite and highly competent. He had taken pains to learn about Miles's family, his car, and other personal details and to demonstrate that he had done his homework.

But Dai also revealed constant and zealous concerns for security, which seemed to border on paranoia. Less than an hour after they first met, he suggested that Miles assume a false name and wear civilian clothes. Although Miles never said what he thought of the general's advice, he never took it. However, it may have influenced his decision to have all American SACOs dress in plain army fatigues without rank or insignia.

During the meeting, an astonished McHugh said almost nothing. As the author of some of the scathing reports about Dai's insular world in the State Department file, he was stunned to be seated in the intelligence chief's private quarters sipping tea. Over the years in Chongqing, Dai had been a major roadblock to his work and had certainly never entertained him.

The surprises kept coming. After the doubts about Miles's travels through India were resolved, Dai offered him a lovely house on a hill in Chongqing to replace his shabby hotel room, and Miles accepted. It would be a few days, however, before the house, called the Fairy Cave, would be ready for occupancy. Miles later discovered that the previous tenant, the mayor of Chongqing, had been evicted for his sake.

Miles found Fairy Cave almost embarrassingly luxurious. The hilltop mansion came with a car, a cook, a housekeeper, and a gardener who placed gardenias on Miles's pillow every night simply because he had admired them on his initial tour of the grounds. More importantly, the home also contained a bomb shelter.

Now that the ice was broken, Miles became integrated into Dai's daily schedule. Miles and McHugh were invited to Dai's staff meeting the following day, Miles's first opportunity to describe what the navy hoped to accomplish through his mission, then called the Friendship Project.

During this first meeting, Miles decided not to put forward a complicated agenda that might evoke a picture of legions of American sailors and officers descending on China and making demands. It had taken him only a couple of days to realize that the prevailing Chinese view of foreigners had shifted dramatically since his last tour of duty in 1939. The Chinese had formerly deferred to Westerners, assuming that they knew best, owing to superior education and experience. But after the Americans and British had taken severe beatings from the Japanese in December 1941 even as the Chinese, with far fewer resources, had been fighting them off for four years, the general attitude toward foreigners became one of contempt. "No more outside bossing," as Miles later wrote.[4]

With that in mind, he trod lightly in his presentation, focusing on the navy's need for weather reports, manned weather stations to collect them, and radio transmitters to send them. The navy would have to count on China to support and protect the system the United States intended to build.

To his surprise, the Chinese officers debated his argument point by point. He had expected a staff of yes men who would listen to what the boss had to say before daring to posit an opinion. But what happened was just the opposite. Dai listened to their analyses and took them into account before stating his decision.

Miles knew he had won the day when the discussion shifted from what to how: the number of navy personnel expected and the quarters they would need.

As on the previous day, McHugh could do nothing but watch in astonishment. After more than a decade in China and three years in Chongqing, he had never met this group. Three months later he would write to Navy Secretary Frank Knox:

> Commander Miles has gotten off to a flying start and has been taken completely into the confidence of the Chinese Secret Service. He has seen and done things I never thought any foreigner would be able to do.[5]

High on Miles's immediate agenda was to see the coast of China for himself and make a report to Admiral King. He needed to observe the strength of the Japanese occupation, scope out locations for coast watches, and get a fresh overview of the terrain for a future invasion by U.S. forces. He had dropped a few hints about the trip, and though Dai had responded casually, no specifics had been mentioned.

McHugh warned him that, as gracious and cooperative as Dai appeared to be, he would never let Miles out of Chongqing.

Again, McHugh's prediction proved to be wrong. The night after the staff meeting, Dai gave a dinner in Miles's honor to which McHugh was invited. Miles, confident in his quickly growing rapport with Dai, decided it was time to stop dancing around his planned tour of the coast. He announced his wish to make the trip, and Dai instantly agreed. In fact, had the general's staff not reminded him of other business, he and Miles might have departed the next morning. Instead, plans were set to start the trip the following week.

Those plans were put off, however, because the Japanese were on the move again, and General Dai had to tend to military matters. McHugh and Ambassador Gauss had the pleasure of saying, "I told you so." No foreigner had ever been permitted to travel through China in the manner Miles had intended.

Miles was frustrated but not discouraged because Dai did all he could to help Miles get settled in Chongqing. For instance, he provided Miles with an excellent interpreter, Liu Chen-feng, who went by his mission school name "Eddie" to English speakers. Eddie Liu did more than translate Chinese to English and vice versa. He also served as something of a cultural ambassador, explaining the finer points of Chinese military manners so that Miles's intentions were never misunderstood.

Dai also gave Miles a Chinese name, Mei Lo-ssu, which, when spoken quickly, sounded something like "Miles" with an extra vowel at the end. It also had a fortuitous meaning. Mei means "winter plum blossom," a flower that blooms in late winter on bare branches still covered with snow, an inspiring sight just when one despairs that spring may never come. It symbolizes perseverance, courage, and the ability to overcome hardship. Lo-ssu may be translated as "you like this place" or "you stay here."

Dai Li had to put off the coast trip several times during the next two weeks. When plans finally fell into place, Dai could not travel with Miles after all. He had to go ahead on his own to join a column of his guerrillas as the Japanese pressed inland. Miles and Dai planned to meet at Pucheng in coastal Fujian Province ten days later.

Miles and nine other men climbed into a Dodge truck in Chongqing on May 26, 1942, bound for the coast, eleven hundred miles away. The party included Al Lusey, who had given Miles a ride from the airport that first day in Chongqing.

Lusey was a former American journalist in China who worked for the U.S. Office of the Coordinator of Information, soon to be the Office of Strategic Services. SACO and the OSS would have some rocky times ahead, but at that moment, Miles found Lusey very helpful. He had expertise in radio communication and intelligence that Miles lacked, and even though Miles had years of experience in China, he must have appreciated another American as a companion. Dai's policy was "any friend of Miles is a friend of mine," and he was happy to have Lusey included in the party.

The others in the group were Eddie Liu, Miles's cook Liu Shih-feng, four armed guards, Miles's personal bodyguard, whom he had nicknamed "Speed," a general fix-it man, and the driver.

Seated in wicker chairs bolted to the truck floor, they bumped along over rugged dirt roads through the terraced mountains for two weeks. As they traveled east, the reality of war became evident. They passed through towns that had recently been bombed, meeting bundle-laden refugees walking in the opposite direction to escape the advancing Japanese. At most stops, they found accommodations in hotels and guesthouses, but in the city of Kukong, they had to sleep in sampans on the river because all the hotels had been destroyed. Their route was diverted hundreds of miles to the south to avoid enemy movements.

They finally arrived at Pucheng, situated in a lovely landscape of rice paddies, crop fields, and woodlands. The only evidence of war in the peaceful town was an ancient, crumbling wall that had protected it from other enemies centuries before.

Though Miles and his party were a couple of days late, so was Dai. After reaching the general by phone, he arrived in Pucheng looking dead-tired. He hadn't slept in several days and had gone to check on his mother, children, and grandchildren, who lived in a town now occupied by the Japanese. Miles couldn't help but think of the intelligence file that claimed he had executed his mother twice. In fact, each day that he spent with Dai in Pucheng, he grew more impressed with him, and the Washington dossier seemed more ludicrous.

Miles was invited to Dai Li's meetings with a stream of agents who came in from Hong Kong, Shanghai, Xiamen, and even the Imperial Palace in Japan to report what they had learned about the Japanese. In Miles's eyes, Dai's intelligence network equaled or surpassed any in the West.

Though the general must have been concerned about his family and under great pressure from the war, he never seemed preoccupied. He worked efficiently and showed the utmost respect to the agents. No one seemed to be afraid of him. Observing him in action bolstered Miles's confidence that he would be able to work with Dai to achieve the navy's goals.

However, the peace was broken in Pucheng soon after Dai arrived; Japanese planes dropped bombs two days in a row, sending the village's residents scrambling to take cover.

With spies, enemy movements, and plans for radio transmitters spinning in his head, a restless Miles was up at 4:00 a.m. on June 9. While shaving beside an open window, he heard hurried footsteps in the street and a soft but intense voice say, "Jing Bao," meaning "urgent alarm." Moments later, a pair of white lights, the public alert signal for Jing Bao, pierced the darkness from atop the town wall. Perhaps the person he had heard had been on his way to hoist the warning lights.

Dai, Lusey, Liu, and Miles met at the door of their quarters and ran down the cobblestone streets toward the edge of town, joining the crowd of villagers, from crying babies in carts to bent old women tottering along on bound feet.

Dai and his friends took cover among the bushes growing between dry rice paddies and watched the most intense attack on Pucheng yet. Eleven Japanese planes roared over the town dropping bombs and strafing the streets with machine gun fire.

"They know you are here, you and General Dai," said Liu. Spying, after all, worked two ways. The Japanese must have had a local informant.

With enemy planes circling overhead, Dai seized the opportunity to speak his mind to his new American friend. He asked Eddie Liu to tell Mr. Winter Plum Blossom that he would like the navy to arm fifty thousand of Dai's best guerrillas and train them to fight the Japanese.

Although Miles thought he understood Dai's astonishing words, he took advantage of the delay imposed by translation to mull them over.

Dai ticked off a list of what the U.S. Navy was seeking in China—weather reports, coast watches, radio stations, intelligence about Japanese forces—all requiring Chinese military protection. By training and arming Dai's guerrillas, Miles would get the support he needed for these operations and simultaneously create a stronger force to fight their common enemy. Miles would receive a commission as a general in the Chinese army so that he and Dai could manage the force together.

Miles instantly grasped the magnitude of this moment. Dai Li had a reputation for avoiding relations with foreigners, and yet he was offering Miles everything he wanted, plus an army of fifty thousand, in exchange for training and arms. Although his acquaintance with Dai had been brief, Miles believed he understood him well enough to recognize a turning point in their nascent relationship.

Despite the State Department's appalling portrait of Dai, Miles had seen no evidence of the purported ruthless killer. Watching for signs of intimidation among the general's subordinates, he had detected only mutual respect. Moreover, the impressive management skills Dai had displayed under the most challenging circumstances indicated that he could deliver on his end of the bargain.

The success of the Pacific war depended on the weather reports Miles had been sent to obtain, and he needed Dai's support to get them. Besides, his orders from Admiral King included a charge to make trouble for the enemy in any way he could. This guerrilla force could certainly do that, and more.

Miles weighed all these factors in an instant and gave what for him was the only logical response.

"O.K.," he said. No translation necessary.

Dai extended his right hand, and Miles took it.

Al Lusey was shocked. Later, he would urge Miles to check with Washington before charging forward with such a bold step. But Miles brushed it off. He was trained to make independent decisions, a necessary skill for a naval officer at sea. He had sensed that any hesitation would have broken the trust Dai had in him and thus in the United States. Had he hedged on the request, the plan might have evaporated, along with all the navy's hopes in China.

For Dai, the handshake meant he had replaced the ill-fated Commando Group China, the training and espionage operation he had attempted with Great Britain but with disastrous results. But this time, Dai expected a better outcome. First, Commander Miles had a totally different attitude from his British counterparts. He utterly respected the sovereignty and the people of China. Second, Dai knew exactly what the Americans wanted. His agent Xiao Bo had been in on the navy's clearly articulated agenda from the start, going back to the coffee chats two years earlier, and Miles had stuck to it. And most importantly, this time around, Dai would not let control slip through his fingers. He was determined to make Miles a partner, but not an independent agent.

When the attack was over, the party returned to a town in flames. Dai organized bucket brigades to extinguish fires, and Miles's legs were badly burned when a roof collapsed nearly on top of him. After three more air raids that day, town authorities caught a local physician with a radio transmitter, accused him of informing the enemy that Dai Li was in town, and arranged a trial. Miles had expected Dai to have the doctor shot at once with no formalities, but Eddie Liu said the general never had anyone executed "without proper authorization." Miles later pointed to the incident as proof that Dai was not the ruthless killer depicted in the Washington dossier.

In spite of the burns, which became infected, and a bout with malaria, Miles continued his tour of the coast, but without Dai and Lusey. Chiang Kai-shek had called Dai back to Chongqing, and Lusey was summoned to Washington.

For the next month, the group proceeded south by truck, sampan, and on foot. Miles, weakened from his burns and illness, reluctantly accepted a sedan chair until his strength recovered enough to walk with the others, donning a Chinese suit and balancing a yo-yo pole with baskets at each end on his shoulder to blend in with the landscape. They slipped in and out of enemy territory, moving hundreds of miles south along the coast to Xiamen, where they got into a brief gun battle with a Japanese patrol, and Miles took a flesh wound in the shin. All along the route, Miles photographed clusters of Japanese ships and sites to consider for future coast watches and the U.S. Navy invasion.

Returning by river steamer and truck, he got back to Chongqing in mid-July expecting a pile of mail, but there were no instructions or inquiries from the navy, not even a postcard from his wife. It seemed his country had forgotten him, but Dai Li certainly had not. He was already assembling one hundred thirty crack troops to make up the first class of sabotage training.

It was time for Miles to get busy. He wrote to Washington for two thousand tommy guns, three thousand service revolvers, and ten thousand grenades and began scouting for a place to set up a training camp.

U.S. Army General Joseph Stilwell, a crusty, old-fashioned soldier known as "Vinegar Joe," was now in Chongqing as commander of the Allied China–Burma–India Theater and chief of staff to Chiang Kai-shek. He and Miles hit it off immediately. Though Stilwell's gruffness contrasted with Miles's congenial style, both men were doers, not talkers, and when they spoke, it was frankly and simply.

In characteristic bluntness, Stilwell told Miles that he liked him but not what he was doing. He objected on principle to tactics like sabotage and guerrilla warfare and to having a navy officer on the loose in his theater. But Miles sold him on the budding program with Dai Li as a way to contain the Japanese. Stilwell suggested that Miles go to India to shake loose some guns that were sitting in a warehouse. Stilwell promised to get them onto one of his supply flights "over the Hump" (over the Himalayas to China) and make that a regular arrangement as materials arrived for Miles from the United States.

Miles took his advice and made a quick, though disappointing, trip to India, which yielded nothing but a frightening lesson. As he was returning to Chongqing, a virtually naked man stabbed him in the arm and leg late at night on a railroad platform in Allahabad. After Miles kicked his attacker in the chin, the man dropped to the platform, rolled over the edge and under a rail car, then disappeared into the darkness. The force of the kick had clamped the man's teeth down on his tongue, severing the tip, which Miles found lying on the platform.

The next day, a doctor fished the end of the knife out of the swollen wound in Miles's arm. Miles turned over the tongue fragment and knife tip to Dai Li's agents in India, and the ghastly evidence proved sufficient to capture the assailant, a Chinese Korean who had attended a Japanese assassination school in Shandong Province, China. Dai concluded that the man had acted under Japanese command.

Upon Miles's return to Chongqing in late August 1942, Dai warned him never to go out without a guard, and now the cautions did not seem overblown. It appeared that the Japanese had targeted him because of his association with Dai.

Another thing was apparent: Dai Li had abruptly and mysteriously turned chilly toward him. It wasn't until Miles received a cable from Washington in mid-October that he found out why. He had been named Far East Coordinator of the Office of Special Services, but the cable did not reveal any details about his new post. Only when Al Lusey got back in November did Miles understand what the title entailed. Lusey brought with him written orders from Washington placing Miles under Colonel William Donovan in the newly created intelligence agency, the OSS, which had split from the Coordinator of Information Office. Lusey was also now with the OSS as an assistant to Miles.

The appointment was a complete surprise to Miles, but Dai had known about it since early September through Xiao Bo. Dai had been furious that OSS agents were already operating in China without informing Chiang's government, and he had assumed Miles had authorized their activities while trying to conceal them.

Although the confusion was resolved and the two returned to their former friendly relationship, the incident convinced Dai Li that a handshake was not enough to form the cooperative operation he envisioned with the U.S. Navy. Eager to avoid repeating his failed attempt to work with the British, he wanted to spell out in writing exactly how the joint project would work.

Chiang Kai-shek summoned Miles and Dai for a meeting. He told Miles that given the new complexity of his responsibilities, an official agreement was necessary, to be signed by Chiang and President Roosevelt.

Thus began a two-month ordeal for Miles and Dai, who worked together to produce the document that formally created the Sino–American Special Technical Cooperative Organization. (In common parlance, the words "Special Technical" were dropped, and the group became known as SACO.) The two men concurred from the start that the sun would never set on a disagreement during the process of writing it, but as Miles recalled, sunset was sometimes ignored until after midnight.

The first draft was written in Chinese. Working section by section, the document was translated into English and back into Chinese by a different interpreter, sometimes producing a different result. They would then rephrase the passage to make it precise in both languages. As obstacles cropped up, Miles worked through them without consulting anyone in Washington. Seeking approval would have delayed progress for months, and his sense of urgency was mounting.

Dai's top priority for the agreement was to make sure the navy couldn't do anything without his approval. To ensure that, he was designated director of SACO, and Miles was deputy director, but to equalize their authority, each had veto power over all decisions. This key provision later caused friction for Miles with U.S. military officials who frowned on his subordinate position, but it seemed reasonable to him because they were working in Dai's country. He couldn't imagine the United States entering into a similar project at home with a foreign government without having ultimate control. Miles viewed these objections as examples of American disrespect for China's sovereignty, which in turn inspired xenophobic attitudes in China.

Though Miles was number two, he got what he wanted most: the right to fulfill his orders to gather weather data and intelligence and to bring in the personnel and set up the infrastructure necessary for that purpose with full Chinese logistical support.

The agreement took the form of a treaty creating a joint United States Navy–Chinese Guerrilla Army force for sabotage, raids, and guerrilla military operations in addition to weather forecasting and intelligence. The navy would supply materials and training while China provided personnel, facilities, and security.

It also authorized another pet project for Dai, a school to teach his police force modern investigation techniques. This provision also caused problems later. During the war, the U.S. State Department and the U.S. Army objected to training police officers who seemed to serve no military purpose in the war against Japan. Long after the war was over, the People's Republic of China would use the school as a propaganda tool for "evidence" that the United States had aided Chiang Kai-shek in the oppression of his own people through Dai Li.

The SACO treaty was completed in time for Lusey once more to serve as courier when he left Chongqing for Washington on New Year's Eve, 1942. Miles optimistically imagined that it would be returned with signatures in a matter of weeks.

WHILE CRAFTING THIS DOCUMENT occupied much of their time, it wasn't all the two were doing during the last quarter of 1942. Dai was fighting an enemy on his home soil, and Miles was taking the initial steps to establish SACO.

At the top of Miles's agenda was to develop a facility where SACO could operate, and a major requirement for its location was access to abundant water. Dime-novel-worthy adventures in China notwithstanding, Miles was still a buttoned-down naval officer who kept things ship shape. He wanted his men to be able to bathe twice a day. Dai offered Miles two hundred acres of his personal compound in the hills eight miles northwest of Chongqing, which became known as Happy Valley.

The first eight American SACOs, all radio experts, had arrived in early September, living and working at Fairy Cave until October, when they moved to Happy Valley. By November, their number had grown to fifteen.

They were the first to adopt SACO's required unadorned army khakis, but they still wanted an official symbol to identify SACO even if they were not going to wear it. The first version was a military-clad mosquito named "Socko," an irreverent nod to the voracious pests that plagued them in Chongqing. Miles then suggested the gag pennant he had designed to hoist during maneuvers eight years earlier as executive officer aboard the USS *Wilkes*. With three question marks, three exclamation points, and three asterisks in red on a white field, it meant, "What the hell?"

The group agreed. The pennant was raised over Happy Valley and flew until the end of the war. It decorated embroidered patches, was stenciled onto SACO shipments in Kolkata bound for Chongqing, and was still used on the cover of the SACO Veterans' newsletter as of this writing.

The Japanese Navy had seen the pennant years earlier. In 1939, stationed in China as captain of the U.S. destroyer *John D. Edwards*, Miles was ordered to check on some American missionaries on Hainan Island, where the Japanese Navy was preparing to land.

When the destroyer arrived at the island, a sizable Japanese fleet was bombarding the port city. Seeing the American ship, the command vessel sent up international signal flags meaning, "turn around and go away." Determined to contact the stranded Americans, Miles hoisted his "What the Hell?" pennant in reply and proceeded cautiously into the bay. A confused Japanese admiral, unable to interpret the pennant, halted the bombardment and sent a reconnaissance craft, whose officer shouted, "You can't anchor here!"

Miles answered, "You're right, I'd rather anchor closer to shore," and continued to make his way toward land. As the frustrated officer raced back to report to his commander, the *John D. Edwards* dropped anchor, and Miles took a party ashore to complete his mission.

Before leaving, he made the customary courtesy call to the Japanese admiral, who asked him the meaning of the unfamiliar signal flag he had raised. Miles would only reply that the admiral's codebook must be out of date.

But the story didn't end there. Six months later when stationed in Washington, Miles received an inquiry about the strange pennant. Originating with the Japanese admiral, it had bounced from desk to desk through the navy and the State Department and randomly landed at the Interior Control Board. Miles's reply never made it back to the admiral.

Given the pennant's storied history and the seat-of-the-pants conditions under which the new outfit was formed, it seemed a fitting symbol.

WITH SO MUCH TO DO in early 1943, the SACO men were frustrated that promised supplies were not arriving, and they had to wait for the agreement to be signed before starting large-scale training sessions with Chinese troops.

Miles went to India in February to try to get some of his equipment flown over the Hump. While there, he received a message from Washington that he was needed there to ferry the SACO treaty through the bureaucracy, so he immediately flew back to the States.

Had he not gone, the agreement might have languished unsigned until the war was over. It needed the initials of the Joint Chiefs and the President, but none of them had approved it. Three things had kept the document at the bottom of Washington's in-baskets.

First, the wartime workload was overwhelming, and without someone pushing it, the agreement remained a low priority.

Second, President Roosevelt and the Joint Chiefs attended a ten-day Casablanca conference in January with Prime Minister Winston Churchill and French generals Henri Giraud and Charles de Gaulle. None of these key endorsers would even look at the treaty until the meeting was over, fully digested, and written up.*

---

* Incidentally, the conference was another incident that aroused Dai Li's suspicions. Owing to his hypersensitive prejudice against the British, he feared that it was an occasion for Churchill and Roosevelt to discuss the SACO arrangement. He cabled Rear Admiral W. R. Purnell, Jeff Metzel's superior in Washington, that the British were to have no input in the SACO Agreement and that he would not accept any material changes to it. Purnell assured him that it would remain intact as written and that the British had no connection with SACO.

Finally, the navy and the army had objections to certain details. The navy's issues were technical, and Miles successfully and quickly cleared them up, but the army was another matter.

Army Chief of Staff General George C. Marshall disapproved of the treaty on grounds that it violated the military principle "continuity of command" on several fronts. Dai Li's designation as director of SACO unacceptably placed American servicemen under the command of a foreign officer. In addition, allowing Miles to report directly to Admiral King and the Joint Chiefs bypassed CBI Theater Commander Stilwell. Dai had insisted on this provision to avoid a "too many cooks in the kitchen" scenario that might wrest control of SACO out of Chinese hands.

Similarly, the treaty created an inconsistent command structure for the OSS. In all other parts of the world, the OSS was under the region's theater commander, and although SACO was not part of the OSS, Miles was. Marshall therefore concluded that continuity required Miles, SACO, and the OSS to be placed under Stilwell's command.

Jeff Metzel had anticipated this argument before Miles left Chongqing and had encouraged him to get Stilwell on SACO's side. Thanks to Miles's friendly coaxing, Stilwell wrote to Marshall that SACO's success depended on complete cooperation from Dai Li, who would never accept having a U.S. Army general between himself and Miles.

To overcome the dilemma Marshall had pointed out over the OSS command structure, the Joint Chiefs attached a directive that the Far East would be the single theater in which the OSS would report to the Joint Chiefs. In the rest of the world, it would remain under the theater commander.

While these efforts seemed to smooth the way for Marshall's approval, he still hesitated before putting pen to paper in his office as Miles, Metzel, Purnell, and Xiao Bo anxiously looked on.

According to Maochun Yu, a professor at the United States Naval Academy who has written several books about United States–China relations during the first half of the twentieth century, Marshall's technical objections were merely props to cover the root of the problem: interservice rivalry.

In Marshall's eyes, the document gave the navy undue precedence over the army. It placed Miles under Dai Li, who reported directly to Chiang Kai-shek.

This chain of command gave Miles access to the highest authority in China without Stilwell's involvement, allowing the navy to leapfrog over the army. But more importantly, SACO activities would prepare for the navy's coastal invasion of China, a plan promoted by Admiral King over Marshall's objections.[6] Marshall thought this should be the army's job. Furthermore, army officers from Washington to Chongqing frequently wondered aloud what the navy was doing on the ground in China in the first place.

Therefore, when the time arrived to make the commitment, Marshall told his anxious visitors that he would like to make some "minor changes" before initialing it.

Miles and Purnell were stunned speechless. They had spent months lobbying for SACO and overcoming objections throughout the military bureaucracy. Marshall, whose stated issues with the treaty had already been satisfied, was the last stop before the President. Any change could potentially add months to an already protracted process.

Jeff Metzel rose to the occasion, advancing an argument that he knew Marshall would find irresistible. Knowing the high priority Marshall placed in preserving Stilwell's authority and leadership status, he reminded Marshall that Stilwell specifically supported having Miles work under Dai while answering to the Joint Chiefs. Moreover, Stilwell was counting on information and support from SACO.

Metzel's reasoning did the trick. Marshall reluctantly added his initials, and the treaty sailed through Roosevelt's office, although the President made a pragmatic change that the Chinese readily approved. Instead of a "treaty," the administration designated the document an "agreement" to avoid the necessity of Senate ratification. Even in time of war, that would have delayed the document and potentially compromised the secrecy of SACO.

Two navy typists produced the final, clean copies in English, and Xiao Bo wrote the Chinese version in his own hand. The navy Photostat department then made copies of both documents, and Miles remembered that the typists made sure the Chinese photostats were arranged in the proper order and right-side up.

On April 16, 1943, Captain Milton E. Miles (recently promoted) and General William J. Donovan signed the SACO Agreement on behalf of the United States. Dr. T. V. Soong, brother-in-law of Chiang Kai-shek, and Colonel Xiao Bo signed for China, representing the Generalissimo and General Dai Li, respectively.

The agreement became effective immediately, although Dai did not personally sign it until July 4.

The Friendship Project, originally conceived as a small band of weather technologists, radio operators, cryptographers, photographers, and coast watchers, was now to be all of that and much more. The Sino–American Cooperative Organization planned to unleash a campaign of sabotage and guerrilla warfare that they hoped would cripple the Japanese occupation in China.

PART 2

A Strange Cast in a Strange Drama

CHAPTER 3

China in Turmoil

MILTON MILES HAD FIRST ARRIVED IN CHINA in 1922 as a young ensign aboard the USS *Pecos,* an instrument of U.S. gunboat diplomacy. The *Pecos* was part of a U.S. Navy fleet cruising the coasts and rivers of China, answering appeals from the American Chamber of Commerce in China for protection of American commerce, shipping, and citizens during a period of political upheaval. Successful naval officers needed courage, tact, and patience for this duty. They negotiated with local authorities, rescued Americans from battle zones, and fended off pirate attacks. Under these relentless, taxing conditions, Miles emerged from eight years in China with his respect for the Chinese people and interest in their culture intact. It was no wonder that Vice Admiral Willis Lee tapped him for the Friendship Project that became SACO.

SACO was born during one of the most volatile periods in China's four-thousand-year history. While Chiang Kai-shek was the recognized leader of China in the eyes of the outside world, the picture was far less clear within China. Chiang headed the central government and the Nationalist party in Chongqing, but the Communist party did not recognize him or his government.

Since the fall of the Qing Dynasty in 1911, China had struggled to recreate itself as a modern republic after thousands of years of imperial rule. Though Chiang Kai-shek had emerged as the country's leader in the eyes of the world by the time World War II began, he held only tenuously to power, having reached a fragile peace with his Communist rivals while fighting a war with Japan.

Since ancient times, the Chinese people had viewed theirs as the supreme culture of the world. Then as now, the country's age-old name, the Middle Kingdom, proclaimed its place at the center of the civilized world.

This worldview was not wholly unjustified. For millennia, the Chinese culture and government had outshined those of all their neighbors in sophistication and effectiveness. The Chinese had pioneered thousands of world-changing technologies, from paper and printing to porcelain and restaurant menus. For more than two thousand years, the Confucian meritocracy based on a civil service examination supported a government administration system that created and maintained a remarkably stable and prosperous social order. Although effective, however, its bureaucracy lacked the nimbleness required to adapt to change. The problem rested in part on the exam and the education system behind it, which emphasized memorization of Chinese classical literature over original thinking. Always looking back instead of forward, it limited government's ability to devise new solutions in a changing world.

DURING THE NINETEENTH CENTURY, China under the Qing Dynasty descended toward chaos as foreign governments infringed on its territory and sovereignty, and its angry people staged uprising after uprising.

The outside world forced itself into the long-isolated country. Following the midcentury Opium Wars of the 1800s, Great Britain and France compelled a weakened monarchy to open China's markets and allow foreign traders to operate under their own rules in port cities. These agreements were the first of the "unequal treaties" that became a rallying point against foreigners in the twentieth century.

The changes rocked the people of southern China and helped ignite the Taiping Rebellion, the largest revolt in China's history. It began in 1850 with thirty thousand revolutionaries and ended fourteen years later after twenty million had died in the struggle.

In 1875, the ultraconservative Empress Dowager Cixi installed her four-year-old nephew Guangxu as Emperor as a means to conserve her power. But her plan went wrong when Guangxu reached majority in 1889 and began making changes to modernize China that flew in the face of her beliefs.

China's 1895 defeat in the first Sino–Japanese War fully exposed the government's weakness and incompetence to its citizens and to the world. Guangxu responded with the Hundred Days Reform of 1898 that promised immediate sweeping changes, from creating a constitutional monarchy to abolishing the antiquated civil service examination. But a coup led by Cixi squelched the program. She had its architects executed and forced Guangxu into hiding.

Western and Japanese opportunists moved in on China, negotiating for territory and expanding business operations. In 1900, the Righteous Harmonious Fists, a secret organization that aimed to eradicate foreign influence from China, retaliated, attacking foreigners and Chinese Christians and laying siege to a multinational embassy compound in Beijing. The imperial court supported their campaign, known as the Boxer Rebellion, but a military alliance of seven Western countries and Japan put it down and forced the government to execute the rebellion's leaders and pay reparations. China emerged even weaker, and Chinese resentment of these payments would inspire a challenge to U.S. presence two decades later.

When the Russo–Japanese War broke out in 1905 in northern Manchuria, the Qing Dynasty withdrew from the region and let the two combatants slug it out over the territory. This infuriated the people, and their anger spelled the demise of the Qing when revolution exploded six years later.

The revolt began in Wuchang, the capital of Hubei Province, on October 10, 1911, over nationalization of the railroad, but that issue was merely the spark that ignited a tinderbox of discontent all over the country. The imperial family and most of the bureaucrats were minority Manchus, and the majority Han saw them as incompetent, corrupt outsiders who had destroyed their once-great country.

The Wuchang uprising marked a profound turning point between ancient imperial China and the modern republic. As of this writing, the Nationalist government in Taiwan celebrates October 10 as Double Ten Day, the nation's birthday, with all the flourish of the Fourth of July in the United States.

As protests broke out in Wuchang and beyond, revolution had been fomenting among Chinese students abroad. For more than a decade, tens of thousands of China's most gifted young people had been studying in Japan, France, and the United States, and there they discovered how truly backward their own country had become compared to the rest of the world. After 1900, they began to organize and make plans to reshape their homeland.

In Japan, Sun Yat-sen formed the Revive China Society with Chinese students and expatriates, and in 1905, the society joined other underground political groups to become the United League, or Tongmeng Hui, under Sun's leadership. The Tongmeng Hui aimed to overthrow the "northern barbarian" rulers in favor of ethnic Han Chinese, establish a republic, and institute land reform.

By the time of the Wuchang revolt, the Tongmeng Hui had branches in Singapore and throughout China. These cells served as catalysts to spread the uprising across the country. In the third month of the rebellion, Sun Yat-sen came back to China from the United States and assumed leadership of the new republic. He was inaugurated as president in Nanjing on January 1, 1912, even though the Qing had not relinquished power. His presidency, however, was short lived.

On March 10, 1912, Sun gave up the office in favor of General Yuan Shikai, the military governor of northern China, who a month earlier had negotiated with Empress Dowager Cixi for child Emperor Puyi to abdicate. Yuan was popular with the people and the military for this and for modernizing the Northern Army and civil institutions. Sun said he was stepping aside to avoid a civil war and to give the republic a chance to take hold.

But Yuan did not live up to popular hopes. Over four years, he became increasingly dictatorial and eventually declared himself emperor. By the time he died of kidney failure in 1916, several provinces had seceded from the crumbling republic.

With his death, the failing central government evaporated completely, and a series of presidents who followed him functioned more like mayors of Beijing than national authorities.

Dozens of local warlords filled the vacuum. Between Yuan's death and the end of Chiang Kai-shek's first unification campaign in 1928, the warlords were the law and the government in China. They ruled over private fiefdoms acquired and retained by personal armies. Generally free of ideology and motivated simply by financial gain, they included career military officers, local politicians, and crime bosses. They based their power on violence, with residents and soldiers subject to torture and execution. To support their armies, they ran the kinds of businesses favored by thugs the world over: opium, gambling, prostitution, and racketeering, supplemented by heavy taxes.

During the twelve-year warlord period, the armies fought at least one hundred sixty wars that ranged in duration from a few days to two months. Individual warlords formed alliances known as cliques that constantly shifted through conquest and double-dealing so that an individual soldier could end up fighting for a series of leaders without ever changing allegiance.

The soldiers often signed on out of desperation to keep from starving, but many were kidnapped from fields and workshops and forced to serve. Receiving low and sporadic wages, the undisciplined troops resorted to pilfering and looting for survival. They preyed on the most vulnerable in the countryside, raping women, stealing crops, and commandeering livestock.

In Beijing, politicians still struggled to create a republic, but they were building a foundation on quicksand. In just twelve years, they went through eight presidents, four regent cabinets between presidents, a brief return of the Qing monarchy, five parliaments, and four constitutions.

The instability had a devastating impact on food production, business, and productivity, resulting in widespread famine and economic disaster. This atmosphere of hopelessness and disorder produced the prevailing mindset that a political resolution for China was not just impossible but preposterous, further impeding attempts to form a sovereign government.

At the same time, the lack of central authority created unprecedented intellectual freedom. Publishing and the creative arts flourished, and new political movements arose, including the Guomindang and the Communists, who failed in several attempts to unite for the good of China and would eventually fight a bloody war over the country's destiny.

The Guomindang, or National People's Party, was heir to the Tongmeng Hui. In 1912, Song Jiaoren, one of Sun Yat-sen's partners from the early days in Japan, formed the new political party and achieved swift success. To President Yuan Shikai's alarm, the Guomindang, or GMD, won a majority of seats in the General Assembly in 1913.

But just as suddenly as the GMD arose, it was stamped out. In March 1913, shortly after the election, Song was assassinated in a Shanghai train station while purchasing a ticket for a speaking tour to promote government reform that would have checked the growing power of the presidency. The party fought back under the leadership of Sun Yat-sen, who raised an army of eighty thousand with the help of the south China warlords in an attempt to overthrow Yuan, but they were crushed, and Sun fled the country.

Six years later, world politics touched off a youth rebellion, creating another opportunity for the Guomindang to assert itself.

Back in the post-Boxer Rebellion years, Germany had taken China's coastal Shandong Province. When World War I began, Japan had joined the Allies, booted the Germans out of Shandong, and occupied the province. Toward the end of the war, China declared war on Germany, hoping to win international sympathy and eventually get Shandong back. But the Allies let the Japanese keep the province, and a floundering Beijing government signed the Treaty of Versailles that sealed the deal.

When word got out on May 4, 1919, infuriated students in Beijing took to the streets, determined to settle the score with the government "traitors" who had given away a chunk of their country. Mirroring the 1911 Wuchang revolt, the riots evolved into a political movement among China's youth. Intellectual, nationalistic, and anti-Western, they inspired the working class to join them in what became known as the May Fourth Movement.

Into this arena of political evolution stepped Sun Yat-sen and the resurrected Guomindang. Sun recruited the south China warlords and formed a provisional nationalist government based in Guangzhou. By 1922, the party had one hundred fifty thousand members, but Sun's alliance with the southern warlords had fallen apart.

Sun determined that depending on warlord whims would never allow a stable government to grow. The regional rulers would have to submit to a central authority in order for a unified country to be possible. He formulated a plan to build on his southern power base, assembling a strong army with well-trained officers to drive north and oust the northern warlords, bringing their people into the new republic. He had expected that Western democracies would support his ambitions, but his appeals for foreign aid yielded nothing.

The Soviet Union was the only foreign power to respond, and it did so eagerly. Already working closely with the tiny, fledgling Chinese Communist Party, the Soviets offered Sun money and advisors in the hope of uniting the two parties. But Soviet interest in the GMD was merely a steppingstone to creating a communist state. Following a plan posited by Lenin, they intended to prop up China's so-called "bourgeois government" so that it could evict all foreign imperialists. Once that was accomplished, the Soviets' intention was to turn against Sun in favor of the proletariat to instigate a communist revolution.

WHILE SUN YAT-SEN WAS WAITING for an opening to bring back the Guomindang in 1918, Mao Zedong, the son of peasant farmers in rural Hunan Province, was experiencing a political awakening. At age twenty-five, he landed a job as an assistant at Beijing University library and fell in love with new political theory, mixing with some of the most prominent radical thinkers of the day and discovering Marxism.

Bursting with inspiration and ambition, Mao went back to Hunan Province that year and organized students, workers, and shopkeepers around the ideals of anti-Japanese nationalism and radical change. Joining the Chinese publishing renaissance, he launched and edited a political magazine, but his euphoric new life was brief. Amid rumors that the governor was cracking down on radical activists, he fled and eventually landed in Shanghai.

That city became the birthplace of the Chinese Communist Party. In July 1921, Mao gathered about a hundred budding communists at a vacant girls' academy for an organizational meeting. When the Shanghai police came snooping around, the group hurried away from the school and boarded a pleasure cruise on a lake near the city. Safely secluded on the excursion boat, they formed their party and declared its core goals: to organize the workers, dismantle the capitalist system, and establish the ruling authority of the proletariat. A pair of political advisors from the Soviet Union joined the shipboard meeting to guide the proceedings and help draft their declaration.

In stark contrast to Mao's humble roots, Zhou Enlai was born to a family of career scholar-bureaucrats whose livelihoods were shaken by the dramatic changes in China in the early twentieth century. Zhou spent the warlord years studying abroad. He discovered Marxism in secondary school in Japan and continued his political development as a college student in Paris. There he became active in the European Communist Party, organizing Chinese students and working his way up the party hierarchy in Paris and Berlin.

At its second congress in July 1922, the Chinese Communist Party still numbered only about two hundred members, but by then Soviet advisors were heavily invested in the organization. At their urging, the party passed a resolution to join the Guomindang to fight feudalism.

In 1923 as the two parties inched toward union, Sun made a speech in Hong Kong proclaiming the Three Principles of the People that are still admired by Communist and Nationalist Chinese: nationalism, the right of the people to rule themselves without intervention from other countries; democracy, giving every member of society in every region an equal voice regardless of race or class; and the people's livelihood, a concept combining workers' rights, land reform, public welfare, and a strong economy. These broad principles identified ideals under which both parties could unite.

In Berlin, Zhou Enlai took instructions from Comintern, the Moscow-based communist international congress, to call for cooperation between China's Communists and Nationalists. Shortly after that, he was elected to the GMD European Executive Committee. Mao assumed a similar office in China in January 1924 after the Nationalist convention officially made Communist Party members eligible for GMD membership.

With two of China's communist leaders firmly positioned in the nationalist party's power structure, the Soviets appeared to have achieved their goal of uniting the two parties.

DURING THIS PERIOD, the navy as the sole U.S. military presence in China answered the U.S. government's call to flex American muscle in the face of growing antiforeign sentiment. In December 1923, Sun Yat-sen threatened to seize the international customs office in Guangzhou, whose revenues were still paid to Japan and western nations for reparations some twenty years after the Boxer Rebellion. The Chinese deeply resented these punitive payments.

But the international coalition was not about to give up these payments, nor its special status in Guangzhou. Six U.S. Navy destroyers joined a multinational flotilla to quell any Chinese attack while the crisis was resolved through diplomacy.

Navy gunboats also steamed into warlord battles, uprisings, and showdowns between the Guomindang and the Communists to rescue Americans caught up in the battles. Miles's specific role in these events is unknown, but he must have experienced the turmoil in China up close during his service.

AS PART OF SUN'S CHINA UNIFICATION PLAN, the Nationalists set up Whampoa Academy in 1924 to train military officers on an island in Guangzhou, the seat of the provisional Nationalist government. Soviet support helped establish the school where Chiang Kai-shek was commandant and Zhou Enlai was deputy political director. Chiang had been groomed for the post the year before, studying Soviet political and military structure in Moscow as a guest of the Russians.

Sun Yat-sen's death from liver cancer on March 12, 1925, left the Guomindang without clear leadership. Wang Jingwei, a close ally of Sun's for twenty years since the early Tongmeng Hui days in Japan, became head of the party and the Nationalist government. But he did not command the loyalty Sun had, and by 1926, the party was clearly divided into right-wing and left-wing factions. The left wing, based in Guangzhou, included Wang, Chiang, and most of the Communists. The right wing established its own headquarters in Shanghai.

The CCP–GMD alliance had no true basis to begin with, and without Sun's unifying influence, the Soviets could not hold their construct together. Although the parties shared many lofty goals, such as ending racism, ancient superstitions, and the subjugation of women, the core of the GMD got nervous when Mao started making speeches urging the destruction of the "feudal landlord class." Some members of this class were loyal and generous party members.

A year after Sun's death, Chiang received several mysterious phone calls that revealed a Communist plot to kidnap him in Guangzhou en route to the academy and pack him off to Vladivostok. Chiang used the threat to justify an anti-Communist coup. On March 20, 1926, he placed the suspected perpetrators under arrest and had the homes of key Communist leaders and Soviet advisors surrounded. As Wang Jingwei left Paris for "vacation" and Zhou Enlai decamped to Shanghai, Chiang declared martial law and ordered telephone communication to the city cut off.

Though Chiang knew that China still needed the Russians for financial support, the incident put them on notice that he would not tolerate any political meddling. Despite cries of protest from other party members, including Sun Yat-sen's widow Soong Ching-ling, Chiang emerged the head of the Guomindang and commander of the army.

In July, Chiang Kai-shek at last realized Sun Yat-sen's long-planned goal, launching the Northern Expedition to defeat the northern warlords and reunite China. His National Republican Army was well armed by the Soviets, well trained by Whampoa graduates, and well financed by the Soviets as well as funds raised by T. V. Soong, Ching-ling's brother, from Shanghai business leaders.

Within three months, Chiang's army subdued two major warlords and arrived at the Yangtze River, with his army swelled to two hundred fifty thousand fighters.

He then turned east and entered Shanghai in March 1927. Zhou Enlai and Communist workers, elated over their recent overthrow of the ruling local warlord, welcomed him at the train station.

The Communists expected Chiang to celebrate their victory, but if he did, it was only on the surface. Chiang was alarmed by the Communist Party's strength in the city. In his eyes, the armed militia composed of euphoric workers posed a threat to civil order and the Nationalist cause. He declared martial law in Shanghai on April 5, triggering protests from unions and CCP members. He enlisted the Green Gang, an organized crime syndicate with nineteenth-century origins as a secret anti-Qing society, to stage a coordinated attack against union and CCP offices while the army arrested party leaders. Thousands of Communists were killed or arrested, and the purge spread to other cities.

In the aftermath of the Shanghai purge, the GMD was torn apart. Chiang Kai-shek established a right-wing Nationalist capital in Nanjing and headed the new government. Wang Jingwei had returned to China, making a futile call for GMD–CCP unity as tensions mounted in Shanghai. He formed a separate left-wing capital in Wuhan.

China now had three capitals: Nanjing, Wuhan, and Beijing.

Meanwhile, Wang and the Wuhan government came around to Chiang's realization that Russian support of the GMD was only a ploy; that its real mission was to ultimately overthrow the Nationalists in favor of a communist state. In July, the Wuhan GMD demanded that all members renounce Communist Party membership, leading to the final Communist–Nationalist split. The Communists withdrew to reorganize.

In autumn 1927, Wang Jingwei and Chiang Kai-shek reunited the Guomindang at its Nanjing capital under Chiang's leadership. Before the year ended, Chiang further consolidated his power through kinship in the ancient tradition, aligning himself with a wealthy and well-connected family through his marriage to Soong Mei-Ling, sister of T. V. Soong and Soong Ching-ling, Sun's widow.

As 1928 began, Chiang announced a second Northern Expedition. This time he held dual roles as heads of the Nationalist government and the Military Affairs Commission, as well as the Supreme Commander of the Army. The arduous campaign lasted two years, but in the end, China was united, and Chiang Kai-shek emerged its leader on the international stage. The title "Generalissimo" came not from the Chinese, but from the Western press, which had conferred the same title on Sun Yat-sen some ten years earlier.

But even as Chiang struggled to subdue the northern warlords, the tattered Communist Party retreated to inaccessible wilderness areas to hide out, regroup, and wait for their chance to rise again. Thousands of peasants joined the fomenting revolution, replacing the Soviet-backed urban proletariat. Mao Zedong and his followers chose the hills of Jiangxi Province in Southeastern China and established the germ of a communist republic as smaller pockets took root in other parts of the country.

The Nationalist Army under Chiang tried but failed to stamp out Mao's group through a series of thrusts into their stronghold. The Jiangxi terrain and the Communists' guerrilla tactics thwarted them until Chiang changed his approach. In 1934, he systematically constructed a series of blockhouses on hillsides to anchor a ring of troops that began to close in on Mao.

Mao and a host of one hundred thousand escaped through a gap in the encirclement in October 1934 and began the Long March that ended at Yan'an, Shaanxi Province, a year later with fewer than ten thousand. They had trekked six thousand miles, at an astonishing average pace of seventeen miles a day, for an entire year.

During the march, Mao and Zhou Enlai were carried in litters where they slept all day, working long hours every night in conferences and directing the march and the revolution. Mao emerged as the sole leader, with Zhou assuming the role of wise and learned counselor, positions they largely maintained for the rest of their lives. The march established a permanent elite cadre within the Communist Party and the government. Those who reached the end achieved mythological status, similar to the signers of the American Declaration of Independence or the original protestors who went to jail with Martin Luther King in Selma, Alabama. Regardless of later controversy and failures, their prestige and authority remained unshakable.

Although the Jiangxi company was the largest and traveled the greatest distance, other Communist groups converged on Yan'an, which became the seat of the revolution and the birthplace of the People's Republic of China.

As Chiang Kai-shek's armies rolled through the country in an attempt to put down the Communists and maintain hard-fought national unity, the Japanese seized the opportunity to press further into China. In desperate need of raw materials to support its expansion plans, Japan invaded and took possession of Manchuria in 1931 and began pressing south. The occupation rendered grave consequences for China's fledgling Nationalist government. Not only did it have to devote more resources to the military, but it also lost significant revenue from the rich province.

While Chiang devoted his energy to the pursuit of his political foes, the people in the northeast watched in horror as their cities and factories were taken over by foreign invaders.

In 1936, Chiang dispatched a northern warlord, General Zhang Xueliang, to Xi'an in Shaanxi Province to attack the Communist army. Zhang was furious that he was fighting his own countrymen at a time when they needed to unite to beat back the Japanese. He staged a coup when Chiang Kai-shek visited Xi'an in mid-December. Zhang arranged a ceasefire with the Communists and arrested Chiang, demanding that he stop the civil war and focus the military's full force against Japan. Zhou Enlai led a CCP delegation to negotiate with Zhang and Chiang's representatives for the Generalissimo's release.

In exchange for Chiang's liberty, the parties agreed that the Communists and Nationalists would form a united front against the Japanese. The CCP would cease its armed revolution and fold its armed forces in with the Nationalist army for the specific purpose of ousting Japan from China. But the Red Army, though working as part of the Nationalist force, would retain its independence as a unit.

Chiang openly wept when released to Madame Chiang and T. V. Soong on December 24, 1936, and a shaky united front put the civil war on hold. The episode known as the Xi'an Incident ended with Zhang being placed under house arrest for twenty-five years. He moved to the United States after he was freed in 1962.

ON JULY 8, 1937, the Marco Polo Bridge Incident provided the excuse for Japan and China to begin all-out war. A Japanese soldier went missing near Beijing, and his friends went to the walled town of Wanping just outside the city to find him. The Chinese occupying the garrison within the walls refused to admit them. Angry words flew, shots were fired, and a gun battle erupted between the Japanese and Chinese at the nearby Marco Polo Bridge, now called the Lugou Bridge. Miles's wife Billy witnessed the event from a nearby hotel.

With a full-scale war underway, the Chinese government moved its capital from Nanjing to Chongqing. This had disastrous economic consequences for the emerging government because its inland location separated it from important sources of revenue, such as marine customs.

For the next five years, Chiang Kai-shek scrambled for international support and tried to institute modern principles of government and education while fighting an ambitious country that had invaded his soil and watching his back against his bitter enemies turned friends. After thousands of years under monarchs and dictators, China knew no precedent for political consensus, power sharing, and multibranch government. The bureaucracy was grossly inefficient; reform programs would be assigned to committees and then disappear in a vortex of endless planning sessions. Chiang himself called the reform process "lackadaisical,"[7] and the peasantry did not support these projects. To them, crop surveys and even new bus service were ideas dreamed up by city people, bringing nothing but higher taxes to the rural population.

As a result of war and a stumbling bureaucracy, the country's financial condition grew desperate. The invasion had cost revenue, the war drained the treasury, and the country's antiquated infrastructure made everything even more expensive. China solved the problem by printing money, and inflation soared. The peasants liked it at first because they got higher prices for their produce and had little to buy compared to urbanites. But their tax burden soon outpaced any extra income. Local officials collected a seemingly endless stream of special taxes to buy sandals for the troops and to train antiaircraft specialists, among other things.

Like Yuan before him, Chiang soon recognized the country's acute inability to function without a strong hand at the top. He made more and more decisions personally and assumed authority befitting the title conferred on him by romanticizing journalists.

MILES WITNESSED SOME OF THIS tumultuous history first-hand during two tours of duty in China in the 1920s and 1930s. After he came home to Washington in 1939, China remained ever-present for him through his coffee circle at the office and after-dinner conversations with Xiao Bo at home. By the time he returned to China in 1942, the united front was five years old, and suspicions had mounted on both sides. No coordinated military program had been developed. The Communists remained in Yan'an, and the Nationalists in Chongqing. Each side nominally fought the occupation while steeling themselves for the real battle to come.

CHAPTER 4

Dai Li and Milton Miles

THE SINO–AMERICAN COOPERATIVE ORGANIZATION could not have existed without cooperation between its two principals, General Dai Li of the Republican Chinese Army's Military Bureau of Investigation and Statistics and Captain Milton Miles of the U.S. Navy. For both men, everything was riding on the success of the Sino–American Cooperative Organization and therefore on the collaboration. This powerful motivation inspired them to build a genuine partnership without so much as a common language between them.

Before they met, both men received information about the other from a third party, and the manner in which each reacted to it reveals dramatic differences in their characters and environments.

Dai Li had reason to think the best of Milton Miles from the beginning, having learned everything he knew about him from a trusted agent, Colonel Xiao Bo. Xiao discovered in Miles an open-minded, straight shooter with a deep respect for China and an earnest desire to work with the Chinese toward a common cause. But in spite of this glowing report from his own hand-picked source, Dai still dealt with Miles as if he were a scheming, suspicious character. He secretly made Miles prove himself before admitting him into his circle.

In contrast, Milton Miles had to rely entirely on the U.S. State Department's blood-curdling account of Dai Li as a suspicious, implacable killer. But because certain details in the dossier did not ring true, Miles discounted the lot and, though wary, decided to judge Dai on personal experience rather than the reports of others. Observing Dai's intellect, management skill, and gracious manners, Miles soon discarded his doubts and became his greatest champion.

UPON FIRST MEETING DAI LI, Miles was struck by the trait that everyone who had ever described him mentioned: penetrating, wide-set, black eyes. His authoritative carriage conveyed strength far beyond his average height and frame and contrasted with his tiny, absurdly delicate hands. He wore impeccable, high-collared uniforms buttoned to the throat. His wiry hair was tamed with a trim cut combed back from his face, which featured a prominent, wide nose, broad, straight mouth, and dark complexion. His rare smile revealed a row of gold front teeth.

Dai Li was born Dai Chunfeng in the mountain village of Baoan, Jiangshan County, Zhejiang Province on May 28, 1897, the eldest of three children. He changed his name to Dai Li when he entered Whampoa Academy in 1926. His father struggled in business, probably not helped by his proclivities for gaming tables and prostitutes, and his mother, Lan Yuexi, supported the family as a seamstress.

Dai and his mother shared mutual devotion that endured until Dai's death in 1946. By then, she was more than eighty years old. Charles Miles, Milton's son, recounts that no one could bear to tell her that her beloved son was gone. Instead, they said he had gone to America with Miles, who perpetuated the compassionate deceit by writing to her from the United States with "news" about her son. However, among Miles's archived personal papers is a condolence letter that he wrote to her after Dai's death. Either the story is a charming fable or Miles never sent the sympathy letter.

Thanks to his mother's prodding and despite a penchant for getting into trouble, Dai graduated first in his class from elementary school in 1913 and was a favorite among his classmates. By then, he had developed his father's tastes for gambling and sex adventures, but ambition and patriotism would overcome them. The next year, he married at age seventeen and soon had a son and a daughter, but he spent very little time with his wife, who died in 1939.

In later years, he claimed that Communist thugs had kicked his teeth out, but his biographer, Frederic Wakeman, believed it more likely that a youthful Dai was beaten up for cheating in a card game.

After a brief stint in a regional army that ended when he was seriously wounded in a battle between warlords, Dai went to Shanghai to seek his fortune when he was in his early twenties. He slept on the floor of his cousin's apartment and frequently washed his only suit of clothes in the river, hiding his nakedness in the water while his things dried on nearby rocks.

During these years "living off the land" in Shanghai, he discovered the writings of Sun Yat-sen, the founding father of modern China and inspiration of the spirit of nationalism then sweeping the country. The texts awakened Dai's patriotism, forming his belief in a united China governed under Sun's principles. He met a group of Nationalist army officers, including Chiang Kai-shek, who let him hang around and run errands for tips.

A few years later, he took the examination for admission to Whampoa Academy in Guangzhou at a friend's suggestion. Dai was accepted and enrolled in the sixth class as a cavalry officer trainee. He renewed his acquaintance with Chiang Kai-shek, the academy's commandant. Dai was deeply inspired by Chiang's charisma and intelligence and made it his goal to enter the commandant's inner circle.

Communists and Nationalists were equally allowed membership of the Guomindang at that time, and the academy included a significant Communist presence. Dai shared Chiang's intense anti-Communist ideology. He infiltrated the academy's Communist and Russian circles and began feeding Chiang unsolicited intelligence reports about the political leanings of his fellow cadets. A professor complained that Dai seemed to spend all his time writing letters instead of doing his classroom work, unaware that Dai was writing to the commandant, who had come to rely on the reports.

Dai left the academy before graduating to join the Northern Expedition as an advance intelligence officer, writing letters to Chiang in invisible ink about safe travel routes and the political climate of various localities.

After the campaign, he followed Chiang to Nanjing. Through an old friend, he got a job at the Whampoa Academy Alumni Association as an intelligence researcher and became the head of Chiang's bodyguards in the winter of 1927–28.

As he had done at the academy, Dai took it upon himself to spy on Chiang's political opponents and slip reports to him. After Chiang began paying Dai for his "special extra work," Dai recruited agents and paid them with the funds he received from Chiang. His freelance spy agency eventually grew to a hundred employees, forming the Special Services Department within the Bureau of Investigation and Statistics in 1932.

Dai Li joined a small group of star Whampoa alumni who formed the secret Society of Vigorous Practice of the Three People's Principles, or Lixingshe. Based on intense, emotional devotion to Chiang Kai-shek and to China, members swore absolute loyalty to him at inaugural meetings at his residence in February 1932. While other inductees made long, flowery speeches professing their allegiance, Dai Li demonstrated his as head of security, listening restlessly to the orations when not roaming the estate on the alert for possible intruders.

Chiang had intended for the circle to be a source of quality, dedicated assistants, but he was frustrated over three-hour meetings during which the members jockeyed for position with passionate words. Though a junior member, Dai Li rose to the top because he was a doer, not a talker. The Generalissimo saw quickly that Dai accomplished what was needed, often without being asked.

Dai ultimately became chief of the entire Military Bureau of Investigation and Statistics, Nationalist China's number one intelligence kingpin, and Chiang's most trusted deputy. Other Lixingshe members went on to hold key positions of authority in the Guomindang, the military, the government, and commerce, but none achieved power equal to Dai's.

He was the only person Chiang would receive anywhere at any hour and the only one who was permitted to carry a firearm in his presence. Chiang nicknamed Dai "Rain Hat," a nod to his knack for shielding the Generalissimo in times of trouble.

Dai grew the BIS into an international spy organization with agents everywhere China had interests, including India, Indochina, Japan, and the United States. In 1938, the bureau was placed within the GMD as the Military Affairs Commission Bureau of Investigation and Statistics, known as the MBIS.

The MBIS was a unique institution, a combined Secret Service, FBI, CIA, and Gestapo. Estimates of the number of agents run as high as three hundred thousand, but these include anyone who shared information or acted on Dai's behalf, including village mayors who aided traveling SACOs and people like Xiao Bo, who was a diplomat as well as Dai Li's representative in Washington, D.C. While many of these agents had other professional careers, it is safe to say that tens of thousands of people were exclusively on the MBIS full-time payroll.

Dai also headed guerrilla army forces. In August 1937 when the Sino–Japanese war was a month old, Japanese forces pressing on Shanghai had expected to take the city in a matter of days. But Dai Li and his deputies organized shopkeepers, criminal gangs, students, and workers into a force of snipers and urban guerrillas who fought off the Japanese for three months. Though eventually routed, two thousand were reorganized outside the city and trained as the Loyal Patriotic Army. The LPA became a key component of the SACO-trained guerrillas, harassing Japanese forces in the northeast for the rest of the war. Dai built on his experience with the LPA and SACO training to organize specialized guerrilla columns throughout China.

Dai's authority was effective but brutal. He tolerated no insubordination, and with constant enemy infiltration of the MBIS, he was ever on the lookout for traitors. He expected the same uncompromising loyalty to himself as he bestowed on Chiang Kai-shek. Mistakes could cost his agents verbal reprimand, imprisonment, or execution, depending on their severity. The biographer Wakeman estimates that during the course of his reign, Dai had two thousand of his own agents killed. But every agent knew the rules and broke them at their peril; there was nothing arbitrary about these punishments. In a bizarre twist on patriotism, Dai would order the executions and then preside over ceremonies honoring those he had killed as heroes who had given their lives for the sake of the bureau's integrity.

His devotion to the Generalissimo was exceeded only by his love for his country. As long as Japan occupied China, he would not permit single MBIS agents to marry, insisting that they should not know the joyful state of matrimony as long as their country remained in peril. But that did not prohibit sex, which Dai considered as necessary to human existence as food and shelter. Indeed, a string of notorious affairs prompted married male subordinates to keep Dai from meeting their wives. Dai was genuinely surprised when Miles turned down his offer to supply American SACOs with prostitutes.

As chief of the Bureau of Investigation and Statistics, Dai oversaw a staff of assassins who carried out killings ordered by Chiang. A typical target was Zhang Jingyao, a northern warlord who was caught taking bribes from the Japanese in 1933. Dai assigned a highly disciplined, ultrapatriotic Whampoa Academy graduate, Bai Shiwei, to carry out the deed. Bai burst into Zhang's suite in an elegant Beijing hotel and shot him in front of his horrified lover, and then calmly walked away from the scene as hotel employees responded to the companion's screams.

Dai Li's suspicious nature was one detail in the U.S. State Department's profile of him that rang true for Miles, but it served the general well in a chaotic place and time. Growing up under a fragmented government, complete with expedient but rancorous political coalitions and a relentless stream of coups and deadly double-crosses, Dai always suspected that people were concealing their true agendas. To ferret out traitors real or imagined, he assigned some of his employees to spy on others, creating what amounted to an informal secret agency within his official secret agency.

His suspicions prompted him to cultivate an aura of mystery, in part for the sake of his own security, since he was a perpetual target of assassination attempts by the Japanese, Communists, and political rivals. He avoided being photographed, never spoke in public, and refused to speak to journalists. During official meetings, he sometimes sat silently in a dark corner and disappeared without a word. To keep his whereabouts a secret, he owned at least a dozen homes scattered throughout the country, including three in Chongqing, and only a handful of people knew where he was sleeping on a given night.

Although mysterious, Dai Li's reputation for ruthlessness was known all over China. The public also knew him as "the Boss," and his name became a trump card to get thieves to hand over stolen goods or children to behave. In the popular culture, he was the Boogey Man, the universal monster.

Dai possessed tremendous physical and mental stamina, often working for days without sleep, yet remaining attentive and sharp. His prodigious memory, extreme intelligence, courage, and self-discipline fueled his rise from Shanghai street person to one of China's most powerful men.

This multifaceted man struck terror in his political and military opponents, inspired affection and loyalty in his friends, and impressed his American partners with his ability to accomplish near miracles out of nothing.

Maochun Yu, professor of East Asia and military history at the U.S. Naval Academy and a leading expert on twentieth-century China, summed up China's mystery man like this: "Dai Li was not lily white by any stretch of the imagination, but as a military intelligence man, he was very effective."[8] Frederic Wakeman ends his exhaustive biography of Dai with the confession that, after ten years of research, he still cannot categorically state whether Dai was a good or a bad man.[9]

At one of many banquets Dai threw for the American SACOs at Happy Valley, he made an emotional speech about his complicated reputation. Referring to a critical, oft-repeated moniker, "the Himmler of China," and insisting that he believed firmly in democracy, he said, "I am not a Himmler. I am the Generalissimo's Dai Li and nothing more."

WHILE DAI EXUDED AN AURA of intensity to all who met him, Rear Admiral Milton E. Miles struck new acquaintances as a relaxed, pleasant fellow. Even as his brown curls began to gray, he had a boyish look about him. With warm brown eyes that lit up with his ready smile, he looked more like a charming salesman than the leader of a spy network. Though always impeccably groomed, he was most at home in the relaxed, khaki uniform of SACO.

He was born Milton Edward Robbins on April 6, 1900, in Jerome, Arizona, the only child of Louis Robbins and Mae Belle Cook. Mae Belle became a bride at age fifteen and a mother at sixteen, and Louis was more than twice her age. When Milton was a baby, Mae Belle's widowed father and her four younger siblings lived with them. Louis, a sawyer at a lumber mill, had helped Mae Belle's two brothers, ages fifteen and eleven, get jobs there.

Like Dai, Miles missed out on having a steady father figure to emulate early in life. His father drank heavily and died before Milton was five years old. By the time he was ten, he and his mother had moved to San Bernardino, California, leaving the rest of the family behind in Arizona.

As Milton entered his teens, his mother married George A. Miles, and the family moved to Seattle. Though Milton took his stepfather's last name, the two had a troubled start, and Milton ran away at age fourteen, around the time his half-brother George was born. Things must have settled down after that, since Miles went on to attend Broadway High School in Seattle.

But the affairs of the world distracted the adventurous youth from his studies. After teetering on the brink of war for nearly three years, the United States finally joined the Allies in the Great War, declaring war on Germany on Miles's seventeenth birthday, April 6, 1917. Five days later, he joined the U.S. Navy and was stationed at Fort Ward, just across Puget Sound from Seattle. During his first year, he served aboard the cruiser USS *Saratoga* in the Pacific and also got a taste of the war in Europe protecting convoys in the Atlantic on the destroyer USS *Beale* out of Queensbury, Ireland.

Miles must have distinguished himself, because he was invited to attend the United States Naval Academy in Annapolis, Maryland, entering in June 1918. There he received his lifelong nickname "Mary." He graduated in June 1922, commissioned as an ensign, but soon was promoted to Lieutenant Junior Grade.

His first postacademy assignment was with the Asiatic Station patrolling China's coastline and rivers, where he served on five vessels in five years. During his off-duty hours, he explored the port towns and hiked the riverbanks, falling in love with the landscape, the Chinese people, and their culture and learning a bit of Cantonese and Mandarin. He often cringed watching boorish Americans and Europeans who treated the Chinese like unruly children and demanded respect they hadn't earned.

Among his accomplishments was a precursor to the radio network he was to create two decades later. He built the first shortwave radio in China, which was powered by a motorcycle engine and was strong enough to reach Texas.

In 1925, his fiancée, Wilma Sinton Jerman, had just graduated from Cornell when she sailed from California to meet him in Hong Kong, though they hadn't seen each other in three years. Their long, intermittent courtship had begun while he was a midshipman at the Naval Academy and she was a high school girl vacationing with her family on the shores of Chesapeake Bay. They were married with the American Consul as witness on September 4, the day after she landed in Hong Kong, where she lived for the next two years. The couple, known incongruously as Mary and Billy, toured China together whenever Miles had shore leave.

In 1927, Miles was called back stateside to study electrical engineering, receiving a master's degree at Columbia University in 1929. At the same time, Billy got her master's at Columbia in nutrition communication.

After a few years of administrative engineering jobs in Washington, D.C., Miles was at sea again as executive officer of the USS *Wilkes,* where he first flew his famous "What the Hell?" pennant.

That dangerous but effective prank demonstrated his creative thinking, a talent that qualified him for the SACO mission eight years later. Indeed, his willingness to throw out the rulebook would emerge when Admiral King assigned Captain Jeff Metzel as SACO's behind-the-scenes officer in Washington. Miles would heartily approve the appointment because he had admired Metzel's past use of unorthodox methods to accomplish objectives when necessary.

Miles and Billy were delighted when, in 1936, he was reassigned to the Asiatic Fleet. Now the parents of three young boys, they moved to Yantai, China, spending winters in Manila. Billy and the children traveled all over Asia with and without Miles. He was at sea when Billy witnessed the opening salvos of the Sino–Japanese War at the Marco Polo Bridge near Beijing in the wee hours of July 8, 1937.

When Miles was assigned to the Interior Control Board in Washington in 1939, the family decided to make an adventure of the return trip to the United States, taking as much of it as they could overland. Against the advice of everyone they knew, they hired a truck and rode five hundred bone-rattling miles over the newly opened Burma Road between Kunming and Lashio. It was an experience they shared forever.

Miles's record proved to the navy leadership that he was the right man for a job that would have to be invented on the fly. He was intelligent, flexible, and determined, always ready to solve problems with humor, inventiveness, and courage. Xiao saw another quality just as important: his understanding, respect, and even love for China.

DAI AND MILES HAD LITTLE IN COMMON, but the genuine friendship they forged is the miracle that made the Sino–American Cooperative Organization possible.

In the beginning, the alliance was entirely pragmatic. Each man needed something from the other on orders from his superiors, and Miles realized quickly that cultivating a relationship with Dai, who reputedly disdained foreigners, was perhaps his most important task. Even Stilwell, who firmly objected to Dai and his tactics, acknowledged that there was no substitute for the personal connection Miles had achieved with the man. It was absolutely essential to American interests in China.

The first trip Dai and Miles took together in the summer of 1942 laid the groundwork for mutual trust. Miles observed Dai's skill, authority, and professionalism, as well as the surprising kindness he demonstrated while working with his agents in Pucheng and dealing with an enemy spy. At the same time, Miles proved that he could endure hardship graciously and that he was courageous, decisive, and reliable. Dai later told Miles that his brief shootout with the Japanese patrol near Xiamen was "the most important gun battle SACO ever fought." Even though Dai did not witness it, the reports he received assured him that Miles was a man who could be trusted.

Without that groundwork, their relationship might not have survived the nearly disastrous arrival of the OSS. In September 1942, Dai began quizzing Miles about Americans he had never heard of, including OSS agents who had not even arrived yet and two men traveling with internationalist and informal ambassador-at-large Wendell Willkie on a fact-finding mission for President Roosevelt. Accustomed to double crosses, Dai assumed that Miles was feigning ignorance and concealing information.

When it finally came out that Dai Li had learned of Miles's appointment to the OSS before Miles had himself, Miles took quick action to reassure his partner.

OSS chief William Donovan had dispatched China scholar Dr. Joseph Hayden to implement the Dragon Plan, a secret OSS intelligence and guerrilla-training operation that paralleled SACO, though using army personnel. The plan was a slap in the face to Dai and Chiang, who knew about it through their own sources but had been neither asked nor informed by the Americans. Moreover, Hayden had been an invited speaker at the Chongqing headquarters of a Korean group that Dai suspected of collaborating with the Japanese. Dai was furious about it.

Miles exercised his new authority as Far East Coordinator of the OSS by asking for and receiving Hayden's removal and putting a freeze on the Dragon Plan. Furthermore, he let Donovan know that he had to be more careful about whom he sent to Chongqing. White supremacy was out, and so were old China hands. To make sure Dai Li got the message, Miles wrote him a letter with full details.

The incident highlights a difference between Dai and Miles that could have been insurmountable. Miles was utterly naïve of such political underhandedness, while Dai suspected it even when it wasn't there. But once Miles discovered it, he made it his mission to prove which side he was on, and it worked.

Indeed, the whole world of espionage was new to Miles, and he was rather smitten by it. Though exceedingly difficult, the job before him turned out to be fun.

If their life experiences and worldviews were vastly different, Miles and Dai had important things in common. Both were men of action who had overcome seemingly impossible challenges. They also shared a commitment to the job before them.

As SACO grew, Miles and Dai traveled all over China together, often sleeping in the same room. Though they spoke through Eddie Liu, their conversations became intimate. They shared details of their troubled childhoods and worries about their children. Miles was a guest in the home of Dai's mother, whom few people, Western or Chinese, had ever met.

Little by little, Miles discarded the horrific reports he had heard about Dai Li. During the winter of 1945 in Xifeng, Miles went to visit the site of a notorious GMD concentration camp he had read about in the State Department file. It looked more like a refugee camp to him. The people he saw looked healthy and well dressed, and they exchanged greeting bows with Dai. They were allowed to come and go, although they had to identify themselves to get back in past armed guards who claimed to be stationed there solely to keep unwanted intruders out.

Miles acknowledged that the visit could have been a setup, but if so, it was a good one hastily arranged. When he later spoke to Theodore White, a *Time* magazine correspondent who had written about the concentration camps, White said he had never actually seen one but had learned about them from a trusted informant. Miles's critics have often said that he was easily duped, but he witnessed brutal punishments and executions of soldiers and civilians, as did many rank-and-file Americans of SACO. It is probable that he saw much more than he ever revealed, but he maintained to the end that Dai Li was not the monster portrayed in intelligence reports and the press.

PART 3

SACO From the Ground Up

CHAPTER 5

Building the Rice Paddy Navy

THE RICE PADDY NAVY BEGAN a few months after Pearl Harbor as a mission of one. By August 1945, 2,694 members of the U.S. armed forces, mostly navy along with about a hundred marines and a handful of army officers, had served in Naval Group China, the official name of the American contingent of the Sino–American Cooperative Organization. Of these, some thousand men got only as far as Kolkata toward the end of the war.

In fall 1942, Captain Milton Miles thought about the men who soon would be hiking the Chinese mountain paths with him and training Dai Li's army, and he decided to avoid bringing in any "old China hands." These were the Western company men and government bureaucrats who had embarrassed him with their patronizing behavior in the 1920s as he patrolled China's coasts and rivers and toured the countryside with his wife. These men thought they knew better than the Chinese themselves what was good for China, and at one time, the Chinese had believed them.

But the prevailing mindset had completely reversed as China struggled to shake off a century of chaos and build a modern society. With the new patriotism came resentment for these relics of the Opium Wars. Justified or not, the Chinese painted the old hands with a broad brush as exploitative racists.

Now the old China hands were all over Washington, D.C., peddling their expertise and hoping to land jobs in the war effort. And Miles wanted no part of them. He had no doubt that there were plenty of earnest, respectful, talented, and patriotic people among them who could serve SACO well, but he did not believe the Chinese, especially Dai Li, would ever accept them. Moreover, he was not about to risk bringing in experts who might turn out to be know-it-alls capable of destroying the delicate partnership he had forged. Instead, Miles preferred to start with men who had no prior knowledge of China and train them his way.

Captain Jeffrey Metzel, SACO coordinator in Washington, understood Miles's position, but advised him to soften a bit about allowing old China hands into the group. They could be useful, Metzel had argued, and they comprised the majority of the OSS force General William Donovan wanted to deploy. Miles paid lip service to Metzel but ultimately stuck to his original policy, which would contribute to the OSS–SACO rupture of the following year.

Miles described his ideal candidate to Metzel. He wanted to recruit men who were "solid" but "a little crazy." He was looking for adventurous, talented, adaptable people who could withstand both hardship without becoming resentful and frustration without growing discouraged. And they had to do it all willingly.

He needed men who were mission oriented rather than process oriented. Someone who worked best following regulations right out the window would not be able to function in the freewheeling outfit he meant to build.

"No high-hat, red tape clerks allowed," he wrote to Metzel.

Another specification he made at first never held up. Miles had originally planned to forbid drinking alcohol and to recruit men willing to abstain. While he was known to enjoy an occasional drink, he particularly abhorred the phrase "drunken sailor" and hoped to prevent any problems with alcohol. But judging from the stories SACOs told about the cups of wine they were expected to gulp down at Dai's parties, that idea must have been abandoned rather early on. No one ever mentioned hiding alcohol from Miles. In fact, one navy storekeeper was designated official procurer of the beverages at his camp because he knew how to find quality products and had a gift for negotiating prices. Nevertheless, Miles's men would be working too remotely to expect highballs at 5:00 p.m. and nightclubs where they could blissfully fritter away their paychecks; anyone unable to suffer such hardship was better off elsewhere.

Booze and bars weren't the only things SACO men would have to do without. Miles's team would have to go long stretches without coffee, chocolate, and big band music. He needed people who could live in China as it was and not expect America to be flown over the Hump for their pleasure.

Superior job skills were essential, too. Sentinels perched on lonely crags on the coast and technicians launching weather instruments on wind-blown plateaus would need to be resourceful and able to double-up on duties. And with no one to back them up, they would have to be able to deliver results on their own. One qualification, therefore, was for each man to have more than one job skill and perhaps a useful hobby.

In other words, Miles was looking for men in his own image, although he never said so. He was a man who had hoisted a homemade pennant and sailed boldly into a foreign seaport under enemy bombardment, traveled against expert advice with three little boys over the remote Burma Road while it was still under construction, and promised Dai Li that the United States would make an army out of thousands of farmers and shopkeepers without so much as a telegram to his boss in Washington asking for advice or permission. He was an electrical engineer, an administrator, and an amateur photographer who processed film in his bathroom sink. He was irreverent, fearless, versatile, and multitalented, but simultaneously squeaky clean.

With a few hundred more men just like himself, he could deliver everything General Dai Li and Admiral Ernest King had asked for.

Finally, the recruits also had to be congenial: slow to anger, quick to forgive, and willing to tackle any task without bruised egos. Owing to limited personnel and resources, the operation could not afford squabbles. Moreover, given that Chinese culture did not tolerate overt complaints and criticism, they would have to be able to suppress American-style conflict resolution in favor of a more measured and gradual approach.

"One sour grape spoils a whole bowl of rice," Miles said, paraphrasing a Chinese proverb.

MILES TOOK A FRUSTRATING TOUR of India in the summer of 1942 trying to locate his first shipment of supplies, but got little cooperation from army supply managers. The cities were jam-packed with the kind of men Miles wanted to keep out of his outfit in China. In the hotels, American military officers bullied the Indian staff over being served honey instead of maple syrup with their pancakes. The war seemed to be a second or third priority to everyone he met.

While in New Delhi, he took a phone call from Lieutenant Daniel Webster "Webb" Heagy, a radio expert who had just arrived in Karachi with six radiomen and was reporting to Miles for duty. Miles, discouraged by what he had witnessed in India, bluntly told him that they had better expect Spartan living conditions in China.

"There must be a war on," said Heagy.

His sporting, upbeat reply buoyed Miles, and Heagy turned out to be even better than his first impression. He had experience in both radio intercept and medicine, having served in the Navy Hospital Corps. He wasn't a physician, but he had excellent nursing skills, and for the first six months, he was all they had. He took on the challenge with relish. The seven newcomers set up quarters and offices in Miles's house for a few weeks before moving to Happy Valley on October 1, 1942.

On moving day, they set up a radio receiver complete with a direction finder fashioned from extra buggy-whip antennas and oil drums. Within hours, they were monitoring Japanese messages. SACO would later add three more radio direction finders at camps hundreds of miles away, allowing triangulation to identify the messages' points of origin. These special radio stations were closely guarded, allowing only a handful of people access to each, and the camp personnel knew to steer clear.

By the end of November, SACO's ranks had swollen to fifteen, including Lieutenant Commander Edward Gilfillan, a Ph.D. in mechanical engineering with special expertise in explosives and chemistry, on top of being a long-distance swimmer. Three aerologists formed the nucleus of what was to become a network of more than seventy weather stations. One of them, Lieutenant Commander Raymond Kotrla, stayed almost to the end of the war and made himself useful nearly every waking hour. When he wasn't gathering weather data, he took over Miles's bathroom darkroom and later trained Chinese recruits in aerology and marksmanship. Nearly every SACO became a teacher in one way or another.

Each new arrival had the skills necessary to perform one of SACO's missions: weather reporting, radio and ground intelligence, coast watches, mines and sabotage, and training Chinese recruits. Eventually, physicians and chaplains arrived to tend to the medical and spiritual needs of the men, but after the war, Miles regretted that he had not included them in that first handful in 1942. The first three navy doctors made it to China in May 1943, but en route, their plane had crash-landed in Nigeria, and all their medical equipment was lost.

By war's end, SACO included an astonishing array of exceptional men with multiple skills and outstanding physical fitness. Lieutenant Seth I. Morris served at first as executive housekeeper at Happy Valley, supervising everything from installation of bathroom fixtures to a Christmas party for orphans. Later, he established surveillance operations along the coast and taught Chinese radiomen to separate the chaff from the wheat in Japanese code interceptions. An architect in peacetime, he designed the buildings and layout for SACO's sixth training camp, which he commanded. On top of all this, he was a navy-trained underwater demolition expert.

Lieutenant Dr. Lloyd McPherson Felmly was perhaps the Navy's only physician who was also a certified deep-sea diver. Motor Machinists Mate First Class Irvin Sheffer knew many trades, but contrary to the old saw, he was master of them all. In addition to being a first-rate mechanic, he was an electrician, carpenter, machinist, and horseman. He traveled all over China to keep SACO's precious generators running. Although Lieutenant John Ryder Horton claimed to have only average talents in his memoir, *Ninety-Day Wonder*, he served as a supply officer, managed the communications office in Chongqing, trained Chinese troops, planned and executed sabotage raids on Japanese targets, and commanded a SACO camp. He went on to a career in the CIA after the war.

As the group grew, Miles established a code of conduct that would become an integral part of a training program in Kolkata and at Happy Valley. It was primarily a list of don'ts that, while covering only a handful of situations, offered a model for appropriate behavior in China. The men were forbidden to say "Chinaman" or "coolie." They were not to shout or use "pidgin English" to break language barriers. Wisecracks referring to American food and utensils as "civilized" were neither funny nor accurate, and the Chinese did not read "from the back of the book."

But perhaps most important, the Americans were never to display any form of anger or impatience with the Chinese. There was always another way to get the job done, and it was up to the SACOs to find it. The few men who couldn't get along with each other and the locals were sent back to India or the United States. Miles was proud that SACO never needed a brig.

These rules opened a window to cultural sensitivity that seems obvious in the twenty-first century, but in the 1940s, it was unheard of. Most of the recruits had never encountered a Chinese person before, other than perhaps in a Chinese restaurant or in an urban Chinatown. SACO's critics—and there were many, as later chapters will show—accused Miles of being naïve to China's political intrigues or of "going native." But in his mind, he was deferring to Chinese values and sovereignty as he believed Americans would expect if, say, a Mexican force were invited to work in Washington, D.C. Miles's mission and the lives of his crew depended on complete acceptance by their Chinese partners. As outnumbered foreigners, he reasoned that it was his group's job to adapt.

Another thing the men were taught was absolute secrecy. Their plain army khakis provided anonymity, and they were warned not to discuss SACO and its mission with anyone, including other American service personnel and diplomats.

New arrivals received this cultural indoctrination at Kolkata and Happy Valley. In June 1945, when it appeared that a large influx of new men was imminent, SACO established a special school, Camp Hank Gibbons, for this training. It was designed to teach classes of three hundred men during a twelve-day course that could be condensed to six if deployment was urgent. The camp was twenty miles south of Kunming, where all SACOs landed after flying over the Hump.

In contrast to his strict conduct code, Miles encouraged a decidedly informal tenor within Happy Valley and the later camps. In part to stay under the Japanese radar, he relaxed the normal military discipline with all its attendant differentiations of rank. Officers and enlisted men, Americans and Chinese, were deliberately mixed in the mess hall. Promoted to captain in November 1942 and commodore a year later, Miles still asked the men to call him Mary, although some of them were never comfortable with it and had to fight the urge to salute.

In his book, *A Different Kind of War,* Miles summed up the SACO culture:

We hoisted no flag. We sounded no calls. We practiced no salutes and wore what was handy. We walked, hiked, and scrambled, but we never marched. It was a place to forget spit and polish but never cleanliness, to forget rank but not discipline.

In summer, the men walked around shirtless and in shorts when not teaching. Miles personally led a short fitness ascent up a rocky trail every morning. But contrary to what he wrote, Miles and the SACO men did in fact hoist one flag: The "What the Hell?" pennant flew bravely over Happy Valley for four years.

MEN LANDED IN SACO from naval bases across the United States. Each one volunteered in writing for "prolonged, hazardous, distant duty," although they were well into their preparations before they knew where they were headed and why.

In one instance, a communications officer serving in Washington, D.C., had to pass an interview with the Chinese ambassador to the United States before he was approved. In another, unusual dexterity with the telegraph key earned a seaman at the navy's Memphis radio school a ticket to China with a stopover in Hawaii for a crash course in Chinese.

At the age of twenty-six, a self-taught mechanical engineer from Chicago who had enlisted as a chief shipfitter already boasted nine years of supervisory experience in metal shops. The navy tapped his leadership talents as a company commander for raw recruits at Camp Peary, Virginia, before sending him to Fort Pierce, Florida, to train frogmen in underwater demolitions. There, he stepped up for hazardous duty and, after Chinese language lessons, traveled alone by sea to India. Soon, he was in China instructing soldiers on the finer points of blowing things up.

An ensign from Oklahoma in the navy's exclusive Scouts and Raiders unit, forerunners of the modern Navy SEALs, had already served in Europe when he was asked to report to Washington for a new clandestine and hazardous assignment. He waited at the Ambassador Hotel downtown for a call to the Chief of Naval Operations office. The aura of secrecy was palpable as he walked down a long corridor to a locked door. He knocked and was admitted into a small, sparse room with a single window and another door. Knocking again, he was admitted and given orders for China.

A pair of identical twins, Coxswains Keith Allen and Johnny Lough, volunteered for SACO at age eighteen in hopes of staying together after boot camp. They were both accepted. Having different last names allowed them to circumvent the U.S. Armed Forces rule against siblings serving in the same unit. The twins had been separated as toddlers when their desperately poor family was forced to give them up for adoption. At thirteen, Allen and Lough were reunited at a basketball tournament in their native West Virginia, and after graduating from high school, they joined the navy.

They managed to stay together as far as Kolkata until Allen flew over the Hump in July 1945 without his brother and reported to Happy Valley awaiting a field assignment. Lough went over the Hump a couple of weeks later and was assigned a mission directly from Kunming, but he landed in the hospital with amoebic dysentery. Meanwhile, Ensign Donald Miller, who worked at Happy Valley, had business in Kunming. Upon arrival, he was stunned to find Allen, whom he had just left in Happy Valley, lying in a Kunming hospital. After Lough explained that he was Allen's brother, Miller arranged for the twins to serve together at Happy Valley.

Allen and Lough became personal assistants to Milton Miles at House Number One and served him there until the war ended.

AT FORT PIERCE, THE RIGOROUS TRAINING PROGRAM of the Scouts and Raiders developed the unique skills Miles was looking for. Physical conditioning included swimming, bodybuilding, and running obstacle courses. Trainees shimmied up ropes to the tops of trees and crawled on their bellies through swampy woods. To build strength and teamwork, they lay on their backs in a row of half a dozen men with their heads touching a thick, fifteen-foot log. Together, they hoisted it above their heads, down to their chests, and back over their heads to the ground.

They trained in hand-to-hand combat and stealth, sneaking up behind a lone enemy and "killing" him without making a sound. Communications training included basic signaling and the use of short-wave radios. They studied silhouettes of Japanese and Chinese ships and learned to identify landmarks in the dark. A favorite exercise was to paddle rubber boats out into the ocean at night, then land at a pinpoint location on the beach.

One pair assigned to "take" a beach at night did not count on a coast guard security officer on horseback who had no knowledge of the exercise. The trainees had anchored a kayak offshore and were swimming for the beach when the equestrian appeared. They might have escaped notice, but the horse detected them. The next thing they knew, they were under arrest and being held in the town jail.

The most demanding part of the course was "Hell Week," now a legendary aspect of Navy SEAL training. It consisted of a stepped-up program of vigorous physical conditioning and stressful military exercises in the wild with only four hours of rest per day for five days. After that experience, they were ready to tackle physical and mental challenges in the field, but most of them were never put to the test.

In spring 1945, about a thousand of these specially trained men, known as Amphibious Roger, got only as far as Kolkata, due to political squabbles between the army and the navy.* Of these, a few teams made it to China, where they mapped and photographed the coast and rivers in preparation for the planned invasion of China that became unnecessary when Japan surrendered.

Twenty men from the Navy Storekeepers School in Toledo had already been trained in tasks such as payroll and inventory when they volunteered for prolonged, hazardous duty. Their destiny shrouded in mystery, they flew to Washington and hung around an army barracks for a couple of weeks before boarding a truck. Canvas flaps were secured to the truck to prevent them from seeing where they were going. After an hour's ride, they emerged at an isolated camp in the woods. The only others there were support staff and instructors.

The training program over the next three weeks seemed absurd for a group of men destined for bookkeeping and handing out supplies. They rose every day at 5:00 a.m. for a mile-long run, followed by fitness drills, marksmanship, map and compass reading, snowshoeing, and kayaking. They demolished buildings and uprooted railroad tracks with plastic explosives. They were dropped off in the woods several miles from camp on a moonless night to find their way back, guided only by a compass with a luminous dial.

*Their story is told in Chapter Nine.

When the program was complete, they returned to Washington and were questioned individually by members of the State Department. Only then did they learn that their orders were for Chongqing.

Chief Radioman Edwin Ritter, a volunteer out of Boston, trained later at the same camp. At the end of the course, his group was treated to dinner in a Chinese restaurant in the city, where it was announced they were on their way to China.

Another radioman had a one-day course in parachute jumping in case he had to be dropped from an airplane for duty. His plane landed in Kunming the conventional way, but the shipfitter from Chicago had to parachute in carrying orders with no details other than "Unit Two, China," and instructions to follow his verbal orders.

Secrecy, training, and strange orders were the norm for would-be SACO men. Even the doctors and pharmacist mates destined for Happy Valley learned skills such as hand-to-hand combat, orienteering, and spotting booby traps in addition to field medicine before shipping out for Asia.

For the first two years, new arrivals reported first to Happy Valley, flying from Kunming to Chongqing's sandy island airport in the Jialing River. Replicating his own Chongqing arrival experience, Miles never sent Americans to meet their planes. He felt that figuring things out on their own would boost their confidence and prepare them to make their own way in the coming months. Right from the start, they got a taste of all the walking that lay ahead of them, climbing a long set of stairs from the airport to the street level of Chongqing, where a truck with a Chinese driver waited. When they got to headquarters eight miles outside the city, they faced hundreds more stairs. Dignitaries would make the ascent in sedan chairs, but for all the jostling, those who could make it under their own powers might have found it easier to walk.

Later, as deployment grew more urgent, SACOs reported directly to their field assignments without the stop-off in Chongqing.

Happy Valley became the nerve center for an operation that expanded north, south, and east. SACO added thirteen training camps that doubled as radio and weather surveillance stations, in addition to scores of separate radio and weather sites. The camps were positioned as close to Japanese forces as they could safely operate and yet at a sufficient distance to discourage attack. They had to be within walking distance—though perhaps a walk of more than a day—of enemy positions for launching raids and sabotage, which placed most of them within Japanese-held territory. But lines between the enemy and Free China were porous; many Chinese living under Japanese control were not even aware of it. Most camps had to move at least once as enemy positions shifted. Some moved so often that a plan to use carrier pigeons for messages was abandoned. The birds could not be trained or employed effectively without a stationary home base.

The camps closely coordinated with Dai's nearest guerrilla columns, training their soldiers, working with their officers to plan missions, and eventually joining the troops in the field.

While proximity to the action was important, so was a sympathetic local official. If the nearby mayor or governor was not a staunch Dai Li loyalist, he at least had to be cooperative and trustworthy.

In spring 1943, a half dozen Americans along with Chinese interpreters, armed guards, and a general fix-it man set off from Happy Valley in six old trucks stuffed beyond capacity with gasoline, explosives, arms, and housekeeping supplies to start SACO's first satellite camp. Camp One, established in April in Anhui Province about a hundred miles from the coast, was the first of many to commandeer an empty Buddhist temple for its operations. Though eight hundred miles from Chongqing as the crow flies, it was two thousand miles away by road. The camp became home to the second radio direction finder, which was erected in a cornfield. When they moved it to a more suitable location, the farmer demanded and received compensation for the dozen corn plants she had lost to the tower.

New camps were created as needed and as opportunities arose right up to the end of the war. Camp Two, sited in the center of China near the Yangtze River to mine Japanese shipping lanes and harass enemy troops, had to move twice. Its guerrilla-training program was second only to Happy Valley's, graduating and arming nearly four thousand soldiers who became an effective fighting force and sabotage unit against Japanese supply lines.

A handful of men from Camp Two founded Camp Five to the south near the border with Indochina in August 1944. It was originally built in Nanning and then moved to Bose, both in Guanxi Province. The men experienced some of the most serious hardships in all of SACO while in Bose. Due to bad water and clouds of infected mosquitos, so many suffered from dysentery and malaria that there were periods when only three Americans were healthy enough to work. Food was scarce; at times there was nothing to buy, forcing the men to survive on K rations.

Two members of Camp Five were among SACO's heroes because of their grueling workloads due to lack of personnel. Chief Radio Mate Clinton Landreth, succeeded by Radioman R. T. Cunningham, worked the radio station alone from 7:00 a.m. to midnight every day, intercepting heavy traffic of Japanese messages and relaying them to Chongqing. They had no aerial meteorology instruments, but they fulfilled a special request of Chennault's Flying Tigers, making ground observation reports to the Air Force unit every three hours.

Illness also plagued Camp Ten with an outbreak of typhus while several hundred Chinese were in residence for training. The commander suspended all operations for a week to delouse every person at the camp, thoroughly clean every building, and steam treat all clothing and bedding. The measures did the trick, and work resumed.

Though several camps had to work through such challenges of illness, lack of food, and other outside factors, two developed problems from within. Trouble at Camp Seven arose from having too many Americans without enough to do. The camp was organized quickly in September 1944 as Miles scrambled to prepare for a U.S. Navy invasion that Admiral King had warned could be only months away. Due to hasty preparations, the camp somehow ended up with one hundred forty-seven officers and men who had bypassed the usual SACO cultural training. This group had gone directly from Kunming to the camp about thirty miles from Jianyang in Fujian Province, thereby skipping informal indoctrination from Miles and other SACO leaders.

The men had disciplinary problems uncharacteristic of SACO. They acted like a bunch of college kids on spring break instead of men on a secret mission, repeatedly slipping into town without permission. Their behavior improved after their commander organized football and basketball leagues and assigned more work, but for a few men, the bad habits were hard to break. Miles decided to send the troublemakers to exemplary Camp Six about a hundred fifty miles to the south, but the transfers had limited success. Camp Six commander Lieutenant

Robert Jantzen later wrote to Miles requesting more men as long as they were not from Camp Seven.

At the other trouble spot, Camp Three, the problem was not discipline, but rather friction between Americans and Chinese. The northernmost camp until Camp Four was founded, SACO established it in August 1943. In short order, the Americans fell into criticizing the Chinese troops and complaining that Dai Li provided his men with inadequate nutrition and clothing. The Chinese grew resentful of the bossy Americans and withheld intelligence from them. Miles traced the problem to a proverbial sour grape, a U.S. Army captain from the OSS who served as second in command.

The officer's expectations of the Chinese, in Miles's view, were unrealistic and failed to take the country's grave challenges into account. His remarks had infected the camp with distrust of Dai Li in particular and of the Chinese in general. New leadership took over the camp in January 1944, but it took another year and a third set of commanders to turn the camp around and make it as productive as the others. Miles blamed himself for not detecting the problem sooner and for not preventing it to begin with. After that, newcomers received more training in how to get along with their Chinese partners.

Camp Three was the only unit where cooperation with the Chinese utterly failed. But these men there were not the only ones frustrated by the Chinese and suspicious of Dai Li, although most had the sense to keep quiet and find ways to make their relationships work. Several SACOs observed that Dai manipulated every situation to require more American arms and equipment and seemed determined to keep Americans safely in the camps under Chinese protection. Motor Machinist's Mate First Class Salvatore Ciaccio laughed that Americans could sometimes barely move for all the Chinese soldiers guarding them. He had heard rumors that explained it. Dai had warned his men that if an American were killed, the soldier responsible for him would also be killed.[10]

For Storekeeper First Class Clayton Mishler, Dai's protective zeal resulted in a unique war story. An adventurous man touched by wanderlust and an uncanny ability to navigate new places and situations, Mishler would often volunteer for solo procurement missions, buying eggs, candles, gasoline, and other necessities for the camps.

On one such mission, out for an evening stroll in the northern city of Xi'an, he noticed that a man was following him. After confirming that he was being tailed by abruptly changing direction and seeing that the suspicious man followed suit, he walked deliberately to a crowded plaza where he had seen a police officer earlier. Mishler maneuvered so that the officer stood between himself and his pursuer, and then tried in a smattering of Chinese to explain the danger to the officer, but the policeman did not understand. In desperation, Mishler pulled out his trump card: a special blue and silver badge recognized all over China that identified the bearer as Dai Li's associate. The badge cleared everything up. The mystery man had indeed been following Mishler under orders from Dai Li himself. He was a secret security guard charged with protecting Mishler, who was alone in the city.

DAI LI'S DETERMINATION to keep Americans safe proved frustrating for men like Ensign John Ryder Horton and Captain Theodore Cathey, who were itching to wreak a bit of havoc on the Japanese with the men they had trained. They mapped out specific missions, such as destroying a key bridge to cripple Japan's supply lines, and Miles proposed them to Dai, who exercised his veto power to nix every idea.

Miles was never sure why Dai so staunchly resisted risking American lives, but he speculated that the general feared compromising Chinese sovereignty by allowing his troops to be commanded by foreign officers. Or perhaps he worried that the navy would pull out if they sustained too many casualties.

The issue reached a crisis when Stanley Hornbeck, director of the State Department's Office of Far Eastern Affairs, accused Dai of using SACO to hoard American arms and equipment rather than to defeat Japan. Rumors had been flying that Dai Li did not want Americans out in the field because they would discover his deceit. In a heated conference with Miles, Dai finally agreed to send SACO teachers out with the troops as an extension of their instruction. The Americans would plan missions and work with the Chinese field commanders to carry them out. To prove his earnestness, Dai offered to execute any Chinese officer who refused to take direction from an American instructor, unaware of how preposterous and even horrid his proposal sounded to his partners.

But overblown commitments or not, in October 1944, Dai ordered all Chinese SACOs to include Americans in their operations. Thus began a new phase of engagement for Naval Group China.

CHAPTER 6

Happy Valley, SACO Headquarters

As NIGHT FELL, a group of SACOs sipping tea on a stone terrace high on the hillside at Happy Valley spotted a pair of flames far below zigzagging along the path, their wavering orange light reflected on the black surfaces of rice paddies. As the fiery plumes drew nearer, the tea drinkers could make out the dark shapes of torchbearers lighting the way for a newcomer trudging up behind them.

Upon arrival, the hungry and exhausted sailor was welcomed with a hot, damp towel and a glass of boiling-hot water, no matter the season. Thus refreshed, he awkwardly tried his hand at a pair of chopsticks to wolf down a bowl of rice and fried eggs before crashing for the first time in his bunk.

The next day, he awoke to a lovely landscape of whitewashed, tile-roofed buildings clinging to green terraces on the steep hillside with mountain peaks towering behind. On every stone footpath lined with thornless, pink and white roses stood an armed Chinese sentry.

Discounting the guards, the compound seemed like an antique painting of a Chinese village come alive, but within the walls, a modern military machine staffed by Americans and Chinese was conducting secret operations. They monitored Japanese radio traffic, sent coded radio messages to Washington

73

and the Pacific Fleet, collected weather data to compile pan-Asian forecasts, developed photos furtively snapped by spies, and tracked the progress of supplies making their way around the globe to equip the program.

HAPPY VALLEY SAT HIGH ABOVE CHONGQING, China's wartime capital, about eight miles northwest of the city. It met Captain Milton Miles's chief criterion for SACO headquarters: an adequate water supply to allow his men to bathe twice a day.

After Miles returned to Chongqing from his tour of the coast with Dai Li in the summer of 1942, he began a fruitless search in the city for a place to set up the nerve center for his mission that could double as a training school for General Dai Li's guerrilla army. None of the sites available had the necessary capacity, security, or water access.

Gesturing to the beautiful mountainside beyond the city, Dai asked Miles how he would like to locate his operation there.

To the astonishment of Dai's staff, the general gave two hundred acres of his personal compound to SACO with the stroke of a magistrate's pen in July. The acreage, adjacent to Dai's private villa, was a fiefdom containing an orphanage and school for the children of soldiers and agents who had died in his service, as well as small industries such as papermaking and garment factories to employ families of the fallen. It had also housed a former prison where errant military officers and MBIS agents had been punished, but that cement building, called the White House, was repurposed as the radio center after SACO took over.*

There is no record of how the headquarters came to be called Happy Valley, a misnomer because the site is not a valley but a cluster of rocky swells on a mountainside. Accessible only on foot, one arrived at the bottom of the slope by truck or by sampan down the Yangtze River and then climbed hundreds of steps to get there. Its very inaccessibility and the protections already in place made it a secure location.

Miles and the seven SACO pioneers, Webb Heagy, Chief Radioman Kenneth A. Mann, Ensign Lashley Mann, Lieutenant Jr. Grade Robert L. "Buck" Dormer,

---

* Claims by the People's Republic of China that Dai Li ran a death camp there in cooperation with SACO have been discredited. Officials backed down from the story in 2008 when it came out that atrocities they described occurred there long after Dai Li had died and the Americans had left. See Chapter Twenty.

Lieutenant Jr. Grade Clarence P. Taylor, Ensign Theodore Wildman, and Yeoman First Class Terrence J. O'Neill, moved from Fairy Cave in Chongqing to the new quarters on October 1, 1942. When they arrived, the compound consisted of a farmhouse, an outbuilding, and a cave for storage.

With every man a radio specialist, it took them only an hour to set up a radio receiving station made of equipment borrowed from Dai Li. They were thrilled to intercept hundreds of Japanese radio messages the first day.

But beyond taking turns monitoring and decoding radio traffic, there wasn't much to do the first few weeks because they had no equipment. Without so much as a typewriter, Miles wrote memos to Washington by hand, requesting nails, electric switches, and carbon paper, all nonexistent or prohibitively expensive in Chongqing. For recreation, they wandered the footpaths and sat together watching night descend while drinking tea straight from the spouts of single-serving pots. After dark, their quarters were illuminated by candles and flashlights, stingily used because batteries were in short supply.

Seven more men arrived in October and November, including the first three Navy aerographers who established the initial weather station at Happy Valley and started making plans for training Chinese to collect meteorological data in the field.

Supplies from the United States began to trickle in, but the excitement of receiving the first shipment evaporated as soon as they opened it. While the group was in desperate need of just about everything, the case contained two things that were totally useless: empty oilcans and collapsible antenna poles. They ended up using the cans as components for a radio receiver, but they were already making antenna towers from China's unlimited supply of bamboo. An eagerly anticipated field radio transmitter-receiver arrived in time for Christmas, but it was full of seawater. Fortunately, the moisture had not damaged it, and the radio crew got it working.

Dai Li had initially objected to the Americans transmitting radio signals because he thought it would be too great a security risk, but Miles convinced him that their work could not be done without it. By degrees, Miles would later win approval to establish a countrywide SACO communications network rather than relying on China's patchwork, overtaxed system.

Having transmission capacity at Happy Valley had become essential. Miles could send radio messages to Washington at the naval attaché's office in Chongqing, but it took him a whole day to make the round trip from headquarters, walking down the tortuous path to the road and then finishing the trip by truck using precious gasoline that cost $39 a gallon, equivalent to about $550 in 2012.

After overcoming the shipping damage and Dai's objections, Miles faced problems powering the transmitter, which required 120 volts of electricity to work properly. They had no gasoline generator, and even if they had found one, it would have cost a fortune to run it. Instead, they turned to the Chongqing power plant, an imperfect source that put out an unpredictable supply of electricity ranging from three hundred volts to none at all. They took to calling the power plant to find out the current voltage and then adjusting the set before transmitting each message.

They made do with this preposterous workaround until 1944, when SACO created what the men affectionately called the Happy Valley Light and Power Company. They generated electricity from a bank of diesel engines modified to run on specially refined tung oil. It took a team of porters four days to carry the massive engines suspended on ropes and bamboo poles up to Happy Valley.

THE DEARTH OF SUPPLIES became Miles's biggest challenge. Every battery, radio tube, and thermometer had to be flown from India over the Hump to Kunming, where it would finally be trucked to Chongqing and carried by human pack train up to Happy Valley. In spite of General Stilwell's promise to include a few pounds of SACO supplies for Miles on every supply flight over the Hump, almost nothing made it to Chongqing, and with so many transfer points along the route, it was no wonder. Each transfer created an opportunity for the goods to be misdirected or even stolen. Miles came up with a partial solution, sending navy officers to east India for the express purpose of getting shipments out of warehouses and onto planes and trucks.

Lieutenant John Ryder Horton was the first to tackle this job. Shortly after reaching Happy Valley in February 1943, he was dispatched to Assam with orders to locate equipment detailed in a stack of shipping invoices. Though not a trained shopkeeper, he was resourceful. He made friends with army supply officers at military airfields in Assam, Jorhat, and Dinjan and finally found some of the shipments hidden in warehouses around the Chabau airfield. For weeks, he hung around the field cajoling supply clerks by day and playing poker and sipping gin with pilots by night. These personal connections got enough navy materiel onto planes and into a warehouse in Kunming for a truck convoy to Chongqing. He flew to Kunming, arranged the last leg of the shipment, and returned to Happy Valley.

Soon after Horton's successful mission, SACO assigned permanent storekeepers to Kolkata, Assam, and Kunming to keep the equipment moving. But this proved to be only a partial solution. Army–navy rivalry and disagreements within the U.S. government entangled SACO's supply line through the end of the war.

AS HORTON WAS SHAKING SUPPLIES LOOSE in India and Miles was in Washington pushing the SACO Agreement through the military bureaucracy, Happy Valley was growing. Fifteen men increased to eighty, and eight new, mud-walled buildings sprang up in Miles's absence. He returned in May 1943 to find that the darkroom had finally moved out of his bathroom and into a new photo lab. The technicians now had proper equipment. Months earlier, they had used a duck named Harvey to stir the chemicals in a steel tub, releasing him in a nearby rice paddy for the occasional breath of fresh air, but now an automatic processor did the job. A new barracks featured a colonnaded terrace made of stone quarried right at Happy Valley a short distance above the compound. There were classrooms, a medical clinic, and a radio repair shop. By then, Miles had virtually abandoned Fairy Cave in favor of Happy Valley for the sake of convenience and to be near the men. House Number One became his home and office.

Specifications for the largest building, the new mess hall, baffled the Chinese construction crew. It was designed with the kitchen in the same building, but they were used to cooking in one place and carrying the food to another to be served. Miles insisted that the food be prepared and consumed under one roof to ensure that meals were served hot. In the interest of sanitation, he had ordered that the kitchen walls be constructed so they could be washed every day, but they did not hold up to his cleaning method. With no disinfectants available, he had the cooks douse the walls with boiling water, which liquefied the dirt walls into puddles of mud on the floor. Dai Li came up with slabs of terrazzo, a composite of stone chips embedded in concrete, for flooring and to cover the walls up to six feet, so that the kitchen could be cleaned to Miles's standard.

Unable to get enough toilets flown over the Hump, Miles managed to obtain one that had been made in India and hired a Chongqing ceramics factory to replicate it. They had plenty of water but no pipes, so they used bamboo. The men had a wonderful time ribbing Chief Shipfitter William Shelley for the constant leaks, claiming that he had forgotten to bring his bamboo wrench.

WITH NO MOVIES and a short supply of books and electricity, the expanded team continued candlelit tea parties as the primary form of evening entertainment. The gatherings gave the swelling ranks of newcomers a quick indoctrination into the ways of the Chinese and of SACO. When they had had enough tea and chitchat, they played cards and studied Chinese language.

Documenting life at Happy Valley was Romanian-born cartoonist Saul Steinberg, who became a United States citizen and received a commission as an ensign in the U.S. Navy Reserves the same day. Steinberg, whose cartoons graced ninety covers of *The New Yorker* magazine over fifty years, served at Happy Valley from June 1943 to March 1944. In his sparse, whimsical style, he captured endless terraced hills, a Chinese sentry in straw sandals, and an August day so hot that drops of sweat poured off everyone, including a dog.

But even in this tidy, idyllic setting with its unique spirit of camaraderie, the men of Happy Valley suffered from the primitive conditions. Most stayed isolated in the compound and surrounding hills because Chongqing was too far to walk over the rough terrain, and gas was too expensive to go by truck. Though cooler than the city below, the temperature topped a hundred degrees Fahrenheit in the summer and coupled with extreme humidity, plaguing them with prickly heat. Despite all the precautions, many suffered bouts of diarrhea, and though they ate voraciously, nearly everyone lost weight.

They slogged through mud and fought off rats and mosquitos. One man woke to find a fat, brown rat tangled in the mosquito netting above his bed. In a panic, he pulled out a pistol and shot it, splattering blood and guts all over himself and his bedding and blowing a hole through the roof to boot.

Nothing cheered up the men like letters from home, but mail delivery was a chronic problem. Letters and packages could take months to arrive at Happy Valley, and from there, they went by truck, sampan, and foot to the camp or remote station where the sailor was assigned. The shipfitter from Chicago never received any of his wife's letters, and she never heard from him until he got home after nine months in China. SACO had no regular delivery schedule; mail languished at Happy Valley until supplies or personnel were headed for its destination.

Handling improved with the arrival of Mailman First Class Eddie O'Toole in November 1943, soon followed by construction of a new post office building. He had a unique method for distributing packages of food. He simply sent them on the next truck out regardless of where the intended recipient was stationed, especially if that camp had not seen mail in a long time. It was better for Aunt Ethel's homemade cookies to be eaten by strangers than never to be eaten at all.

Despite these hardships, complaints were almost entirely of the good-natured, boastful variety. Miles wondered how the place had come to be called Happy Valley at first, given its discomforts and inconveniences. But he realized that the men were genuinely happy to be back after an outside assignment. And he made it a policy to send every man on a remote mission if he could. He believed that witnessing conditions in the field made for a better desk officer. He wanted them to experience the hardship of travel in the broken-down country and to discover the courage and resourcefulness of the Chinese people.

DAI WAS SO ANXIOUS for training of Chinese troops to begin that Miles started a program on a small scale late in 1942, even though he had yet received no guns, radios, or weather instruments, and without them, instruction was limited. As part of their training, Lieutenant Commander Ed Gilfillan took a small group of Chinese out to plan and execute a raid on Happy Valley to "capture" Miles. Other officers taught hand-to-hand combat and used their own guns to demonstrate cleaning and loading techniques.

When the convoys of supplies finally started showing up, school began in earnest. The first full classes started in May 1943. In addition to arms, fighting, and demolitions, Happy Valley specialized in teaching technical skills such as radio, weather data collection, and medical care so that the Chinese could work with the slim ranks of Americans in the field.

Roger Moore, Miles's personal photographer, taught photography and wrote a user's manual for Kodak cameras that was translated into Chinese. The navy had intended to use this new pool of skilled photographers to document the planned U.S. landing in China.

Happy Valley ran SACO's largest school, graduating classes of several hundred Chinese fighters every two months, and eventually turning out some fifteen thousand field-ready guerrillas.

Camp Nine, a special school for police officers, opened on a separate campus about a mile from the main Happy Valley headquarters in June 1944. The school had been a key negotiation point for China in the SACO Agreement, and Dai Li made sure that no expense was spared. Its elaborate campus made the other men at Happy Valley feel like stepchildren. Fifty new buildings were clustered around a large parade ground. Thirty-six Americans, including retired police detectives and FBI agents, came to Chongqing to teach courses such as crime detection, special driving techniques, photography, and unarmed combat. For firearms training, SACO imported a superstar instructor, USMC Captain Harry W. Reeves, a national competitive shooting champion.

WEATHER FORECASTING BEGAN in earnest in August 1943 with the arrival of Captain Irwin Forest Beyerly, a brilliant navy meteorologist who had coauthored a technical weather treatise published by the Massachusetts Institute of Technology. He created a pan-Asian weather data collection system staffed by SACO-trained Chinese, Thai, and American aerologists who transmitted reports to Happy Valley three times a day. It took a little more than a year to build the network of weather stations and deliver the first detailed forecast to the Pacific Fleet. Soon after that initial forecast went out, the Happy Valley weather center moved into a new building worthy of its growing role perched on "Beyerly Hill."

As aerology grew, so did radio communications. The radio shack and repair shop expanded into the White House in 1944. In addition to monitoring and decoding enemy messages, Happy Valley received radio intelligence from SACO coast watchers and monitors all over the country. The headquarters staff synthesized the information and relayed it to Washington and Pacific Fleet Command. An enemy ship location report went to the submarines in the Pacific three times a day.

Radiomen pulled twelve-hour shifts in the shack, often treated to a late-night visit from Miles, whose passion for radio never faded.

MILES ENCOURAGED THE MEN to get to know Chinese civilians in Happy Valley and the surrounding villages. The houseboys who swept floors, served tea, and mended mosquito nets became friends with the men they served. On free afternoons, the SACOs might hike down to the bottom of the hill to visit the friendly coffin maker who spouted Chinese philosophy. The orphans accompanied the Americans on their hikes and entertained them with songs so often that every man in Happy Valley could sing "Old MacDonald" in Chinese. The highlight of the calendar was a big Christmas party SACO threw for the orphans, complete with presents, funny hats, and a visit from Santa.

Happy Valley rarely saw visitors by mutual agreement between Miles and Dai due to the security risk, but an exception was made when a USO troop came to Chongqing in October 1944.

Actor Pat O'Brien, actress Jinx Falkenburg, and a host of "USO girls" were carried up the winding footpath in sedan chairs by torchlight and marveled at what O'Brien dubbed "Shangri-la." Their show was held in the auditorium in the orphanage school. Before they took the stage, the children delighted them with songs and gifts of chrysanthemums. Although O'Brien had told Miles that the cast would be too tired for anything but a good night's sleep, they all attended Dai Li's signature banquet and opera. When Miles dragged himself out of bed on a couple hours of sleep the next morning, he found O'Brien still up talking to American and Chinese officers.

Before he left, O'Brien heartily thanked Miles for the hospitality. It was the only place on their tour where they had met any locals and eaten local cuisine, and where the women had been treated with respect rather than fighting off groping hands. He was genuinely glad they had come to Happy Valley. At his next show at an army base, O'Brien appeared on stage wearing a navy windbreaker, a nod to his new SACO friends.

IN THE COOPERATIVE SPIRIT on which it was founded, SACO appointed one Chinese and one American director to head each department such as supply, transportation, and communications, but the system was seriously flawed. For the first eighteen months, Dai Li's staff worked out of the MBIS office in Chongqing, and the distance between the city and Happy Valley proved to be a profound obstacle. The city's antiquated telephone system necessitated a lot of shouting, and a translator or even two was required for every conversation. Documents had to be translated as well, and they took too long to go back and forth.

Dai Li was often away seeing to other duties within the Nationalist government. General Pan Qiwu, a brilliant, soft-spoken former monk who was also a poet and a calligraphy artist, represented Dai when necessary and spent the better part of a year shuttling between the offices. Once while dashing to Happy Valley to resolve some dilemma, Pan cracked up his car, prompting him to suggest that the Chinese should move up to the American headquarters. Miles was relieved. He had long believed it was the best solution but had hesitated to suggest it, not wishing to come off as a know-it-all American. But once Pan brought it up, Miles pushed for it, and Dai Li agreed.

Communication did not improve as much as it should have after the Chinese came to Happy Valley in August 1944. The staff from each country worked in separate buildings. Meetings were easier to arrange, but memos still had to be translated, and in the case of English-to-Chinese, hand written by calligraphers. Under these absurd working conditions, deadlines were missed, hundreds of eager students showed up without warning, and the Americans never knew the Chinese were running low on batteries until there were none.

The solution was found in a rambling, broken-down farmhouse on the grounds large enough for the entire staff to work together. Dai Li relished the renovations in spite of construction problems. A new wing extending beyond the hillside on stilts collapsed twice before they got it to stay up with the help of an American engineer.

Miles wanted a proper map room in the new headquarters. It was to be windowless for security with wooden walls and no corners so that maps could be tacked up easily. The Chinese architect appeared puzzled and asked Miles questions that did not seem relevant, but it wasn't until Miles saw the first sketch that he understood the designer's problem. It revealed a spherical room like the inside of a wooden globe. The architect had probably been ordered to give Miles anything he wanted and had struggled mightily to fill the foreigner's strange request. Miles graciously explained that it was okay for the floor and ceiling to be flat and have corners where they met the walls, but he would like a curve where the walls met each other.

The map room turned out exactly as Miles had hoped with one significant exception. The only available wood was camphor, from the tree that secretes the substance commonly used to keep moths away and as a chest rub to treat a cold. Conferences in the map room were necessarily interrupted by frequent fresh air breaks.

The combined staff moved into the new building in January 1945. Department heads and their assistants occupied one large room instead of separate offices, but having two directors per department proved unworkable. Instead, each section was led by the person who had the most expertise, while his counterpart was second in command. For example, a Chinese directed transportation, while an American was the head of medicine.

The desks for each department were arranged in a square with the men facing the center and Americans and Chinese in alternating positions so that they could not literally "take sides." The result was transformational. Communication took minutes instead of weeks. A pool of translators stood at the ready, but the partners often got by using gestures, drawings, and facial expressions to convey their ideas.

And an amazing phenomenon began to occur with regularity: they argued. Instead of politely saying yes when they meant no and waiting for the issue to go away, the Chinese asserted themselves. The Americans responded with more reserve than they might have at home, but they stood their ground. These open disagreements led to small negotiations whose cumulative effect resulted in resolution and action. Management and teamwork subtly replaced sidestepping and stagnating fear of making a mistake. Things got done.

Miles could hardly contain his pride. Back when he was first assigned to China, every expert had told him that he would never be able to work with the Chinese, that they were lazy, apathetic, dishonest, guarded, and suspicious. But he and Dai Li had figured out how to work together despite extreme differences in personality and experience, and now their men were a unified team. They were SACO.

CHAPTER 7

Backstage SACO: India and Over the Hump

WITH WAR CHURNING UP THE PACIFIC and the coast of China occupied by the enemy, the only way into China from the United States was through India. Kolkata, already bursting with humanity, filled with Indian and Burmese refugees, European Jews, freelance reporters, adventurers, and soldiers and sailors from every Allied country. The city became a way station for military men headed further east, an earthly limbo where men waited restlessly for a flight over the Hump. Fortune tellers and street vendors conspired to part bored, guileless soldiers from their pay.

During the first months of the operation, the handful of SACOs stopping over in Kolkata stayed in hotels. But as their numbers increased to dozens each month, SACO opened hostels throughout the city to provide them with lodging and security.

After the first hostel opened, strangers kept ringing the doorbell all night and asking for Susan, Agnes, or Betty. After the third night, the SACO organizers finally realized that the nocturnal visitors were looking for prostitutes. The team had unwittingly established the hostel in a former whorehouse in the middle of a red light district. After that, SACO found more suitable quarters in private, walled-in homes, each large enough to accommodate ten to fifteen men, in upperclass sections of the city. Miles chose these unlikely garrisons to avoid the notice of spies on the Japanese payroll who combed the city.

In 1943, three officers and nineteen enlisted men were stationed near Kolkata to take care of SACOs heading for China and to keep supplies flowing. Equipment arrived in India by sea and might be offloaded at any port and warehoused all over the country. Miles worked with his own men and navy liaison officers to get the materials by train to Kolkata and on to the airfields in the eastern province of Assam so it could be flown to Kunming over the Hump. Before being airlifted, SACO repacked shipments into porter-sized parcels of less than fifty pounds in lighter-weight packing materials with the "What the Hell?" pennant stenciled onto each package. The gear was then ready for pack trains of men on foot in China.

During the war, India had to contend with multiple troubles in addition to the strain of the Allied military presence and its demands on the infrastructure. It suffered severe famine, threat of Japanese invasion, and social upheaval borne of the political transformation from a colonial to an independent state. These events had the potential to place SACO supply lines in jeopardy. To keep Miles apprised of the changing state of affairs, naval attaché Phil Talbot organized a news clip service in Mumbai. He hired several disabled, well-educated Indians to read fifty daily newspapers and provide clips and summaries of the most important stories to Kay Stimson, an American writer living in Mumbai with her British journalist husband. She created a daily digest of India news called "What the Hell," which was shared with the U.S. Office of Naval Intelligence. In the spirit of Allied cooperation, ONI passed it on to British intelligence officials, who wondered how the navy could have dug up such detailed information. They were incredulous that the intelligence was simply gleaned from newspapers.

OVER TIME, INDIA GRADUALLY BECAME much more than a place for men and supplies to wait for transport. It developed into backstage SACO. Miles became a small-scale industrial baron overseeing several factories established specifically for the needs of his outfit.

Printing materials in the United States and shipping them to China proved futile. By the time they got to Chongqing, they would be a year old and likely out of date. Instead, SACO opened its own printing plant in Kolkata, fitted with a four-color press, graphic arts camera, and bindery equipment. The navy-staffed print shop provided the most secure way to produce secret documents as well as the posters, maps, forms, and manuals Naval Group China needed quickly. The shop's hottest product was a previously published, full-color Chinese atlas with an English index that became a coveted item for SACO and other armed forces in China. Despite chronic paper shortages and technical problems due to humidity, Lieutenant Vivian H. Ellis and Ship's Clerk Frank Dennis cranked out a steady stream of printed matter from late 1943 until the end of the war.

Miles procured the entire output of Eveready Industries Kolkata to fill SACO's voracious appetite for batteries—at least twenty tons a month to run radios, weather equipment, and lighting. Without the Kolkata factory, SACO would practically have ground to a halt. Batteries took so long to get to China from the United States that they arrived dead.

SACO depended on the army's Air Tactical Command to transport every battery, atlas, and bullet, but ATC was chronically behind in its shipments. A hundred planes often sat idle on the ground for lack of oxygen, essential to flight crew and passengers during high-altitude flights over the Hump. ATC had a small, trailer-mounted oxygen compressor near an airfield in Assam, India, but the need far outstripped its capacity, and the compressor was constantly breaking down. Miles had heard the "no oxygen" excuse for waylaid shipments repeatedly when an opportunity to do something about it fell into his lap.

While in Washington on SACO business in 1943, Miles had dinner with Captain John Bay, an old friend from graduate school. Bay was responsible for the setup and operation of plants to produce compressed oxygen, required for ship repair, on island navy bases in the Pacific. The dinner conversation led to creating a SACO-run, high-capacity oxygen plant in Jorhat, Assam, India, a three-hour flight northeast of Kolkata.

The army had initially planned a similar facility of its own, but the idea had to be scuttled. The company that manufactured the equipment would not sell it to the army for fear of having to send a technician to India each time a problem cropped up. But company officials had confidence in the navy, which had its own experts. The navy had been running oxygen plants in shipyards and aboard ships at sea for years with minimal assistance.

Working with Bay, Miles procured two industrial oxygen-compression units and a trained crew to run them. Naval Group China set up the plant in a large Quonset hut hidden in the jungle outside Jorhat within easy trucking distance to Hump airfields in Chabua, Jorhat, and Dinjan. The oxygen units, tools to maintain them, and buildings to house them, some 525 tons in all, were shipped by sea to Kolkata and then to Jorhat by rail. Staffed by twelve experienced machinists and a yeoman, the oxygen-condensing plant was the largest in Asia. It went online in October 1944 and was cranking out the gas at full capacity by November, prompting a second plant with two more compressors to be added in January 1945. Six enormous diesel generators supplied the electricity. At first, oxygen needed on the other side of the Hump went over as compressed gas in bulky brass tanks, but they soon switched to making liquid oxygen, saving precious Hump tonnage. It was easily converted to gas near the site of use.

Thanks in part to this new oxygen supply, the army was able to increase Hump tonnage from 3,500 to 22,000 tons a month, but SACO's monthly allowance of 150 tons never increased, much to Miles's chagrin. He had made an informal deal with ATC for more tonnage in exchange for the oxygen, but political squabbles got in the way.

In addition to oxygen, the navy also made acetylene, a gas used for welding, lighting, and manufacturing batteries, in Jorhat. The trailer-mounted plant arrived in Jorhat by barge on the Brahmaputra River. About a hundred miles to the west in Tezpur, they set up a mine factory. Mines were stored, armed, and prepared for shipment to China, where they were planted in Japanese shipping lanes in rivers and along the coast. SACO built smooth, concrete roads between the plant and the nearest railroad depot to minimize the risk of explosions during transport. During India's blistering summers, they covered the mines with tarps fitted with pouches full of water to keep them cool.

Army and air force personnel at the air bases in Northeast India scornfully dubbed their SACO counterparts the Assam Navy. SACOs were the stepchildren of the region, a small cadre of landlocked sailors placed in the degrading position of having to ask for support as if it were a personal favor instead of a contribution to the war effort. They were the only military personnel at the bases with no insignia, so they created their own: a peg-legged parrot in eighteenth-century naval officers' garb with the word "Miles" inscribed beneath his feet.

But the SACOs in Assam nevertheless proved to be useful friends. As Lieutenant Commander Charles Johnson was escorting precious supplies for the secret police school he was to establish in China for Dai Li, he was delayed at an Assam airfield. During his stay, a Japanese force was discovered some twenty miles away, and, suddenly, the unprotected airfield felt vulnerable. Johnson loaned some of the guns intended for the police school to the air corps maintenance and technical crew and gave a quick tutorial on how to use them. The Japanese never attacked, but neither did Johnson get his guns back.

SACO had other operations in addition to manufacturing in Kolkata. An antenna farm collected and transmitted radio signals from all over Asia, and a specialized direction finder antenna worked with the four others SACO had erected in China. The data from direction finders spaced hundreds of miles apart could pinpoint the origin of intercepted enemy code using triangulation. The hydrographic office compiled and interpreted data from men in the field to chart the navigable waters in the Far East. A motor pool and vehicle repair shop kept the other services connected.

Like its hostels, SACO's offices, scattered quietly throughout Kolkata in plain-vanilla buildings, were designed to be invisible. Navy personnel waiting for flights over the Hump served as couriers, circulating documents between offices by motorcycle, but perhaps not as discreetly as their superiors would have liked. Chief Signalman Guy Purvis made a sport of clearing paths through streets clogged with rickshaws, fruit stands, and livestock with the help of his uncanny vocal imitation of a police siren.

AS OPERATIONS GREW MORE COMPLEX and the flow of personnel and materials increased, Miles placed Lieutenant Commander Francis H. Smith in charge of SACO India. Smith set up Camp Schmidt, a tent compound in a park-like setting in the Kolkata suburb of Tollygunge, where men waited until passage over the Hump was imminent, at which point they moved into one of the urban hostels. Gurhkas, the notoriously fearless warriors from Nepal with enormous, curved knives at their waists, guarded the camp and other SACO facilities in India. Men passing through noted that their guards could decapitate an intruder with a single knife blow.

Smith began construction of Camp Regent in Ballygunge, a south-side suburb of Kolkata, to offer more comfortable and secure quarters to men in transit.

He overcame his limited labor budget by commandeering SACOs with civilian construction experience, who were happy to do something useful while waiting to go to China. The facility was commissioned as Camp Frank Knox in April 1945, named for President Roosevelt's secretary of the navy, who had died in 1944. The heavily guarded, walled compound of Quonset huts was designed to hold four hundred fifty people and included a gunnery school to keep marksmanship skills sharp while staving off boredom. While Camp Knox was under construction, some SACOs stayed at Camp Kanchrapara, an army base near Kolkata.

THE MEN ARRIVED restless and eager in India after complicated, hopscotch air journeys over the Atlantic Ocean, North Africa, and the Middle East or following months at sea via circuitous routes designed to avoid the Japanese in the Pacific. In India, they at last received a taste of the exotic that seemed fitting to the prolonged and hazardous duty they had taken on. They rode around in rickshaws, visited the Taj Mahal, watched elephants hauling timber and monkeys swinging over the rail lines, and smelled the pungent, cow dung-fueled funeral pyres that burned along sacred rivers every day.

For most, the experience in India was as gut wrenching as it was fascinating. They witnessed abject poverty beyond their imaginations and saw more people than even those hailing from New York or Chicago had ever seen in one place. Every city was a roiling flow of humanity oozing through the streets. Children, naked except for the girls' earrings and bracelets, begged incessantly with cries of "baksheesh." A navy storekeeper escorted weather equipment by train across India in a rickety boxcar fitted with a hole in the floor rimmed with a pair of painted footprints to indicate the right squatting position while relieving oneself. On brothel patrol, a mission to control venereal disease by keeping servicemen away from prostitutes, Lieutenant Charles Gutch visited prostitution houses that were nothing but piles of filthy mattresses and rags screened from the street by burlap curtains.

In the disease-ravaged country, SACO worked to keep the men healthy with chlorinated water, carefully screened food service workers, medical supervision of food preparation, and a well-supplied and -staffed sick bay. But despite these precautions, some men also had their first taste of exotic ailments, especially dysentery and malaria.

Upon arrival in Kolkata, the men reported to Camp Schmitt or, later, to Camp Frank Knox under protection of the Gurhka guards. They exchanged their navy uniforms for SACO's requisite unmarked khakis. Instructors repeated cautions not to answer questions or tell anyone, including another American, where they were headed or the outfit to which they were assigned. While waiting for a seat on a Hump flight, they took classes in riding and shooting, helped coordinate transportation, inspected the guards, and served as officer of the day, but the idleness could still be excruciating, especially with a mysterious assignment waiting on the other side of the mountain range. A group of four SACO communications experts traveling together spent the wait plotting how they would set up a radio station behind enemy lines when they got to China.

Motor Machinist Mate Second Class Matthew Komorowski-Kaye, a member of Scouts and Raiders who had served in Italy before joining SACO, found the wait at Camp Knox almost intolerable and eagerly accepted an assignment. He was to oversee the transport of four rail cars from Kolkata to the oxygen plant at Jorhat and make sure they were not separated or raided by black-marketeers. Riding on top of the train to keep his eye on the cars, he tingled with suspicion when it stopped abruptly in the middle of a swamp. Dropping to the ground, he raced to the front of the train, only to find the engineers squatted on the tracks in a circle around a bucket of water. A tube connected to the engine was immersed in the bucket and releasing steam to heat the water. It was teatime.

With no officers' clubs or entertainment, those awaiting transport tried to amuse themselves by swimming at the British club, shopping, and playing cards. Finally one day, often after weeks of waiting, an officer would quietly direct a man to a warehouse to select a sleeping bag, underwear, blankets, and uniforms. The man would pack up his new gear and board a jeep with no time for goodbyes and move into one of the urban hostels. His stay there might be two nights or two weeks, but he would maintain a low profile when venturing out. He then got the nudge in the wee hours that it was time to move on. He was quietly slipped out to a plane, train, or truck for Assam, where he boarded a plane for the five-hundred-mile flight over the Hump to Kunming and SACO.

IN JANUARY 1945, the U.S. Army, after brutal fighting through the jungles of Burma and two years of perilous construction, opened a new road through Burma to China. Chiang Kai-shek suggested that it be named Stilwell Road despite his contentious relationship with the American general who had left China in disgrace but whose vision and tenacity had made the road possible. A ceremonial army convoy of one hundred thirteen vehicles was to make the first trip over the new road, but a pair of SACOs beat them to it. Lieutenant Conrad A. Bradshaw, who went AWOL from his post in Jorhat, and Storekeeper William White slipped onto the new road at Ledo in a jeep and completed the eleven-hundred-mile trip to Kunming four days before the convoy, claiming bragging rights for SACO.

Nine months later, another team of SACOs traveled Stilwell Road in a convoy full of war materiel bound for Chiang Kai-shek's army. The war was over for the United States, but for China, the worst was yet to come. Aerographer's Mate Third Class Nobel Shadduck had spent a month in Kolkata sweating and doing odd jobs for SACO when the long-awaited call came to move out. In September 1945, he and more than a hundred other SACOs packed up cold-weather gear for use in China and boarded a train bound for their jumping-off point in Burma.

For four days, Shadduck, a native of the north woods of Minnesota, watched India, Nepal, and Bhutan pass by, marveling at exotic birds, boatmen rowing dugout canoes with their feet, and emerald-colored tea plantations that looked like ornamental gardens. The rail journey ended at a vast complex of row upon row of warehouses stuffed with the makings of war. While selecting items for Chiang's army and loading them into a truck, Shadduck noticed a stack of cartons marked for Rev. W. C. Austin of Kunming. A military warehouse depot struck him as a peculiar location for the belongings of a man of the cloth, and the idea of an American preacher in Kunming captured his imagination. Impulsively, he piled the reverend's cartons into the truck on top of several cases of bazooka rockets for the Generalissimo.

When the one hundred forty-truck convoy arrived in Kunming weeks later, Shadduck spotted a man in the crowd wearing a cross around his neck and asked him if he knew Rev. Austin. He did indeed. He and Austin were members of the China Inland Mission, an ecumenical missionary association. Shadduck delivered the cartons to a stunned Reverend and Mrs. Austin, who had shipped their worldly possessions to Kunming before the war and had long since given them up for lost. Invited to the mission headquarters, Shadduck discovered that the missionaries were practically starving. He gave them a case of Vienna sausages, the sight of which moved some of them to tears.

PART 4

SACO's Battle Within the U.S. Military

CHAPTER 8

SACO and the OSS: A Shaky Alliance

As Mary Miles and Dai Li toured coastal China together in the summer of 1942, they made a strong impression on their traveling companion, Alghan Lusey, a new friend of Miles's who had come along to offer radio expertise. Not only did the trip give Lusey a rare glimpse into the inner workings of General Dai's efficient intelligence network, it also revealed Miles's growing access to the mysterious general's inner circle.[11]

Lusey had been in Chongqing since April, officially as a communications engineer for the U.S. Coordinator of Information, soon to be the Office of Strategic Services, but he was secretly doubling as an intelligence agent. His boss, General William "Wild Bill" Donovan, had been trying to set up shop in Asia but had been thwarted by the Chinese and his own military.

Lusey immediately grasped that the relationship between Miles and Dai had the potential to open a new door for Americans in China, where Dai held a tight grip on all activities of foreign governments. Perhaps the COI could walk through that door with the help of Miles. Moreover, Dai's sophisticated intelligence service could provide vital information to the COI if the agency could offer him something valuable in return. Lusey broached the subject of such an exchange with Dai, dangling an enticing plan for a worldwide radio surveillance network before him. Dai was intrigued and asked his agent Xiao Bo in Washington to check out the COI as a potential partner.

Lusey was called back to Washington unexpectedly during the coastal tour and had to cut the trip short. He arrived at Donovan's office flush with enthusiasm for Dai and Miles and their budding Friendship Project. Xiao Bo eagerly accepted an invitation to meet with Donovan and Lusey, during which Lusey proposed working with Miles to make a COI deal with China parallel with the navy's. COI could supply the Nationalists with radios and expertise in exchange for intelligence and permission to launch missions within China's borders. But the key, he cautioned, was to include Dai Li and Chiang Kai-shek in every plan. It was also essential to keep their British allies out of the picture entirely.

Donovan practically salivated over the idea. A decorated World War I hero, he had a deep yearning to charge up San Juan Hill for his country. He had tried unsuccessfully to get a post leading a guerrilla mission at the dawn of World War II, and after an injury in a car accident, it was clear that his battlefield days were over. But through the COI, he had a chance to direct saboteurs and guerrilla units all over the world, even if he could not perform the heroics himself. Immediately after Pearl Harbor, he had even considered approaching Dai Li about working with his guerrillas, but Stilwell had utterly rejected the scheme. Now, with Miles and Dai planning a guerrilla training program, Donovan could conceivably commandeer its graduates for OSS missions.

Back in July 1941, President Roosevelt had tapped Donovan, a gifted attorney with a passion for politics and foreign affairs, to improve America's scattershot intelligence efforts. Intelligence was spread among the State Department and the separate branches of the military with no coordination or central analysis. Despite turf-protecting challenges from the FBI, State Department, and military, Donovan doggedly built the agency that became the Office of Strategic Services in June 1942 and would boast thirteen thousand employees at its peak. By the summer of 1942, the OSS's work had developed into four groups: secret intelligence; special operations—propaganda, guerrilla, and sabotage missions; research and analysis; and foreign nationalities—the use of patriotic American immigrants and ethnic clubs for gathering information.

Though the COI/OSS had made amateurish blunders during its first year, its operatives in North Africa provided critical information to the Allies for Operation Torch, elevating the agency's reputation. It was also working well with British intelligence in Europe.

But Donovan could not get any traction in Asia. Neither Admiral Chester Nimitz, commander of the Central Pacific theater, nor General Douglas MacArthur, chief in the South Pacific, saw any need for intelligence services. They both believed that the war was entirely about military might, and they preferred not to have an untested undercover group to keep track of.

Donovan badly wanted to get into China. Long before Lusey brought Miles to his attention, he had crafted the Dragon Plan, a comprehensive intelligence operation to be headed by C. V. Starr, an American businessman with more than twenty years of experience in that country and exactly the kind of person Miles wanted banned from his group. The plan called for Starr's employees at American International Underwriters in Shanghai and several newspapers he owned in China to double as intelligence agents. But the plan got caught up in the century-old rivalry between the army and the navy and therefore never got past the Joint Chiefs of Staff.

But Donovan didn't give up. He sent Joseph R. Hayden, a political science professor from the University of Michigan who had served as vice governor of the Philippines in the 1930s, to Chongqing to get General Stilwell and Ambassador Clarence Gauss on board with the Dragon Plan. They wanted no part of it.

Despite these rebuffs, Donovan forged ahead, adding OSS operatives in addition to Hayden and Lusey, with the launch of two new programs in September 1942.

First, the OSS dispatched Army Major Carl Eifler and a contingent of guerrillas to India to start implementing the Dragon Plan. They converted a tea plantation in Nazira, Assam, into a commando camp and began scouting and sabotage missions in Japanese-occupied Burma.

Second, Donovan sent a pair of agents on a scouting trip dubbed "the Tolstoy Mission" to Tibet with the direct approval of President Roosevelt. Ilya Tolstoy, grandson of the Russian novelist, and Brooke Dolan of the Academy of Natural Sciences left New Delhi for Lhasa, Tibet, in September to explore a possible path for a road to China and to gauge popular and official sentiments toward the United States. The pair would make important contacts for the United States and even meet the ten-year-old Dalai Lama. Tibet was a complete mystery to the West at that time, and China was making territorial claims to it.

With these two missions underway, Donovan went to work in Washington to get Miles assigned to the OSS. Since Dai Li had already accepted Miles, making the navy captain an OSS officer would finally give Donovan a key to China. Meeting with Xiao Bo, Metzel, and Miles's superior, Admiral W. R. Purnell, Donovan used his masterful powers of persuasion to win their approval to appoint Miles as Far East Coordinator of the OSS, citing the agency's deep pockets and the many benefits if could offer the Friendship Project. He drafted a plan that would place the navy over the OSS in China with Miles at the helm of both in alliance with Dai's MBIS. On September 21, Purnell formally wrote up Miles's orders, giving him authority over Eifler's group, the Tolstoy Mission, Lusey, and John Fairbank, an OSS operations agent already in Chongqing. Donovan wrote to Fairbank that he now reported to Miles, and Xiao Bo radioed Dai Li about the appointment.

But nobody told Miles.

Hence, as we have seen, during the critical first months of their relationship, Dai Li became highly suspicious of Miles, who seemed to be keeping secrets. Dai knew about the American poking around in Burma, and he didn't like it. Chiang Kai-shek, Allied military commander of the Far East, had not approved it or even been informed. Dai and his staff repeatedly questioned Miles about an American named "Major I Flew," but a befuddled Miles had never heard of such a person. Miles received a cable from Washington on October 12 announcing his new OSS title without explaining anything about his duties or OSS activities. Miles, busy setting up his headquarters at Happy Valley, did not grasp the appointment's significance. It wasn't until Lusey returned to Chongqing in November with Miles's written orders in hand that he learned any details. That was when he found out about Eifler and the Tolstoy Mission. Suddenly, the strange questions Dai had been asking made sense. The mysterious "Major I Flew" was Major Eifler spoken with a Chinese accent. Miles immediately shared everything with Dai.

Once Miles had restored Dai's trust, he was optimistic about his new job, which he believed would lend more authority to his expanding but still only verbal mission. He promised Donovan that he would do everything in his power to deliver for the OSS, but from the beginning, he adamantly asserted that no "old China hands" were to be part of the OSS/Navy operation.

Back in Washington, Metzel was delighted with the way the new partnership was working out. Donovan had already deposited at least $80,000 cash in Far East bank accounts in Miles's name, and the OSS was shipping everything from jeeps to wristwatches to Chongqing for the navy.

But even though Dai Li accepted the OSS alliance, he remained wary. For one thing, the OSS was getting mixed up with the British, whom he distrusted. John Keswick, the British businessman he had kicked out of China along with the Chinese Commando Group in 1942, was now in Washington as British SOE liaison to the OSS. Dai also feared that inviting the OSS into China would grow to multiple American agencies running all over the country unchecked. He made it clear to Xiao Bo that he would not tolerate such a situation. He wanted a single unit under a single authority, and that had to be Miles, whom he knew and trusted.

Finally, Chiang Kai-shek was furious that the Tolstoy Mission was making overtures to Tibet, tacitly encouraging its growing independence movement at a time when Chiang was trying to assert authority over it. The mission was ostensibly under Miles's direction, but he had no control over two men journeying through an uncharted country with no communication system. These problems led to Chiang Kai-shek's insistence on the formal agreement between China and the United States that created SACO.

Dai Li's suspicions of the OSS turned out to be well founded. In fact, SACO scholar Maochun Yu called SACO's partnership with the OSS "a debilitating birth defect."[12]

But the impending trouble had nothing to do with the British. Rather, it was Donovan who was plotting to deceive both Miles and Dai even before the orders were signed. On paper, Miles headed all of OSS in the Far East with Al Lusey as his assistant. But in practice, Miles would only run Special Operations. Donovan gave Lusey a secret dual role. He would direct Secret Intelligence, which would be entirely concealed from Miles, Dai, and Stilwell.

Lusey objected. The plan would require bringing in personnel without clearing them with Dai and the Generalissimo and then hiding their activities. Although

Lusey emphasized his loyalty to Donovan and the OSS, he warned that his secret duties could not remain secret from Dai Li, and when the general found out, it would all blow up in their faces. Ernest Price, an OSS Secret Intelligence manager in Washington, was genuinely confused about who was to be in command of whom in Chongqing, and a memo to Donovan with pointed questions about it got him fired.[13] Price was so worried about the Lusey–Miles implications for Sino–American relations that he went directly to Roosevelt, who ordered a quiet investigation. But Donovan suavely convinced the president's representative that Price was just a bitter former employee trying to get his job back.

Although he managed to get Price's concerns swept under the rug, Donovan still had some fighting to do to keep his plan intact. Colonel Ellery Huntington, OSS chief of Special Operations, also questioned the wisdom of keeping Lusey's real position from Dai and Miles. He soon received an angry, sarcastic memo from Donovan that in essence ordered him to do his job and stay out of it. He did.

Despite advice to the contrary, Donovan honestly believed that Miles would never know the difference and perhaps would not even care. But the secret did not last long, and when it got out, Miles in fact cared very much. In early December, Lusey mentioned to Miles a new OSS man, Arthur Duff, who was on his way to Kunming. Miles knew nothing about him, and questions led to the discovery that he was a Secret Intelligence agent reporting to Lusey. A livid Miles fired off a protest to Washington, reminding them that the Chinese would not permit an SI agent working outside SACO, and that it was foolish to try to sneak one in. Prodded by Miles, Metzel in Washington discovered that Lusey was actually on the SI payroll, reporting to Norwood Allman in New York, who was working with C. V. Starr to implement the original Dragon Plan.

Donovan was embarrassed to have been caught and quickly reversed course. By the end of January 1943, Lusey was officially back in Special Operations under Miles, but Secret Intelligence continued without either of them for the next year, and Miles watched it all unfold.

In Kunming, Duff managed Metropolitan Motors Overseas, Inc., a front company owned by Starr that was really in the espionage business. Starr launched New York and Chongqing editions of the *Shanghai Evening Post and Mercury* with secret agents posing as reporters. Their OSS connection was even withheld from the agency staff in order to keep it from Chiang, Dai, and Miles. As Yu wrote, the OSS had spies in China who did not even know they were spies. OSS agents in Kunming and Chongqing entertained Chinese informants with opium and prostitutes, in direct contradiction to Dai's policy. Early on, Miles had suggested procuring cash from Washington to pay informants, but Dai killed the idea on grounds that purchased intelligence was worthless.

Perhaps the most galling to Miles was a suitcase delivered to Happy Valley for Duff. The customs list attached revealed that it contained items such as lipsticks and compacts, presumably to elicit secrets from the ladies. Miles resented having this frivolous cache delivered to his doorstep at a time that he was having trouble getting radio tubes and batteries. He refused the delivery.

Each time Miles questioned Donovan about these unauthorized agents, he was told that they were in China on personal business. Feeling betrayed and humiliated, Miles's commitment to the OSS deteriorated. The original deal had called for Miles to collect information from Dai's intelligence net and feed it to Donovan in exchange for OSS's logistical and financial help. At first, cultural differences frustrated Miles's efforts. Dai's men simply did not understand what kind of intelligence was useful to the United States. They reported internal gossip and political wrangling as avidly as they did movements of enemy cargo ships. Once quality information finally began to flow, Miles passed it on to OSS, but his old professional loyalties prompted him to send it to the Office of Naval Intelligence first. This habit likely fueled Donovan's later claim that Miles's duties to SACO and to the OSS imposed conflicting priorities which one man could not manage.

In addition to logistics, money, and materiel, OSS contributed operations personnel to SACO at several satellite camps and at Happy Valley. Whether fact or perception, Miles found that some of these people did not mesh with SACO as they should have, complaining too often about the food, the mail, and the Chinese. Indeed, at Camp Three, where SACO's only serious morale problems between Americans and Chinese hampered operations the first year, Miles traced the source to the camp's second in command, an OSS officer with a bad attitude.[14]

In another case of bad chemistry, an OSS agent arrived unannounced at the secret camp of Lieutenant Joseph Champe's Yangtze River Raiders (see Chapter Fifteen). The Raiders were achieving stunning success in sabotage and guerrilla attacks, the result of careful risk assessment and planning. Champe attributed the results to the manner in which the Americans and Chinese had learned to take joint ownership of every mission. The OSS man knew none of this, but he certainly knew the Raiders were having swell adventures. Ready for action with his own private arsenal strapped to his body, he told Champe he wanted to take some of the Chinese guerrillas out to see if they lived up to their reputations. As Miles recounted the story, "Here was an officer who referred to the guerrillas as though they were a pack of hunting dogs."[15] Champe kicked him out.

FROM GENERAL DONOVAN'S PERSPECTIVE, he was dumping significant resources into SACO and getting little in return, and though he signed the hard-fought SACO Agreement in April 1943, he did so reluctantly. Those aspects of the Sino–American verbal arrangement that had tied OSS's hands were now in writing. The document expressly prohibited any American intelligence activities without permission and cooperation of the Chinese Nationalist government. Donovan summoned his skills as an attorney and began looking for loopholes that would let him run the Dragon Plan unfettered.

Desire to circumvent the agreement became urgent when an opportunity arose in the spring of 1943. Members of Stilwell's Chongqing staff headed by John Paton Davies hatched a plan to gather intelligence from Communist-occupied China, where they believed they could obtain the highest quality information. They would need direct cooperation from the Communists, so Davies met with Zhou Enlai with promising results. Davies wanted to employ OSS agents for the project, but that would be impossible under the SACO Agreement, which required approval from Chiang Kai-shek, the Communists' bitter enemy.

Davies proposed a workaround: an OSS branch in the China–Burma–India theater located outside China—and therefore outside the SACO Agreement. Donovan tapped Colonel Richard Heppner, also an attorney, to run an intelligence bureau in India. In that post, Heppner was technically working outside the scope of SACO, but he also shuttled to Stilwell's Chongqing office as OSS liaison. In this second capacity, his activities were unquestionably tied to SACO, but no one in the OSS or Stilwell's office informed SACO. By August, Miles discovered not only Heppner's presence but that he was filtering Miles's OSS materiel requisitions. Miles resented this babysitter from Washington, but he tried to play nice and so invited Heppner to Happy Valley for dinner.

Heppner replied that he was not about to go up there and eat with chopsticks "like a god-damned Chinese."[16]

It was clear that the worst nightmares of Dai and Miles were coming to fruition. Heppner and Starr behaved like the worst of the old China hands. Miles had warned Donovan against employing such men, and they and their cronies were running around loose in China without the approval of the government—just as Dai had feared. Miles complained to Metzel, who told OSS officials that Heppner would either have to honor Miles's authority as the highest OSS officer in the Far East or get out of China.

BY THE END OF SEPTEMBER 1943, with Miles's OSS appointment less than a year old, Donovan finally had to acknowledge that putting Miles in charge and then trying to skirt around him had not worked. His advisors convinced him that he could not simply cut ties with SACO and still maintain the OSS in China. He continued to look for a legal way out of his bind. If he couldn't get rid of his dependence on SACO, perhaps he could get Miles out of OSS and work with Dai directly.

Meanwhile, a bitter Miles did little to help his own cause. To the chagrin of Donovan, he told Metzel and others that Dai Li equated the trustworthiness of the OSS with that of the British and included its agents in his little black book of enemies. He let colleagues know that he considered himself a naval officer and deputy director of SACO first. He even said as much to Commander S. David Halliwell, an OSS representative who came to Chongqing on Donovan's behalf in late October to confer with Miles. On the day of his arrival, Miles met with him all night but left the next morning for a meeting in India with Lord Mountbatten against Halliwell's wishes. The commander was indignant, but Miles maintained that Halliwell had come unannounced while the meeting in India had been booked for months.

That was the last straw for Donovan. He wrote in a letter to Purnell on November 3 that Miles had to be removed from his post as OSS coordinator but should retain his authority within SACO. Donovan argued that the conflicts imposed by Miles's dual roles with the navy and the OSS made it impossible for him to function. His personal commitment to the Chinese prevented him from performing intelligence activities, but the OSS could not operate under those constraints. Purnell replied that, on the contrary, Miles performed intelligence activities every day, but he did so in cooperation with the Chinese as specified in the agreement. Rather than supporting his efforts, the OSS had executed intelligence independently, usurping his authority and embarrassing him in front of his Chinese partners. Furthermore, neither Donovan nor Purnell could remove Miles from his job. That required a change in the agreement approved by all its signatories, including Chiang Kai-shek and President Roosevelt.

But by that point, it mattered little what anyone had to say. Donovan wanted Miles gone, and on November 9, he sent him a cable advising him that he was to be relieved of his OSS responsibilities. Later that month, Donovan went to the Cairo Conference, where British Prime Minister Winston Churchill, Chiang Kai-shek, and Roosevelt convened to discuss Japan. While in Cairo, Roosevelt privately agreed with Donovan that the United States needed to have an independent intelligence program in China and authorized Donovan to tell Chiang as much.

Donovan flew to Chongqing with Halliwell after the conference. When he arrived on December 6, Miles, Dai, and Xiao Bo, who had hurried to China to lend his support, met him at the airport with an entourage, whisked him up to Happy Valley, and feted him with beautiful women and a fitting opera about feuding brothers resolving their differences. Donovan presented Dai with $5,000 for the school for orphans. But after all the smiles and gracious gestures, Donovan met privately with Dai Li.

Donovan said the quality of information he was getting was not good enough, and that if things did not improve, it would be the end of the OSS gravy train. Moreover, he was under orders from his president to collect intelligence in China, and he intended to follow those orders with or without Dai Li's cooperation.

Then it was Miles's turn. Donovan sat him down in a closed office and told him that he was being relieved of his duties as OSS Coordinator in the Far East effective immediately, but that it would in no other way diminish his position or responsibilities in SACO. There are two conflicting versions of this meeting. According to Donovan biographer Douglas Waller, the two met tête-à-tête, Miles trembling before Donovan as the latter sugarcoated the dismissal, asserting that the joint OSS–SACO post was too much for one man. Miles told a different story in a letter to Metzel, that he sat in a chair smirking like a smart-alecky school kid as Donovan, Halliwell, and Major Carl Hoffman of the OSS stood around him yelling accusations. Miles took particular pleasure in Hoffman's role in this drama because when Miles had first met him a year earlier, the brand new attorney-turned-army-officer was wearing his insignia upside-down. But regardless of what happened during the meeting, the result was the same: Donovan fired Miles.

That evening at a banquet in Dai Li's home, Donovan repeated that the OSS was going to operate in China whether Dai liked it or not. The party deteriorated into a shouting match during which Dai threatened to kill any unauthorized OSS agents in China, and Donovan threatened to retaliate by killing Nationalist Chinese generals tit for tat. Even the gentlemanly Xiao Bo joined in the yelling.

To Miles, the night was like a bad dream. Donovan's behavior flew in the face of everything Miles believed in and had possibly undone everything he had accomplished with the Chinese. In Donovan's view, Miles's acquiescence to Dai and over-the-top adoption of Chinese ways had undermined the United States's intelligence operation. Donovan believed he had firmly put a stop to it.

The next day, Donovan went to Chiang Kai-shek's home, fully prepared to state the American case for unfettered intelligence gathering in China, knowing that he had the full support of Roosevelt. But the Generalissimo was ready for him. Serene but firm, he told Donovan that China could no more tolerate an unauthorized American intelligence operation in China than the Americans would accept the same from the Chinese in the United States. It was a rare moment in which neither bullying nor persuasion would get Donovan what he wanted. He realized that in order to achieve his aims in China, he would have to do so behind the Generalissimo's back.

But figuring out how to maneuver around Chiang Kai-shek would have to wait for another day. Donovan's immediate problem was to establish a new workflow for the OSS within SACO—without Miles and the navy.

Before Donovan left Chongqing, he, Miles, and Dai divided SACO's activities between the navy and the OSS, with the OSS in charge of intelligence, counterespionage, and special operations, including propaganda and land missions. The navy would oversee weather, maritime operations, aerial reconnaissance, mining, and radio interception. In addition, the two groups would have overlapping duties such as communications and training. Miles cabled these details to Metzel in Washington. Colonel John Coughlin arrived in Chongqing on December 14, 1943, to take over OSS China.

Rear Admiral Purnell, who had been in the hospital while all this was happening, got back to his office in early January 1944 and exploded when he saw Miles's cable. He immediately told Donovan that he had no authority to remove Miles and that Miles had overstepped his own authority when he agreed to the OSS/Navy division of duties. Admiral Ernest King shared Purnell's outrage. The navy had conceived, created, and managed SACO as the Friendship Project before the OSS had ever entered the scene. Although the OSS had sent men, money, and equipment, the navy had contributed more than ninety percent of SACO's resources. The new division of duties unacceptably stripped the navy of control over its own personnel and materials. In addition, it was unclear to whom Coughlin was to report. According to the SACO Agreement, it should have been Miles, but Donovan had left this matter deliberately ambiguous.

Miles was called back to Washington to help sort everything out. In another round of meetings with navy brass and the OSS, no one seemed to agree on what had been settled in Chongqing, despite a blizzard of papers produced by the OSS. Admiral Frederick J. Horne, vice chief of Naval Operations, sat the parties down in his office in the belief that he could discern who had promised what and come to some kind of consensus, but Miles, Donovan, and everyone else dug in their heels and refused to budge. Horne gave up and adjourned the meeting in disgust.

Miles left Washington for China in January 1944 suffering an ear infection, a bruised ego, and an uneasy feeling about his own fate and that of SACO. But during a stopover in India, he received a phone call that restored his confidence and good cheer. He had been promoted to commodore, and his operation was elevated from a nameless outfit to Naval Group China, of which he was commander. King hoped the promotion and the official designation of the group would solidify SACO's position against future attempts by others to take over or dismantle it.

WITHOUT OFFICIALLY AGREEING to anything, the Office of Special Services and the U.S. Navy simply steered clear of each other in China. OSS operatives under Coughlin worked directly with Dai Li. OSS members in the SACO satellite camps were pulled out suddenly, leaving the navy scrambling to replace them. At Happy Valley, the OSS men moved into a separate house and started serving their own mess, all the while making the dreaded remarks about "civilized" food and utensils.

As two of the world's most powerful spymasters, Dai Li and William Donovan enjoyed mutual respect, but Dai had found the power struggle between the American agencies confusing and was never satisfied with the separate OSS in SACO. To begin with, he was never sure who was in charge. In contrast to Miles, who worked out of Happy Valley most of the time, Coughlin was rarely in Chongqing. SACO was not his highest priority, and he missed important meetings.

Soon after the new arrangement took hold, OSS opened an intelligence school to train Dai Li's most promising new agents. The Chinese were initially delighted, but their hopes turned to disappointment. The OSS could not supply instructors and ended up borrowing personnel from the navy. A similar lack of manpower hampered a joint plan for Chinese and OSS experts to go through a vast stockpile of Japanese documents Dai had stored in caves. After starting the project with enthusiasm, the OSS provided only one researcher for the team. The Chinese were surprised and insulted by this lack of commitment.

Finally, the OSS continued to bring in old China hands as secret intelligence agents who did not work within SACO and had not been approved by the Chinese. Donovan believed he was getting away with it, but Dai Li's agents always identified and reported them. Like Miles before him, Major Hoffman, temporarily OSS chief within SACO, complained about the embarrassment these men caused him. The worst example was William B. Christian, former manager of the British–American Tobacco Company in China. His British connection made his presence particularly offensive and suspicious to Chiang and Dai.

In October 1944, Donovan sent an OSS officer, Brigadier General Lyle Miller, to Chongqing to discuss some of Dai's concerns with the OSS–SACO arrangement. Their conference was fruitful. Miller compiled a ten-point list of Dai's issues for Donovan's consideration, including a replacement for Coughlin, an end to any OSS connection with CBI Theater command, and clarification of the OSS's future commitment to SACO. He also emphasized that Miles's performance was exemplary for China and, from Dai's perspective, for the navy.

But that evening, the spirit of the meeting was entirely undone during a banquet Dai hosted in Miller's honor. Miles had sullenly refused an invitation because the dinner was OSS business. Miller appeared to have suddenly undergone a personality transplant from sensitive envoy to ugly American. He repeatedly demanded that Dai Li bring out the "sing-song girls" for his entertainment and asked if the Generalissimo had new women while Madame Chiang was out of town. He referred to the Chinese as "Chinamen" throughout the evening and called China a "twelfth-rank power."[17] Eddie Liu stopped translating as the racial slurs and national insults continued for two hours.

Dai canceled his meeting with Miller the next day and told Miles what had happened. He said he would not immediately inform the Generalissimo, who had more serious matters on his plate in the wake of Stilwell's recall. Neither Miles nor the OSS staff notified Washington. Dai brooded for four days and finally spoke up. He confronted Major Arden Dow, an OSS trainer who had attended the banquet because he happened to be the highest-ranking member of the agency present in Chongqing that evening. Dai told Dow that he held Donovan personally responsible for the insult as head of the OSS and that Chiang Kai-shek would surely expel the OSS from China when he learned of the insults. He also told Miles that as American head of SACO, he, too, was responsible and that Dai might be forced to shut down SACO and expel all Americans.

When Donovan found out about the incident, his primary concern was that Miles would use it to undermine the OSS and promote himself. Official apologies were made, Miller was sacked, and it blew over.

But the Miller debacle focused Dai Li's growing disenchantment with the OSS. Nor did the agency ever get what it had hoped for from SACO. Donovan had expected a flood of intelligence from the Chinese once Miles was replaced, but the change had the opposite effect. As the relationship soured, the Chinese shared less and less. The OSS relationship with SACO became a sham, and Donovan eventually bypassed it altogether.

CHAPTER 9

A Landlocked Navy in Stormy Seas

YEARS AFTER THE WAR WAS OVER, with the Communists ruling the People's Republic of China, Chiang Kai-shek heading a second China in Taiwan, and SACO long dissolved, Rear Admiral Milton Miles was fond of quoting a letter he had received from General Claire Chennault in 1958. The general reflected on his own experience in China:

> I always found the Chinese friendly and cooperative. The Japanese gave me a little trouble at times, but not very much. The British in Burma were quite difficult sometimes. But Washington gave me trouble night and day throughout the whole war![18]

Chennault's words perfectly summed up how Miles had felt running SACO. The profound obstacles of rickety infrastructure, disease, language, cultural differences, enemy gunfire, and even attempts on his life were nothing compared to his precarious position as a landlocked naval officer caught in jealous competition between the U.S. Army and Navy. And it wasn't just the military. The State Department never warmed up to the idea of the United States working with Dai Li, and General William Donovan never stopped trying to take over SACO through the back door.

And, although General George Marshall had approved the SACO Agreement under pressure, he was never comfortable with its command structure. Having Miles report to the Joint Chiefs instead of the theater commander defied the army's time-honored continuity-of-command principle. In his view, it left Miles on the loose, potentially causing conflict with the theater agenda. Moreover, it placed Miles and all other American SACOs under the control of a foreign military command. To Miles, Marshall's objection on this last point was a double standard because he certainly expected all Allied forces, not just Americans, to answer to General Dwight Eisenhower in Europe, and Miles did not see why Americans under General Dai Li were different.

General Joseph Stilwell, U.S. Commander of the China–Burma–India Theater, never liked the Friendship Project from the beginning, and he didn't like it any better when it became the Sino–American Cooperative Organization. But he did like Miles, and he therefore made the pragmatic choice to approve the agreement's specified chain of command. He had been in China long enough to know that if Dai Li didn't approve of the arrangement, the whole project was doomed, and since the Joint Chiefs had authorized it, he saw no point in fighting it.

Stilwell's blessing foiled Marshall's plan to block the agreement. Marshall had said he would accept it only with Stilwell's approval, fully expecting Vinegar Joe to say no. As discussed earlier, approving the agreement meant that Marshall had to swallow the navy's preparations for an amphibious invasion of China.[19] Hydrographic surveys, coast watches, and photo reconnaissance were all included in the document, and they would lay the groundwork for the navy to sweep into China in glory. Stilwell had already suffered a humiliating defeat in Burma in July 1942. A flashy landing by the navy with guns blazing would make the army look even worse by comparison.

The army–navy rivalry repeatedly reared its head in China. It even became entangled in General Donovan's failed Dragon Plan, the sweeping OSS China intelligence proposal. General George Strong, head of G-2, the army's intelligence service, asserted that the plan should be a job for G-2 and the Office of Naval Intelligence. But his argument was a sham, according to scholar Maochun Yu.

In reality, Strong wanted the Dragon Plan suppressed because it placed too much emphasis on matters that naturally fell to the navy, such as surveillance of maritime activities. With most of the fighting against the Japanese already a navy affair, the army wanted to keep China to itself.[20]

Intelligence became a perpetual bone of contention between the army and the navy, just as with the OSS. Few Americans trusted Dai Li, who remained aloof to most foreigners, spawning general suspicion that he was withholding intelligence from the army with Miles's complicity. Stilwell's deputy chief of staff, Brigadier General Benjamin G. Ferris, asked Miles in September 1944 what was happening to all the information he was gathering, and Miles replied with twenty-eight typed pages itemizing three hundred eighty-eight reports he had sent to China–Burma–India Command over the previous ten months.

Distrust between the army and the navy was a two-way street. It was not unheard of for SACOs in the field to come across U.S. Army intelligence personnel who struck up friendly conversations leading to probing questions. But all SACO men had strict instructions never to discuss SACO or the Japanese with anyone outside SACO, including Americans and especially the army.

Interservice rivalry worked two ways, and Miles was not immune to jealousy himself. By March 1944, the navy had begun formulating serious plans for a fleet landing in China as early as December, and Admiral King told Miles to put coastal preparations on the front burner. Since his first journey with Dai Li in early summer 1942, Miles had done little on the coast, but now he swung into hurry-up mode. In May, he mounted a second coastal scouting expedition to provide King with more details about geography and enemy activity. The trip also prepared for setting up SACO's long-planned coast watch network and a chain of camps on the fringes of Japanese territory that were to train Chinese troops in support of the invasion. Miles and a handful of other American SACOs spent several weeks with a Chinese general as their guide walking hundreds of miles in the hills above the sea and rivers, taking photos and notes, particularly around Xiamen at King's request.

Meanwhile, Admiral Chester Nimitz, commander of the Pacific Fleet, sent U.S. Navy Captain Wilfred L. Painter to China to survey the coastline. Earlier in the war, Painter, a Seabee, had won accolades for similar work in Australia, at Guadalcanal, and on islands throughout the Pacific. Upon arrival in China, he reported to the army, which assumed supervision of the expedition and added its own engineers to the party. Immediately after Miles's jaunt along the coast, he ran into Painter in Kunming. Learning of Painter's plans, Miles's hair stood up on his back. He didn't see what right the army had to commandeer a navy mission, and he was a bit miffed that his own work seemed to have been forgotten. He told Painter that he was already in charge of a survey under orders of the Joint Chiefs, and he had Painter placed back under navy command. But jealousy aside, Miles was an old-fashioned military man trained to be cooperative and knew nothing was to be gained by starting a fight with the navy. He turned all his photos over to Painter and arranged for the new expedition's final report to be printed at the SACO plant in India.

The survey captured the attention of General Daniel Sultan, Stilwell's new deputy commander in Burma and India, who called a private conference with Stilwell and Miles at Myitkyina in northern Burma. The two generals were keen to know if it was true that the Joint Chiefs had Miles collecting data along the Chinese coast from Shanghai to Xiamen. Miles replied that it was one of his primary missions, and that what he had discovered was encouraging. He saw an opportunity for the United States to capture a Chinese port, which would provide both a base for attacking Japan and an entry point for supplies.

Sultan and Stilwell were dismissive yet appalled. To them, the only way for large-scale penetration into China was through Burma. Stilwell had devoted every ounce of his energy—and every ton of materiel he could squeeze out of the tortuous supply chain—to taking back Burma ever since he had lost it to the Japanese in 1942. He had even warned Miles from the beginning that SACO's Hump tonnage would be severely limited because Burma had priority over everything else. His fixation had cost him respect and would ultimately cost him his job.

The army generals argued that Japan's strength in eastern China would render taking and holding a Chinese seaport impossible. The only viable option was to break through Burma, creating a corridor to transport troops and supplies from the west to push the enemy out to sea. But Miles countered that his Chinese SACO troops alone could hold the enemy at bay along the coast to support a landing. Once a port was secure, more Allied men and tonnage could be delivered by sea in a day than could come by truck in a week.

Thus the old army–navy rivalry had wormed its way into an office in the Burmese jungle. Even though Miles reminded them that he had no role in these decisions, Stilwell and Sultan seemed determined to suffocate his heretical ideas lest they be unleashed.

Quizzing Miles about the navy's plans for the coast was only part of why Sultan had called the meeting. What he really wanted to know was what the navy was doing in China in the first place. According to Miles, upon discovering the existence of Naval Group China a few weeks earlier, Sultan had "dug up all the complaints that had ever been made … and sent them to General Marshall, requesting clarification of my status."[21] That had touched off an interservice skirmish within the Joint Chiefs in Washington. Marshall demanded to know just what Miles was up to, and King dashed off a five-page report of glowing successes, concluding with his own charge that Sultan was deliberately blocking SACO's supplies without reason or authority.

King's complaint about supplies was true. Without even knowing what Naval Group China was, Sultan had canceled its June Hump allowance on grounds that the Japanese were on the move. Miles was furious and seriously inconvenienced.

Before the meeting in Burma ended, Sultan and Stilwell agreed to make sure Miles's Hump tonnage came through uninterrupted, at least for the next several months, and they parted on a cheerful note. But though it ended well, it had opened rather awkwardly. The three officers had no sooner said their hellos than Sultan brusquely told Miles that he had no right to come into the theater and start operating without Stilwell's permission. Stilwell stepped right up to explain that Miles indeed had his permission and had been working in China for two years. Miles must have been privately grateful that he had made it his business to become Stilwell's friend regardless of their professional differences.

SULTAN'S ARBITRARY CANCELATION of SACO's monthly Hump tonnage was just the latest in Miles's unending struggle to get materials. He called supply trouble the "single biggest headache" SACO faced.[22] Logistics played a large part in the problem. The Japanese occupation made it impossible to bring materials in through Chinese seaports, and between the Japanese in the Pacific and the Germans in the Atlantic, American shipping was forced to take extended, indirect routes to India.

Despite these precautions, many ships fell victim to German and Japanese attack en route. While only four U.S. Navy cargo-class ships were sunk during the course of the war, the U.S. Merchant Marine lost more than fifteen hundred, including freighters, tankers, and liberty ships. Fifty went down in the Indian Ocean, one hundred thirty-four in the Pacific, and seventy in the South Atlantic.[23] More than once, SACO-bound supplies were lost at sea to enemy torpedoes and air attacks.

Furthermore, India's unstable political climate and ramshackle transportation system, as well as the U.S. military's complex supply chain, conspired to effect the disappearance of materials onto roadsides and into warehouses and the black market.

Adding to the problem, cargo flights over the Hump were entirely under U.S. Army control: army planes flown by army pilots. No matter what orders the supply men received, they were not likely to leave army cargo on a loading dock in India to make space for the navy, especially for an obscure outfit no one ever heard of. Hence SACO had to have men in Assam to help shipments along through a combination of administrative skill, pleading, and old-fashioned bribery. American cigarettes and whiskey bought a lot of goodwill.

The SACO supply system had begun as a gentleman's agreement in autumn 1942 between Miles and Stilwell, who had promised to throw a few hundred pounds on every flight over the Hump for SACO. But Stilwell's transportation officer frequently put off special requests from Miles because there were not enough planes.

T. V. Soong, the Generalissimo's brother-in-law, representative in Washington, and signatory to the SACO Agreement, anticipated serious problems for SACO if it had to depend on the army for transport of materials. He attached to the SACO Agreement a letter to Admiral King, advising that the document would be worthless unless the navy established its own transportation system, including cargo planes over the Hump. King concurred, but when Miles went to Stilwell offering four navy planes for Hump shipments in exchange for a guarantee of one hundred fifty tons for SACO per month, Stilwell said they had too many planes already. The obstacle, therefore, was not the number of planes, but the number of flights.

Stilwell ultimately agreed to the monthly SACO allowance, and that eased some of Miles's pain, although his supplies were still subject to the caprice of many unseen hands and clipboards. One hundred fifty tons may sound like a lot of material every month, but in reality, it wasn't much. Out of that came eighteen tons of batteries alone. In addition, there was radio and weather equipment, a new firearm presented to every graduate of SACO's guerrilla training schools, and items that were unavailable or prohibitively expensive in China. In addition, Miles had promised to reserve ten of those tons for the OSS, and he stood by that pledge even after they kicked him out. Unlike the army, Miles did not sacrifice one ounce for anything to comfort the men and officers, such as American food, toiletries, and clothing. The policy of doing as the Chinese thus served a second purpose, in addition to building communication and trust: It saved space on cargo planes for other things.

But beyond the usual problems any military outfit anywhere faces dealing with vehicles, paperwork, and mix-ups, SACO also had to contend with decision makers in the supply chain who either objected to what SACO was doing or didn't understand it. While Miles was in Washington lobbying for the agreement during winter 1943, he overheard a newly commissioned army officer dictating a letter canceling his requisition of single-shot rifles languishing in a warehouse. While under normal circumstances they were of little military use, they were destined for a group of Indian guerrillas working with SACO who had no guns at all except ones they had made themselves that kept blowing up in their faces. Although Miles got the cancelation reversed, the incident served as an example of the bottlenecks that occurred because of seemingly arbitrary decisions out of SACO's control.

Once the one hundred-fifty-ton deal was made, Miles could not get it increased. SACO had fewer than three hundred men on the ground when it was made, but by 1945, they numbered thirteen hundred, plus tens of thousands of Chinese troops under SACO's control. Miles was particularly resentful of this when SACO began producing the oxygen for the Hump fights and still got no increase. And once the Burma Road reopened and SACO began to receive supplies overland, the army wanted to deduct that tonnage from the Hump allocation. It seemed Miles couldn't catch a break.

SUPPLIES AND ARMY–NAVY SQUABBLES cast Miles on stormy seas, but they were by no means his only problems. Dai Li, the source of Naval Group China's unique access to China, also became the source of controversy, repeatedly putting

Miles on the defensive. The U.S. State Department and many others in government and the military had serious objections to the navy being mixed up with Dai, who was implicated in everything from kidnapping to assassinations to drug smuggling.

When Miles had first run into U.S. Ambassador to China Clarence Gauss in Kolkata on his way to Chongqing in 1942, the ambassador had come across as a sour mood on two feet, and that first impression never altered, even as Miles got to know Gauss in China. Miles's initial appointment as naval observer to the U.S. embassy in Chongqing was only a cover for his secret mission, which he had made clear when reporting to Gauss upon arrival. Miles explained that he had received secret, verbal orders from the Joint Chiefs, and he rarely returned to the embassy thereafter. Gauss resented that he was somehow responsible for Miles and yet had no control over him, and that the embassy was now connected to the unsavory Dai Li.

The embassy's protests grew louder in the summer of 1943, when SACO organized a small FBI-style training program, the Police and Investigation Unit, at Happy Valley for Chinese police officers. Students learned skills such as fingerprinting, handling evidence, and using lie detectors. The courses had been near the top of Dai Li's wish list during negotiations for the SACO Agreement. Dai controlled most of the police force in Free China, and many puppet police under the occupation were on Japan's payroll but secretly worked for Dai. He argued that China lacked knowledge of modern crime detection and would need a competent police force after the war. But until then, the police were among his most reliable intelligence agents, and he wanted them to be properly trained.

John Paton Davies, who had grown up in China as the son of Baptist missionaries and was serving as Stilwell's political advisor, warned Miles that he and Stilwell found it inappropriate for the United States to be involved in police activities in China or any other country. He said the State Department had been informed and did not approve of it.

Miles believed Davies was speaking only for himself, but the embassy was not the only group that was uneasy about it. Donovan and Stilwell also chimed in against the school because it had nothing to do with prosecuting war and was an improper use of American resources. SACO dropped the word "police" from the name of the program at the request of its critics.

That did little to ease Gauss's mind. The more SACO expanded, the less he liked it. In January 1944, he wrote Secretary of State Cordell Hull that Dai Li was the most hated and feared man in China and that SACO was engaged in activities that flew in the face of democracy. At the same time, Stanley K. Hornbeck, the State Department's director for the Far East, said Dai Li was only out to get as much equipment and supplies as he could from the United States and was giving nothing in return. That complaint caused a fight between Miles and Dai, prompting the latter to let American guerrilla instructors get into the fight as proof that he truly was using American resources to defeat the Japanese. Until then, Dai had resisted allowing Americans to be included in any field missions, insisting on limiting American SACOs to teaching and technical roles for reasons Miles never fully understood.[24]

Davies spoke with Roosevelt's personal advisor, Harry Hopkins, about the Dai Li situation later in the year. He painted Miles as a naïve renegade who was completely taken in by his Chinese partner, and though Stilwell agreed, he was loathe to stop him because it would only get Stilwell sucked into an army–navy fracas. Hopkins thought SACO sounded un-American.[25]

The complaints intensified over the FBI school at Happy Valley after it blossomed into Camp Nine, a full-blown secret police academy a mile from SACO headquarters that looked more like an American college campus than a military camp. With courses in everything from Chinese criminal law to handling police dogs, its instructors included retired FBI agents and New York police detectives. The State Department and the OSS asked Miles to remove the words "traffic" and "police" from the titles of three courses to play down their civilian connotations.

In addition to the school having insufficient military purpose, the State Department did not want the United States teaching interrogation techniques and providing weapons and police dogs that Dai could use against his political enemies. It was tantamount to sanctioning political terrorism. But the school had been part of the SACO Agreement from the start, and Miles never received orders to cancel it.

Suspicions of Dai Li came to a head in March 1945 with the disappearance of Professor Fei Gong, an American-educated historian and prominent liberal from Zhejian University. He was on sabbatical in Chongqing but was keeping a low profile in fear of reprisals from Chiang Kai-shek after signing a statement against the current dictatorship. He nevertheless accepted an invitation to a conference a four-hour ferry ride from Chongqing and brought a student along for security. As the pair waited at the dock for a 4:00 a.m. ferry, the student dashed off to get breakfast. When he returned, the professor was gone. The student assumed that he had missed the boat, but Fei never turned up at the conference. He had vanished.

Forty of Professor Fei's colleagues who believed Chiang Kai-shek's secret police had nabbed him signed a letter of protest and delivered it to General Albert Wedemeyer, who had taken over for Stilwell. He ordered Miles to investigate and complained directly to the Generalissimo. Dai Li appointed an international team, Lieutenant Commander Clark, a former New York detective teaching at Camp Nine, and Shanghai detective Shen Zui to lead the investigation. Their exhaustive search included jails, prisons, and hospitals. They viewed the bodies of at least ten drowning victims that washed up downstream of the dock. They even visited a dozen monasteries after a student claimed he had seen the professor wearing a monk's robe.

Rumors flew around Chongqing that Dai had had the professor killed and disposed of the body in a pool of nitric acid. Clark and Shen failed to turn up any useful clues. Decades later, Shen, then living in the People's Republic of China safe from remnants of the Guomindang, betrayed no suspicion that Dai or Chiang had any connection with the case. He said it was a mystery that would never be solved.[26]

Miles had known before he first left Washington what the State Department thought of Dai, but during three years of working closely with the man, Miles came to believe that the accusations were untrue or mischaracterized. He knew that Dai was responsible for many killings, but they were part of China's brutal system of justice. One night when the two SACO leaders were on the road together, Dai returned from an absence of several hours in a black mood and uncharacteristically suggested that he and Miles get drunk. After several drinks, he confessed that he had been forced to order the execution of a childhood friend.

As to smuggling, a rumor in Chongqing in 1943 said the Generalissimo had caught Dai in large-scale opium smuggling and was soon to be dismissed, but Miles never saw any change in his status. Miles knew that Dai regularly sent agents to Shanghai to exchange contraband for contraband. It was the only way they could get such essentials as wool, radio tubes, and tires, and the Chinese often paid the Japanese with counterfeit Japanese currency printed by Dai's network. Smuggling played such an important part in China's wartime economy that there was a smuggling and antismuggling course at Camp Nine taught by Chinese instructors Dai appointed.

None of this absolves Dai Li from the accusations of his worst critics, but it does place them in context. Even his most heinous crimes were at the behest of Chiang Kai-shek, and although the Generalissimo had his detractors among the Allies, he was not maligned by American military officers and diplomats the way Dai was. Chiang was a handsome man made more attractive to Westerners by adopting the Methodist faith and pleasing manners and marrying a glamorous, American-educated woman, Soong Mei-ling, known in the States as "Madame Chiang." In contrast, Dai had a rough-hewn look, an intense, watchful air, and a reputation for despising foreigners. He was much easier to hate.

GENERAL STILWELL WAS RECALLED from his post in October 1944, and General Wedemeyer arrived in Chongqing to take his place a month later. Stilwell's departure was not unexpected. T. V. Soong representing Chiang Kai-shek had asked the United States that he be removed as early as July 1942. In addition to commander of the China–Burma–India Theater, Stilwell was chief of staff to Chiang and had made it no secret that he expected complete control of China's armed forces. But Chiang Kai-shek, who was supreme Allied commander in China, had never agreed to this and had no intention of permitting it. This and Stilwell's emphasis on Burma placed him frequently at odds with the Generalissimo, who wanted more resources devoted to air power. Stilwell got so frustrated that he actually considered having Chiang killed, according to William Donovan's biographer, Douglas Waller.[27]

When Wedemeyer got to Chongqing, he found an administrative mess left by Stilwell, and he resolved to clean things up from top to bottom. To that end, he needed to get some kind of control over the helter-skelter, quasi-military activities in the theater. He called a meeting a couple of months after his arrival that included U.S. Army and British intelligence, the OSS, Xiao Bo, Miles, and Dai Li. Wedemeyer assumed a stance of authority over all, displaying the very attitude Miles had worked to avoid with the Chinese for nearly three years. Wedemeyer asked all present, including Dai, to submit weekly reports of their clandestine or quasi-military activities to army intelligence at his headquarters. Dai made no objection during the meeting, but in a private talk with Miles that night that lasted until 3:00 a.m., he said he had only appeared cooperative because the British were present. He would take orders from no one but the Generalissimo, nor did he intend to ask permission to do his job in his own country as he saw fit. Furthermore, he would not make written reports that could be leaked to the Communists or the British.

As part of his housecleaning, Wedemeyer set out to end SACO's special status outside CBI Theater command. He could not tolerate Miles operating outside his authority and particularly under the Chinese. Miles explained that the chain of command was necessary because of the nature of his work, and in any case, it could not be changed without changing the SACO Agreement with the approval of President Roosevelt and Generalissimo Chiang Kai-shek. But unlike Stilwell and Donovan, Wedemeyer was not willing to work around the situation or just look the other way. Any document could be changed, and he set out to do exactly that.

During a trip to Washington in March 1945, Wedemeyer pleaded his case to Roosevelt, and the navy got wind of it. Eager to protect the outfit from army control, the navy called Miles to Washington to lobby once again for SACO's status quo. But this time, it didn't work. The Joint Chiefs voted to support Wedemeyer and amend the SACO Agreement, unambiguously placing every American person and thing, clandestine or not, under the authority of the commander general, U.S. Forces China Theater. King, the lone vote against it, merely shrugged. The fight was over.

Dai Li and Chiang Kai-shek never approved the change, but Wedemeyer did not trouble himself with this technicality. He had the support of the Joint Chiefs and conducted business as if the amendment were in full force; King conducted business as if it were not, continuing to communicate directly with Miles as his superior. Miles was left to flounder between the army and the navy and was squashed flat.

Wedemeyer acted immediately. During the first week of April, he canceled SACO's Hump tonnage altogether and cut off all transport of personnel for SACO into China except as replacements.

The lack of supplies did not shut down SACO. SACO already lived off the land, not by pilfering and commandeering food, but by purchasing it locally. However, the cutoff did create desperate conditions. In the summer of 1945, a small company of Chinese SACO guerrillas led by an American navy officer broke into a U.S. Army warehouse in central China and helped themselves to enough ammunition and food to complete a mission.

The personnel cutoff left about nine hundred SACOs stranded in Kolkata at Camp Knox, which was designed to hold half that number. These were Fort Pierce-trained Scouts and Raiders specially groomed for SACO duty along the coast. The handful who got to China before the suspension wowed Miles with their superior skill and physical prowess, and he began to reshape his plans to make the most of them. He was frustrated that hundreds of such men were stuck playing cards in India.

Miles was not the only one upset about it. In late June, Congressman Harry R. Sheppard of California, chairman of the house subcommittee on naval appropriations, stopped in Kunming on an inspection tour of Asia, meeting with Wedemeyer and U.S. Ambassador Patrick Hurley, and then went on to Kolkata. (Kunming was the chosen rendezvous point because Chongqing was in the midst of a cholera epidemic; Miles and Dai were in the field.) What Sheppard saw in China made him worried that the army had marginalized the navy, but when he saw the crowded, idle navy men waiting to go over the Hump and learned that the army had stopped personnel transports for SACO, he became livid. Some men had been stuck since February. Sheppard wrote to Wedemeyer demanding that four hundred fifty men and a hundred vehicles be transported immediately, or he would inform the President.

Miles had no hand in this but feared that he looked like a tattletale. He wrote to Wedemeyer that, while he was grateful to have these men, he would never have involved politicians to resolve military matters. By the second week in July, it mattered little how it had happened. The Fort Pierce men began arriving in China, but before they could unpack their sea bags, the war had ended without them.

SIMMERING BENEATH ALL THE CONFLICTS and power plays among the U.S. actors in China was the unresolved struggle between the Communists and the

Nationalists. Their 1937 commitment to fight the Japanese together was a truce, not a peace agreement. It put their inevitable showdown on hold without ending their mutual mistrust, animosity, and determination to prevail in the end.

The United States was committed to supporting Chiang Kai-shek's government for the duration of the war, but sympathy was growing within the U.S. government and among the public for the Communists, who were often called "agrarian reformers" in the American press. To many, the Communists promised hope for democracy, while the Nationalists represented the last gasp of the warlord era's oppression and dictatorship. SACO critics in the U.S. Army and the State Department asserted that the very existence of SACO was tantamount to the United States choosing sides in a civil war. These objections were just one more obstacle for Miles to surmount in his ongoing battle for SACO.

PART 5

Operations and the SACO Experience

CHAPTER 10

Teaching: A Learning Experience

CAPTAIN MILTON MILES arrived in China in May 1942 with a blank slate before him but with a firm idea of what he intended to achieve. He had orders to create a weather forecasting service and an intelligence network for the U.S. Navy and to investigate conditions on the coast in preparation for a large-scale invasion to come. Although he had not yet discovered the vehicle for carrying out his mission, he never dreamed it would include running a school, let alone a dozen of them. Yet that was the commitment he made during the air attack outside Pucheng when he agreed to train and arm fifty thousand Chinese soldiers for Dai Li.

As SACO developed, training Chinese soldiers came to occupy a major portion of the organization's time and resources. Nearly every American in the group, whether storekeeper, photographer, or aerologist, doubled as a teacher. These young men found themselves in an extraordinary position. Few had any experience teaching. They knew their specialties inside and out but little of the wider world. Most had never even been out of the United States, let alone had a one-on-one relationship with someone of an alien culture. The student-teacher relationships posed equal challenges for the Chinese as they worked through conflicting national sentiments. Teachers held positions of highest respect in China, but at the same time, the country had recently cast off former notions of western superiority. But these Americans had the blessings of Dai Li, who had sent the students to the schools. Moreover, Miles's instinct to demand of and nurture in his men respect for China, its government, and its people set the stage for success.

Dai Li had made the proposal for the school in the first place because he needed a modern fighting force. The Nationalist Chinese troops were poorly trained and poorly armed, a patchwork of experienced professionals, local militias, and recent recruits with nothing but their hatred of the Japanese to qualify them. He maintained that, man for man, they were the equals of any soldiers in the world. But unlike Americans, they lacked the ability to work together in larger groups or make impromptu decisions in the confusion of battle. Just as importantly, the Chinese had insufficient guns and other equipment. A coordinated training and equipment program would produce soldiers fully ready and able to fight the Japanese, which was in China's—as well as America's—interest.

In addition, Chinese personnel could be trained to help carry out Miles's primary, noncombat missions for the navy. Farmers and factory workers could be transformed into aerologists, radio operators, and medics and also provide security for the navy establishments.

Dai was anxious for the training to begin and already had students waiting while Miles was still working out of Fairy Cave during that first summer in Chongqing. The Americans had barely settled in Happy Valley and had received no supplies when they accepted their first small group of trainees in October 1942. These men became guinea pigs for a training program destined to grow to thirteen camps that trained a combined forty thousand soldiers, technicians, MBIS agents, and police officers.[28]

THE FIRST STUDENTS TO ARRIVE at Happy Valley were hand-selected by Dai Li, intelligent and eager to learn. They were physically much smaller than Americans, which at first led their instructors to treat them like precocious children rather than adult soldiers on a serious mission. The first few weeks resembled a Boy Scout outing. But with the help of translators, better supplies, and experience, the instruction became more sober and professional.

Demolition was a favorite subject; the students enjoyed the drama of blowing things up and relished the sound of an explosion. Left to their own devices, they would waste explosives simply for the thrill of hearing the "bang." Slow-burn fuses that detonated charges hours after being set were not as impressive until the Americans explained their purpose, letting the saboteur remove far from the site by the time it went off.

Demolition training produced immediate results. One student, a Chinese police officer on Japan's payroll in occupied Shanghai, delivered one of the program's earliest successes. Eager to fight the occupation, he had obtained leave from his duties to attend demolition classes by claiming that he had to go to his great-aunt's funeral. Upon his return to Shanghai, he used one of the new time-delay fuses to single-handedly set fire to three Japanese planes at a suburban airfield.

While this success demonstrated the potential of the Friendship Project soon to become SACO, miscues in the beginning revealed difficulties to come. The Americans did not initially understand that treating students differently could cause public humiliation, or loss of face, as the teachers discovered when they unwittingly offended the first group of aerology students. A class of thirty men began with an eight-week basic course in weather science and instruments in February 1944. The instructors planned to split the group for the final four weeks. The ten best students would learn to use radiosondes while the rest of the class would get additional practice in the material covered in the first section. The plan was logical. A radiosonde, a set of instruments launched in a balloon to take meteorological readings at high altitudes and transmit the data via radio signal to a ground receiver, is a sophisticated device that some students were not qualified to handle. The supply of these instruments was limited, and thus there was no reason for every aerologist to be trained on them. But those who were not chosen felt insulted, and some even wanted to quit the program entirely. The only remedy was to give radiosonde instruction to the whole group, even though it was not a productive use of time and resources. After that, radiosonde was taught as an entirely separate course; those students who took only basic weather training never knew about it.

Unfortunately, some members of the same group received a second insult over their post-training field assignments to Class 1, Class 2, and Class 3 weather stations. No one wanted to go to a Class 3 station because it sounded like an inferior post. In reality, the numerical designations had nothing to do with the importance of the stations, but rather with the types of equipment they had. In fact, the most critical stations in occupied territory were Class 3, fitted with low-profile instruments that could be concealed. To avoid future misinterpretations, the aerology department changed the designations to Class A, B, and C because the alphabetical names did not carry the same connotations of rank to the Chinese.

These were minor problems and were completely overshadowed by the inspiration the students instilled in their teachers. Despite primitive conditions by American standards, the students applied themselves with uncommon diligence without complaints. The classroom was unheated, and the students sat two to a desk on benches taking notes by candlelight. They nevertheless listened carefully and took copious notes for seven hours a day without losing interest and then studied for two hours each evening. They held their teachers in highest regard and were deeply grateful for the opportunity to learn and to serve their country.

THE POLICE-OFFICER-TURNED-SABOTEUR from Shanghai had been lucky to be able to travel almost a thousand miles to Happy Valley for instruction, but to train the numbers of men Dai and Miles intended, SACO would have to expand closer to the guerrillas in the field. Thus began plans for satellite facilities known at first as "camps" and later as "units" after the American side of SACO became Naval Group China in early 1944. Dai's agents scouted locations close enough to the enemy to launch missions from the camps on foot, yet far enough away for safety. SACO built the first of these, Camp One, in the mountains at Hero's Village, Anhui Province, as close as they dared to Shanghai. It was also convenient to the Loyal Patriotic Army that Dai had founded, whose members were to be the trainees. It opened for business in April 1943.

Camp commander Major John "Bud" Masters, USMC, was frustrated by the apparent lack of interest the Chinese had in the school. It seemed Dai Li was the only one in China who actually supported this training. Weeks were wasted waiting for students who never materialized, and they finally showed up unannounced in June.

Masters had dim hopes for the first group of three hundred twenty students. Like a modern corporate manager submitting to yet another professional development program, their commander was not keen on losing men to this training scheme, so he had sent those he could do without, the unfit and incompetent. They arrived in even worse shape after marching for several weeks. They had marched their feet bloody and suffered from exhaustion, malnutrition, and illness. Masters pronounced them "too weak to hold up a gun."[29]

He convinced the students' superiors to provide them with three meals a day instead of the standard two, and after a couple of weeks for rest, medical attention, and nutrition, they grew strong enough to start classes. A student assigned as timekeeper let out a disconcerting blat on a bugle when it was time for breaks or the end of class. The soldiers learned to shoot and maintain Smithfield rifles and .45-caliber pistols and to plan and execute sabotage and demolition raids. They also practiced new techniques for hand-to-hand combat. When the first class graduated some twelve weeks later, each man received a new American firearm. Upon return to their units, these cast-off soldiers exuded confidence and outperformed the best of their peers. After that, Camp One had plenty of students.

SACO learned from experience and set up Camp Two in half the time of Camp One with Lieutenant Merrill Stewart at the helm. Positioned near the Yangtze River and large lakes in central China, the camp took over an empty, two-thousand-year-old Buddhist temple. Its mission was to train guerrillas for Dai Li's Columns Two and Four and launch attacks against Japanese communication and shipping in the region. Stewart, who had trained guerrillas in Australia earlier in the war, had not anticipated the complexity of doing the same work in two languages while trying to comprehend a bafflingly unfamiliar culture. But he and his successor learned along with their students and ultimately cranked out a stream of the war's most successful guerrillas.

In summer 1944, four men from Camp One walked two hundred miles southeast to found Camp Eight near Qingtian, Zhejian Province, working with Chinese General Chow Shih Jeh, who had formed a fast friendship with Miles during the latter's tour of the coast in 1942. The camp was part of Miles's hurry-up plan to get ready for the expected navy landing slated for December 1944. Camps Six, Seven, and Eight trained a combined four thousand Chinese by December to form the rear guard for this invasion.

In the haste to get ready, SACO was growing too fast for every man to receive Miles's signature brand of orientation, and newcomers arrived at Camp Eight too green to work effectively with the Chinese. Camp leaders USMC Lieutenants Alfred Close and Stewart Pittman solved the problem with a mini teacher's school set off from the main camp while seasoned SACOs taught the first classes.

Pirates of the Brethren of the Green Circle, a centuries-old confederation in the Shanghai area, formed the first class. After cooperating with Dai for more than a decade, their leader had cut a deal in spring 1944 to work with SACO. A group of four hundred fifty-eight men had made the trip some three hundred miles in July and August 1944, passing through Japanese territory three times, with fifty-nine killed in skirmishes with the enemy en route. After paying such a terrible price to get there, the pirates' classes were suspended only a week after they began due to security issues. At 2:00 a.m. on August 31, General Chow ordered an emergency evacuation in the face of a Japanese advance. They moved twenty miles south, set up the new camp, and picked up with instruction again on September 9. After intense courses in guerrilla tactics and amphibious operations, the pirates graduated at the end of December, and many joined the newly formed 9th Battalion of the Loyal Patriotic Army the following spring.

TRAINING LASTED EIGHT TO TWELVE WEEKS unless a session had to be compressed for a specific, urgent mission. While the curriculum varied by location, all camps taught small arms, grenades, demolition, scouting and patrol, ambush, close-range fighting, and teamwork in the field. Camps close to water included instruction in coast watching, ship identification, mining, and underwater demolition, while those near air routes added aircraft identification. Soldiers likely to work in urban areas got special training in street fighting.

The Americans taught through translators in what was a laborious process. The translator could not simply parrot the English phrases in Chinese but rather had to fully understand what he was saying. As a result, the instructor had to teach the material to the translator who then taught the students. SACO men learned early on that there were no shortcuts to this teach-and-reteach methodology. The translators at Camp Three were inexperienced, and because there were too few, they rushed through their work with hilarious but unfortunate consequences. In one class, a student was asked, "What is TNT?" and responded, "It is one-third long and yellow."[30]

The translation process strained the patience of the students, whose culture had deep respect for teachers and who were eager to learn from the Americans. In one case, a class of more than a hundred student soldiers became agitated as the teacher quietly explained something to the translator, who then shouted it in Chinese to the class. They wanted to hear the teacher's voice, too, even though they could not understand the words. For the rest of the course, the teacher and the translator shouted themselves hoarse, and the students were satisfied.

But for some subjects, it worked much better to avoid translation altogether. Two Chinese meteorologists were recruited to teach highly technical aspects of weather science. Miles got a kick out of listening to their lectures in Chinese peppered with English terms.

SACO developed specialty programs where needed. At Camp Five, after the fall of the city of Guilin two hundred miles from camp, the instructors taught a select group to perform assassinations in enemy-occupied cities. Happy Valley and other locations had special programs to train aerologists, radio operators, and medics, while several guerrilla programs included basic first aid.

SACO created one program exclusive to Camp Two in response to a field success. An American at the camp had been helping the 5th Fighter Group of the 14th Army Air Force by guiding planes to quality Japanese targets. SACO trained six teams of three Chinese to continue and expand the program. The camp also capitalized on its proximity to the Yangtze River, a major artery for Japanese shipping, with intense training in underwater mining and bridge demolition.

At Camp Five, Ensign John Mattmiller gave students swimming lessons in the Jiulong River and then chose a handful of the best swimmers for advanced underwater demolition training. The group later sunk a Japanese freighter.[31]

CONSIDERING THE ENORMOUS OBSTACLES in its path, from a broken supply chain to malaria, SACO's training program makes for a remarkable success story, but it was not without its problems. No matter how deeply committed both countries were to genuine collaboration and mutual respect, they could not overcome differing world views that had developed over thousands of years just because they wanted to.

Classroom sessions revealed the lack of creative nimbleness that frustrated Dai Li in his soldiers. In fact, improving it had been one of his goals for the American training program. In China at that time, education relied heavily on memorization, a tradition dating back to Confucius. It was the only learning the soldiers knew, and it was what they expected in a classroom setting. The goal of the SACO program, however, was to teach them to think differently, to learn a principle and then apply it to a completely different situation. The instructors achieved this by expanding the lessons out in the field and setting up problems to be solved hands-on instead of on paper. In these war games, the students practiced night patrols, sneak attacks, map reading, and teamwork.

During these field exercises, many students tried to impress the teachers with individual heroics that were sure to get them killed. The instructors had to convince them that they were much too valuable to take such risks. A man could better serve his country by setting an explosive, running for dear life, and doing the same tomorrow than by conspicuously flinging himself at the enemy and getting shot to pieces.

Another cultural obstacle came as a real surprise to the Americans. Educated Chinese men had no experience using their hands. Unlike Americans, they had not grown up tinkering with cars and bicycle chains, building crystal radios, and constructing tree houses. They had to be taught how to hammer a nail.

The Americans also found it difficult to tolerate the treatment the Chinese soldiers received from their officers, who remained their commanders in camp. During training, a few officers would physically punish the students for their performance. A wrong answer in class or a missed bull's-eye on the firing range might earn the soldier a kick in the ribs. In the worst case, a Chinese officer hit a student in the face with a belt, catching his eye with the buckle. The young man nearly lost the eye. The American officers complained passionately to Miles, who warned Dai Li that physical abuse of students was totally unacceptable and had to be stopped. Dai Li agreed, and those incidents ended.

Lieutenant John Ryder Horton, who taught small arms and demolitions, recalled that the bullying officers were in the minority, but their behavior still created a stifling atmosphere of intimidation. The American teachers set an example in their interactions with the students, enhancing the status of those Chinese officers who treated the soldiers well, and making a positive impact on the Chinese military leadership. The best of these officers were recruited as teachers, helping make the camps more productive.

The American teachers often complained that their students were too exhausted when they got to class. In addition to their SACO training, the soldiers and technicians attended daily predawn inculcation sessions on the teachings of Sun Yat-sen, late founder of the Guomindang and Chiang Kai-shek's mentor. Bugles sounded at 5:00 a.m., and soon, the strains of "San Min Zhu Yi," a patriotic hymn about the Three People's Principles, rose in the morning air. By the time the students began their classes each day, they had already been up for hours. And for some, the day did not end after class and evening study. A few generals conscripted their troops for night roadwork, allowing the men only a few hours sleep before the bugle blared again.

Every SACO training course ended with a formal ceremony, and Miles and Dai attended as many graduations as they could. Some instructors thought these elaborate ceremonies with their attendant parades, speeches, songs, and handshakes were a waste of time. There was a war on, after all, and everyone had important business. They asked if they could simply distribute the graduation firearms and send the soldiers on their way. But the Chinese officers resisted, stressing the cultural importance of publicly marking what the students had achieved.

This distribution of arms upon graduation was a linchpin of the SACO Agreement. Although Miles staunchly denied it, American critics of SACO and Dai Li claimed that Dai was using the training program to accumulate arms and equipment for Chiang Kai-shek's coming battle with the Communists rather than to fight the Japanese. Indeed, some of the unfortunate suspicions at Camp Three arose from Dai Li visiting the camp and grilling its commanders about when weapons would be distributed and what types they were.

Regardless of their intended use, the Chinese were desperate for modern arms. Captain William H. Sager, commander of Camp Ten, became suspicious that some of the students who showed up for graduation were ringers slipped in just to procure weapons. After that, he had numbers painted on the backs of students' necks with a violet medical dye that does not wash off, and when graduation came, no number, no gun. More than a hundred students without numbers claimed to have taken the course, but they had to do it over again to get their weapons.

At other camps, the Americans had to weed out potential "soldiers" before classes began, eliminating children as well as men who were clearly too sick, old, or disabled to ever serve in the army. The U.S. Navy had no intention of giving the Chinese any weapon unless it was clear that a trained soldier was ready and able to use it against the Japanese immediately.

Disagreements and letdowns were inevitable, and Americans and Chinese alike confused, offended, and misled their counterparts, more often unwittingly than intentionally. Each side forgave or ignored these slights in the interest of achieving a common goal.

And there were the inevitable accidents of war. One of the worst incidents was no one's fault, but it had tragic consequences for the first class at Camp Two. First Lieutenant Leopold Kawarski, Army of the United States, and Navy Chief Torpedoman's Mate Joseph Bradley were demonstrating a new plastic explosive that could be eaten if the guerrilla were captured. As Kawarski had done at an OSS camp in the United States, he and Bradley each ate a piece, and the students followed suit. They all began to fall ill. Bradley and twenty students went into convulsions, and one student died. No one ever figured out why the explosive had been safely ingested in the United States but turned lethal in China. Having an American among the victims may have prevented the tragedy from spawning suspicions and rumors about the Americans, who were a rarity in central China and still called "foreign devils" by some locals. SACO gave the parents of the student who died 5,000 yuan, and each student who got sick received 500 yuan.

COUNTLESS POTENTIAL PROBLEMS never developed or got out of control because the navy sought out even-tempered men for SACO, and the recruits took Miles's "get along" credo seriously. Miles emphasized that criticizing the Chinese would only put up roadblocks, and a navy physician at a hospital in Hero's Village near Camp One remembered that when he became mired in a confounding situation.

The hospital, staffed by Chinese soldiers, treated about a hundred patients at a time suffering from war wounds and debilitating diseases. When Dr. Alfred Young, lieutenant junior grade, arrived, he was appalled by the lack of consistent patient records. Without them, diagnosis and treatment were a guessing game. He therefore instituted standard hospital procedure, having a medical chart hung at each patient's bed and ordering the nurses to note their temperatures every four hours. But after a week, no temperatures had been recorded despite gentle reminders. Angry and frustrated, Young began wondering how he could fix the problem when the solution fell in his lap. He heard a couple of nurses in a spirited argument and, upon asking a translator what was going on, learned that the men were fighting about how to read a thermometer, and both were wrong.

Young was astonished that men without this basic skill were permitted to work in a hospital. Situations like this frustrated many Americans trying to work with the Chinese and typically led to griping about their hopelessly backward institutions. But Young was not out to fix China. He just wanted to see temperatures on the charts so he could treat his patients, and to achieve that, he had to show the men how to use the thermometers without causing loss of face. He thus gave an impromptu class on the sly, conspicuously taking the temperatures of several patients while describing the procedure aloud as if talking to himself with the translator conveniently on hand. Within an hour, every patient chart had a temperature reading, and they appeared like clockwork every four hours thereafter.

The Americans at Camp One applied a bit of psychology to turn around the first class whose initial appearance had so discouraged Masters. Within the group, a dozen or so students seemed particularly hopeless, including a huge oaf who suffered constant ridicule and physical abuse from his patrol leader. Despite his size, the man perpetually cowered like the runt of the pack. Acting on a hunch, his teacher separated the "losers" from the rest of the class and placed the big, cringing simpleton in charge. Once out of range of their tormentors, the poor performers blossomed, especially the big guy, who discovered his latent leadership ability. In jujitsu class, the instructor taught him a secret move for throwing an opponent and gave the man a chance to show it off in a demonstration with his cruel patrol leader. The victim seized the opportunity to get even with the bully, throwing him to the ground repeatedly in front of the entire class, and after that, the former whipping boy grew even taller and became a star student.

CAMP TWO LED THE WAY integrating its students and instructors in the field. After pushing Miles and Dai relentlessly, Camp Two teacher Marine Lieutenant Theodore Cathey was the first American permitted to join a Chinese force in action in May 1944. General Ho Yuen-ting, commander of Column Four, half of whom had been trained at Camp Two, deemed Cathey's presence a logical extension of that training. Cathey worked with the officers planning and executing guerrilla attacks against a Japanese force of ten thousand that outnumbered the Chinese at least three to one. Over the course of three months and thirty-four engagements large and small, the Chinese killed nine hundred sixty-seven Japanese and lost fourteen of their own. Cathey boasted that the Chinese were as good as any American force he had ever seen.

The experiment transformed Camp Two. Located in the thick of the action, it was frequently threatened and had to move three times. It became a home base and mission control for its teachers, who went out to the troops to train them where they were deployed and then applied the training to live action. When Miles visited the camp in December 1944, it was practically deserted. He walked two days to observe Column Four and was proud to see the Americans and Chinese working together, noting that the American presence demonstrated a level of commitment that gave the Chinese rank and file a real boost. They were no longer alone in the world.

IN THE SUMMER OF 1945, Dai Li witnessed the fruit of SACO training as an exhausted and overextended Japanese Army struggled to maintain its hold on China. For reasons that never became clear, a long-standing Japanese force abandoned Xiamen and began moving one hundred fifty miles south to Shantou. Chinese–American mines and air and submarine attacks frustrated their efforts to make the move by sea. In June, they began the trek overland with four thousand men and a large herd of horses. Americans from SACO Camp Six joined the Chinese 75th Division, split into small companies, and harassed the column from all sides for three weeks, keeping Happy Valley apprised of their progress via radio.

Throughout the campaign, Dai Li was restless and jubilant. Glued to the radio, he grew more excited with each transmission.

"These combined troops—these Chinese with a few Americans—are acting like Americans. They are making decisions and reporting their activities instead of asking for directions!" he exclaimed.

CHAPTER 11

Doing Something About the Weather

LIKE MILLIONS OF YOUNG AMERICANS in December 1941, twenty-five-year-old John Klos of Lancaster, Pennsylvania, answered the passionate call to serve his country immediately after the bombing of Pearl Harbor. Signing on with the navy, he adopted the snappy, square-collared jumper that distinguished that branch of the service from all others. Two years later, however, he had shed his handsome uniform for a set of rumpled army fatigues and found himself in a cave in Northern China collecting weather data to aid the U.S. Pacific Fleet.

Klos had been serving stateside as a chief aerographer's mate when asked to volunteer for top-secret, "prolonged and hazardous duty" overseas, and he jumped at the chance, itching to do something big for the war effort. After he came forward, an officer asked whether he could learn to distinguish edible lice from the poisonous variety and whether he thought he could survive on vermin if necessary. That was the moment Klos realized that he had undertaken a curious and risky business, but if the question was meant to scare him away, it didn't. It only intrigued him.

His adventure began in Happy Valley, where he learned more about the Sino–American Cooperative Organization and was tutored on the social graces needed to work with the Chinese. The lessons proved useful. He ultimately commanded four aerographers—three U.S. Navy-trained Chinese and one other American—in the cave weather station in Ningxia Province bordering Inner Mongolia. Three times a day on a strict schedule, the crew stealthily took readings of atmospheric conditions and radioed the results in code to Happy Valley.

SACO WOULD NEVER HAVE EXISTED AT ALL had it not been for the navy's urgent need for weather forecasts in the Pacific Ocean. As we have seen, it was clear from the war's opening blasts that weather was part of Japan's formidable arsenal. The Japanese had used a cloud front to conceal their planes before the surprise attack on Pearl Harbor and would do so repeatedly during the course of the war. It was therefore essential that the U.S. Navy have access to weather forecasts in order to meet the enemy on an equal footing, and that required tracking weather patterns across Asia as they moved east to the sea.

This focus on weather as an instrument of war was nothing new. Weather has played a role in military strategy since ancient times. Indeed, more than two millennia ago, the Chinese general and philosopher Sun Tzu wrote in *The Art of War*, "Know the enemy, know yourself; your victory will never be endangered. Know the ground, know the weather; your victory will then be total."

The U.S. Navy was pursuing total victory in a part of the world where it had absolutely no meteorological presence and no access to weather information. Correcting this deficiency was one of Admiral King's top priorities for Miles's mission, and Captain Howard T. Orville, the navy's chief aerologist, concurred. He told Miles that even occasional reports from central China would make a difference as the navy developed Pacific weather maps to help the fleet plan attacks. The broader and more frequent the reports, the more useful they would be. For example, knowing the state of the weather in the Gobi Desert today would tell Pacific commanders whether conditions were favorable for planes to take off from Japan's airfields two days later. That in turn would aid in planning attacks and scheduling convoys within Japanese striking distance.

SACO ultimately exceeded Orville's expectations, but the task proved to be arduous. Miles made several false starts in his attempt to create a weather reporting and analysis network that could produce timely, reliable forecasts. He had been in China more than two years before the first comprehensive forecast and Pacific weather map were delivered to Pacific fleet command, although the incremental achievements along the way advanced the war effort for the navy and the air force and buoyed Miles's team to keep at it.

SACO's first two weather technicians, Aerologist's Mates First Class Thomas G. McCawley and Willie D. Flournoy, climbed the steep path to Happy Valley in November 1942, but they had little weather-specific work to do at first for lack of equipment.

Miles had plans to put these men and many more to full use, but meanwhile, he hoped to tap into Free China's existing resources for data. Three groups were already monitoring the weather: the Central Meteorological Bureau, the Combined Organization of Aviation Affairs, and the Chinese National Aviation Corporation. If they could share their findings with Happy Valley, SACO aerologists could transmit the information to Orville in Washington and to the fleet.

Miles began meetings with the agencies in autumn 1942. The Chinese officials responded enthusiastically to his proposal. They agreed to send daily reports from designated stations according to a prescribed schedule. SACO would need to receive them within twelve to twenty-four hours for them to be of any use, Miles emphasized. They understood the urgency clearly and whole-heartedly committed to the plan.

The arrangement was a major disappointment. Reports trickled in incomplete, days late, or not at all. Miles's gentle requests for improvement were met with empty promises. It seemed to him that he was working with too many parties, and no one was in charge. No matter what they said to his face, they obviously did not care about the needs of the U.S. Navy.

Miles finally went to Dai Li for help. In order for the plan to work, Miles said, China would need to appoint a single weather director who would work with an American SACO advisor. He suggested that the three agencies adopt a military-style chain of command, and the entire communication system be structured to give weather data top priority. Dai met the request with his standard dodge: "We'll ask the Generalissimo." By this time, Miles knew that was Dai Li parlance for "no." The only solution was to create the navy's own network of weather stations from scratch. He would need Dai's permission for that, too, but once secured, at least he would be able to control the work himself.

While the attempt to coordinate with the three agencies never delivered any live data, it did yield a valuable asset for the United States. Before Miles had given up, he had sent Lieutenant Commander Ray Kotrla to the Central Meteorological Bureau to set up logistics. Kotrla discovered shelves of heavy, leather-bound volumes filled with weather statistics painstakingly recorded by Chinese meteorologists over fifty years. The Bureau had gone to considerable lengths to preserve them when the government moved from Nanjing to Chongqing in 1937, assigning one man to carry each volume. Miles described the books to Francis W. Reichelderfer, head of the United States Weather Service, and his timing could not have been better. The information was exactly what Reichelderfer needed to plug a big hole in a global weather history project the agency was working on to aid in forecasting. The enterprising Kotrla photographed every page and sent the images to Washington.

Despite Miles's failure to get China's meteorology agencies to cooperate, SACO aerologists began a small program collecting weather statistics and feeding reports to the navy and to General Claire Chennault's 14th Army Air Force in Kunming. By July 1943, two men operated a weather station at Happy Valley and received regular reports from solo stations at Camps One and Two.

The aerology service really began to take shape when U.S. Navy Commander Irwin F. Beyerly arrived at Happy Valley in August 1943. A year earlier, his gutsy weather forecasts had played a key role at Guadalcanal. He had predicted the stormy conditions that had allowed the Allies to slip in unseen. While the experience had won him accolades, it had also taught him that the navy badly needed a weather network in China. His task at Guadalcanal would have been much easier if he could have consulted weather charts from East Asia. Now he was bursting to correct the deficiency.

After a few days' study, he told Miles that he could set up a weather net of three hundred stations—twenty full-blown stations with radiosonde and the remainder more modestly fitted for ground observations—if Miles could get him two planeloads of equipment and a thousand men. Miles wondered if this grandiose plan could be completed, but it was a starting point, and Beyerly dived right in. He and Miles placed preliminary orders in Washington for weather instruments, and then turned to the question of personnel. So far, SACO had a staff of exactly five aerologists, including Beyerly. More would surely be coming, but they needed Chinese volunteers to fill in the ranks.

Meeting with General Wei Daming, Dai Li's chief of weather and communications, they agreed that the navy would train up to a thousand Chinese in aerology. Beyerly emphasized that the training would be for naught unless they could also instill a sense of urgency in every person in the system because old weather information was utterly worthless. The plan was to train military radiomen with standard equipment for use in Free China, and to teach select secret agents to use specially designed clandestine instruments behind enemy lines. Miles believed the job could be done with one man per station, but Dai Li insisted on two or more for safety and to allow them to gather other intelligence.

In September, Beyerly and McCawley taught a course in aerology in Lanzhou, several hundred miles north of Chongqing, to one hundred fifty Chinese radio operators, followed by a class of seven hundred, with the help of six more teachers, two Americans and four Chinese.

When sent out on their own into the field, though, members of this first group proved unwilling or unable to adhere to schedules. Whether owing to their youth (some were teenagers), China's patchy radio communications system, too little training, or the result of growing up in an environment where everything was broken and there was no point in rushing, they simply did not deliver. Miles complained to Wei, who blamed the American equipment.

The general lack of a sense of urgency in China frustrated Americans, and not just those in SACO. Chiang Kai-shek had long bemoaned the lack of progress within his own government simply because no one seemed pressed to move things from discussion to action. Americans were so accustomed to rushing around that they misinterpreted the Chinese sense of time as laziness. In truth, China had not yet undergone its industrial revolution, which in the west had given rise to time clocks and railroad schedules. Life in China's rural areas had not changed in a thousand years, and even in cities, services were so sporadic that people did not synchronize their watches, literally or figuratively. Time in China was a vast expanse stretching to infinity, while in the United States it was a pressing force that called for a task to be completed by 5:00 p.m.

A MONTH AFTER THE LANZHOU WEATHER SCHOOL, Beyerly gave a special course in Hsifeng for young men from Thailand and Indochina to take secret weather readings in enemy territory. Their instruments were small enough to be hidden on their person or in a bag of rice. The aerologists were assigned to their home countries and beyond, as far as Manila and Singapore.

Meanwhile, new weather instruments were making their way around the globe and began arriving in Kolkata in October 1943. To make sure the equipment wasn't lost or delayed, SACO placed two dedicated supply mates, one in Kolkata and one in Kunming, to direct the shipments.

More navy weather personnel continued to fly in over the Hump, and in January 1944, aerologists Lieutenant John Mastenbrook and Lieutenant Junior Grade Donald Harkness joined SACO, raising the quotient of aerology officers to three with fourteen enlisted men. Within weeks, they launched the twelve-week Happy Valley weather-technician training program described earlier. More comprehensive than the courses taught in Lanzhou and Hsifeng, it mirrored the training American navy aerology recruits received in the United States. The second class at Happy Valley, which started in July, covered the same material but mixed classroom and hands-on instruction from the very first day, and the students learned more and faster.

At the same time, thousands of American meteorologists and aerologists were enrolled in navy programs on university campuses in the United States, including the Massachusetts Institute of Technology, whose meteorology department was one of the pioneers of modern radiosonde science. A handful of these men were assigned to SACO.

Twenty-eight graduates from the first Happy Valley class took to the field in April. This time, they were paired with Americans in hopes of achieving punctuality. Stations ranged from two to six men who reached their remote sites via truck, Jeep, camel, water buffalo, and on foot. With Americans and Chinese working together, this group got better results than previous efforts had yielded, but even though they made their reports on time, the data took too long to reach Happy Valley through the Chinese radio communication system. By the time it arrived, it was useless.

It became clear to Miles and Beyerly why Dai and Wei had shrugged off the punctuality problem in the first place. They were shrugs of futility. It was impossible for China's overcrowded radio circuits to relay the data on time. When Miles asked about delays in the radio system, he was assured that there was no problem because the Nationalists had plenty of runners. To the Chinese, a network of foot messengers was a perfectly acceptable supplement for a dysfunctional radio communication network, but it was too slow for delivering the weather data from remote stations within twelve hours.

As ridiculous as the runner system seemed to Miles and Beyerly, for the Chinese, it was the only option. Their outdated radios were patched together using spare parts from other broken ones, and the system lacked organized frequency assignments. The weak, short-range signals made many relay stops, each an opportunity for messages to be delayed, garbled, or lost. And no amount of explaining and coaxing could convince every operator at every relay station to consistently give American weather data top priority in an overloaded system.

The only solution was to build a separate radio communications system exclusively for the navy as SACO was doing with its weather stations. Miraculously, Miles got Dai Li's swift approval without the latter having to "ask the Generalissimo." Miles made it his highest priority. Each weather station, eventually numbering more than seventy, received a high-power radio transmitter and an expert to run and maintain it, with robust relay stations positioned in between where needed. Now weather reports came in three times a day exactly on schedule to Happy Valley, giving Beyerly and his staff the tools to provide genuinely useful information to the navy.

SEEING OFF A NEW WEATHER CREW became a regular ritual at Happy Valley. Chinese and American aerologists with their guards, interpreters, and equipment set out in truck convoys for locations Beyerly selected, adding new pinpoints to his weather net map month after month. At some sites, Dai Li's agents had already secured spaces for the stations, but at others, the men found their own workplaces in office buildings, caves, abandoned schools and monasteries, cottages, and chicken coops.

The weather stations served a second, unplanned purpose. They became travelers aid stations for SACOs, Chinese Nationalists, Americans, and allies of every stripe. Where there was a weather station, there was a radio and an operator who could get help for broken-down vehicles and medical emergencies.

SACO built its northern-most outpost, Camp Four, primarily as a weather station at the edge of the Gobi Desert outside the town of Xamba in Inner

Mongolia. This site, four hundred miles north and seventeen hundred miles west of Tokyo, gave the United States weather data days ahead of Japan as air masses swept across Asia from the northwest. A party of twelve Americans and eighty Chinese said good-bye to Happy Valley on November 18, 1943, and reached their destination exactly two months later. They sent the first aerology readings to Happy Valley two weeks after they arrived.

In September 1944, after receiving intelligence that a Japanese offensive threatened to cut off China's coast completely, Miles rushed to send in aerology teams while he still had the chance. Aerologist's Mate Second Class Robert M. Sinks, toting a full radiosonde station, and fourteen navy-trained Chinese aerologists equipped with portable instruments struggled to push on to the east while it seemed that the entire country was fleeing west. At Guilin, they caught a U.S. Army transport plane that turned out to be the last flight east. Landing in Ganzhou, they were still about two hundred miles from the coast. They forged ahead in borrowed trucks and on foot to Camp Six, where Sinks established a station that provided a steady stream of data until the end of the war.[32]

The Chinese fanned out with instruments concealed under their clothing to take secret readings along the coast, but they were less successful because their portable radios proved inadequate, a problem the navy never fully solved. They still managed to transmit information, but not with the regularity of permanent stations. When their kit radios could not get through to Happy Valley, they transmitted the data to the nearest navy coast watcher, and when that failed, they walked to the coast watch station to deliver it in person. From there, it was relayed to the nearest camp weather station. It all made for a lengthy process, and often by the time Happy Valley received it, it was too late.

Chinese were chosen for this mobile duty behind enemy lines because they could remain inconspicuous. Weathermen certainly do not fit romantic notions of wartime spies, but SACO's undercover aerologists faced grave danger. Given the great military value of weather information, the Japanese fought hard to keep the Allies from gathering it. Four of the Thai aerologists sent to Southeast Asia were captured and killed. Like all intelligence, the data were transmitted in code, and the navy developed a written code guide the size of a postage stamp that could be swallowed if the aerologist fell into enemy hands.

The permanent stations in occupied territory were also at risk. SACO used camouflage and other techniques to hide weather towers and limited the use of weather balloons in areas where the Japanese were likely to take notice. The station at Guilin, about three hundred miles from Hong Kong, was constantly under threat and had to be moved six times by the time the war ended. After SACO had resolved earlier performance problems, the Chinese manned the most sensitive stations on their own and discharged their duties with courage and precision. The only obstacles were translation errors that provided funny war stories. One station's reports repeatedly confused the words "to" and "from," resulting in incongruous observations.

BY 1945, SACO HAD SEVENTY WEATHER STATIONS scattered across China, from the Mongolian plains to the shores of the South China Sea.

The station in Shaanxi Province attached to Camp Three north of Xi'an was typical. A crew of six lived and worked in an abandoned Buddhist monastery at the foot of a mountain, guarded by armed Nationalist Chinese sentries.

Each day, they hauled their instruments, a radio, and a hand-cranked generator up a mountain path to a selected spot on the slope. There they launched radiosonde balloons to measure temperature, wind direction, barometric pressure, and humidity in the upper atmosphere and took the same readings at ground level. One man's sole job was to transport equipment and crank the generator to power the radio transmitter as the operator sent information to Chongqing.

At Happy Valley, a new building housed SACO Weather Central on "Beyerly Hill," where its namesake directed the growing pan-Asian weather net. In mid-1944, three aerology-trained radio operators joined the group to monitor broadcasts from other weather forecasting centers around the globe including India, Pearl Harbor, Central Asia, the Aleutian Islands, and Russia. Plotting the combined data onto maps, the staff could detect patterns and project how those patterns were likely to develop in the near future.

SACO sent its first comprehensive weather map to Pacific Fleet Command on September 20, 1944, marking one of the proudest days of Milton Miles's career. The map had emerged from two years of dead ends, failures, and fresh starts. By then, Happy Valley was sending four daily reports to the fleet command.

After that first map, a new one was delivered every day until the war ended, along with four written reports on current and forecasted conditions in China, Japan, and the Pacific. The first forecast to include the entire China coast and five hundred miles out to sea was delivered on October 7. Later that month, SACO supplied its first specially requested forecast to help plan an army–navy attack on Formosa.

As early as September 1943, SACO had begun feeding weather data and forecasts to General Claire Chennault's 14th Air Force. Around that time, one of SACO's first weather stations went up at Chennault's headquarters in Kunming, and the camps near the coast supplemented that data to aid the 14th's reconnaissance and attack missions.

It was not until March 1945 that the coastal weather net was truly complete to Beyerly's satisfaction. Ten stations near the shore, each with one Chinese aerographer and one American radio operator, funneled reports to two of the coastal SACO camps for relay to Happy Valley.

That month, Miles appointed Captain Beyerly commander of SACO in Eastern China, overseeing Camps One, Six, Seven, and Eight, the coast watch stations, and the coastal weather net. Captain Floyd T. Thompson, a U.S. Naval Academy graduate with a master's in aerology, arrived in Chongqing to take over Beyerly's former post as head of weather operations. Thompson represented SACO at a conference of military meteorologists from the United States, Australia, New Zealand, and Great Britain in Manila in May 1945. There he learned that Allied weather centers all over Asia and the Pacific were sharing and relying on SACO forecasts. The reports had been factors in planning at Iwo Jima, Okinawa, and Leyte Gulf. In the case of Leyte Gulf, SACO weather observers and intelligence had combined efforts without knowing it. Aerology warned of a band of severe storms heading toward the Philippines, and a SACO observer flying on a 14th Air Force reconnaissance mission reported a fleet of Japanese ships lurking behind it. Some of these ships were sunk a few days later in a fierce, tide-turning naval battle in which Japan lost four aircraft carriers.

By July 1945, SACO's staff of American aerologists had reached its peak number with ninety-nine officers and men, remarkably few for all they accomplished. New weather centers in other parts of the world had come online during the war, but only SACO had to build one out of nothing. With no infrastructure in a strange, remote country at war, they established a data collection system, traveling weeks or months over bad roads to erect the stations. They trained hundreds of technicians to run the stations, overcoming language and cultural barriers. They even built a communication system to carry the data to headquarters, and a team of aerologists shaped the data into critical information needed by the navy and the air force.

CHAPTER 12

Intelligence: Radios, Spies, and Coast Watchers

BEFORE MILTON "MARY" MILES ARRIVED in China, he had little knowledge of espionage. A no-nonsense naval officer, his earnest wish had been to serve out the war at sea. All he knew about spies he had learned from books and movies, where secret agents exchanged whispered information for thick envelopes of cash passed under tables in greasy, dimly lit bars.

With this in mind, soon after meeting Dai Li and realizing that his strange mission now included being spymaster for the U.S. Navy in China, Miles drew up a price list for performance of intelligence and sabotage. The navy would pay $500 for blowing up a bridge, $100 for an intercepted military message, and so on. But Dai Li immediately squelched the whole idea, explaining that anyone who could be bought by the Americans also could be bought by the Japanese—at a higher price. There was no end to it, and you never knew who could be trusted.

Dai Li proved every day that he knew whereof he spoke. It was nearly impossible to sneak anything past him, hence he had known of Miles's appointment to the OSS even before Miles himself. He commanded tremendous loyalty and got results.

Dai's effective intelligence network, operating in a country where almost nothing else worked smoothly, made a deep impression on Miles, and the simple naval officer soon became smitten with the spy business. Dai showed Miles his secret spy gadget laboratory, which cranked out such gizmos as an incendiary soap cake and a radio-transmitter-and-antenna set disguised as an inkbottle and an umbrella. He flattered Miles with an offer to appoint him to the lab's board of directors, but Miles declined because some of the devices involved poison gas, whose military use was prohibited by international rules of war. Its use may have been acceptable for spies, but not for the U.S. Navy.

Soon Miles learned from Dai's example and his own experience that effective intelligence was not a game but an essential component of a military arsenal, best acquired through smart, dedicated agents who were well trained and well equipped.

The navy's first intelligence mission in China was to gather basic information about hotels, food, and transportation for personnel traveling in China, a sort of military Fodor's guide. At that time, few Americans had been to China, and the country was almost entirely unknown. Commander David D. Wight, Miles's executive officer, led the expedition in 1943.

IF MILES HAD A LOT TO LEARN about intelligence, he already knew a great deal about radios, having tinkered with them since his teens. It was no accident that the seven pioneer SACO members were all navy radio experts, and their instruments became the foundation of SACO's intelligence program.

From the moment Lieutenant Commander Daniel Webster Heagy and his crew set up the first borrowed radio receiver in Happy Valley in October 1942 until after the war ended, SACO monitored Japanese radio traffic. Radiomen at camps, weather and coast watch outposts, and scores of stand-alone radio stations listened in twenty-four hours a day. Operators worked grueling twelve-hour shifts receiving and decoding relentless messages.

For the first several months, the Americans had to use China's aging radio system, which relied on runners carrying messages on paper to fill in the gaps between stations. As precious Hump tonnage began to arrive, though, American antennas started sprouting up, and by mid-1944, a complete independent network, fed a steady flow of reports to Happy Valley.

A seemingly unintelligible stream of information could alert analysts to imminent Japanese advances simply by an increase or decrease in radio traffic. They could tell when ship convoys along the coast and rivers were on the move because their transmissions would suddenly stop. Over several days, individual bits of information could be pieced together like a jigsaw puzzle to tell a story. SACO operators got to know their Japanese counterparts by their style with the telegraph key and often knew their names.

The radio stations served many functions in addition to intercepting enemy communication. Chinese agents delivered intelligence in person to the nearest radio station, from which it was sent to Chongqing. In the city of Guiyang in central China, Radioman First Class Dean Spaulding did his own ground intelligence gathering. When he wasn't wearing his headset and tapping out coded messages, he made friends with officials, police, and residents, gossiping with them over tea to stay informed about any local developments that could have a bearing on his station or the war effort.

On an early landmark mission, radio and ground intelligence worked hand in hand to stop a spy ring that was wreaking havoc for planes of the 14th Air Force in spring 1943. For months, the Japanese had always seemed to know when the planes were coming and were ready with antiaircraft fire. With the help of direction finders, SACO radio analysts discovered why. They could actually trace the route of a plane by plotting the locations of anonymous radio broadcasts reporting sightings of it. Evidence from the messages pointed to Kunming as the center of the ring responsible for these broadcasts.

Ensign Ted Wildman and a team of Chinese radiomen were assigned to uncover the spy cell. In a cave at Happy Valley where Dai Li stored every cast-off piece of radio or antenna equipment that came his way, they found parts to build three small direction finders. They packed them into a truck and drove to Kunming.

The city had mushroomed in recent years, and business was booming, but the unreliable phone system could not keep up with demand. Unable to function without communication, businesses resorted to radio. Radio transmission required a license in China for security reasons, but the process was cumbersome, so most of these companies operated their radios illegally. Kunming authorities looked the other way rather than stifle commerce.

The air was thick with these unlicensed broadcasts. It took the SACO team weeks of listening in to sort through them and compile a list of suspect broadcast stations. Installing one of the direction finders in an old wooden truck and the other two in stationary locations, they pinpointed the origins of the questionable broadcasts. For the next phase of the investigation, two of the Chinese radiomen impersonated street vendors and began snooping around while selling peanuts and sharpening knives. Their intelligence narrowed the list to five pseudo-financial companies sending coded messages about American air traffic disguised as commodity and currency prices. Dai Li gave the information to his local army general, who unearthed thirty-five Chinese spying for Japan. The 14th's problems stopped overnight.

But radio intelligence worked both ways. Everyone was monitoring everyone else. In the region of Xiamen, a Japanese stronghold and intelligence hot spot, four enemy radio stations appeared to exist solely to interfere with SACO communications. They jammed signals and interrupted SACO messages with fake "Q" codes, a signal asking that a message be repeated. A navy coast watch operator got so frustrated with one such interruption that he tapped back, "Get off the air, you yellow bastard," and received a succinct, two-word reply.

DAI LI'S NETWORK TOOK CARE of most field intelligence, in part because his agents knew the country and the people, but mostly because that was the way Dai wanted it. As much as he trusted Milton Miles and the navy, he had an aversion to having foreigners on the loose in China snooping. His own espionage system reached from Singapore to the Japanese Diet (parliament) in Tokyo, and those agents fed their findings to the navy. But it took more than a year and tremendous patience for Miles to get what the Americans wanted from these spies. MBIS agents were masterful at rooting out counterspies and coup attempts and following political developments, but Miles had no interest in those things unless they threatened SACO or the Pacific fleet. He wanted to know where the Japanese were, what they were doing, who was helping them, where they were going, how they were equipped, and what impact the occupation had on Chinese citizens.

Miles was also frustrated by the Chinese lack of urgency in handling intelligence, just as he had been with the failed weather data cooperative. One agent discovered a fleet of Japanese speedboats along the coast and reported it at the nearest

SACO radio station, but the radio was under repair just then, so the man dropped his report in the mail. Miles was flabbergasted. The agent's decision demonstrated a basic lack of understanding about the importance of time in performance of his duties.

In the face of these problems, General Donovan came to believe that SACO would never yield any useful information, leading to the break-up of the SACO–OSS partnership. SACO intelligence was not very effective for military purposes in the early days, yet Dai had initially impressed Donovan with intelligence suggesting that Japan was preparing to invade Siberia in autumn 1942. Even though he turned out to be wrong, his prediction anticipated conclusions of the world intelligence community by several months.

AS THE WAR PROGRESSED, American and Chinese members of SACO improved their communication and the quality of their intelligence operation, and nowhere was this more apparent—or more important—than in the coast watching program. It was one of the original missions Admiral Ernest King had assigned to Miles, both to observe Japanese naval activities and to prepare the navy for an invasion intended to uproot the occupation. Although the navy learned invaluable information by intercepting enemy radio transmissions and collecting news from friendly local Chinese, these were no substitutes for a trained pair of eyes directly observing ship movements along the coast. Skilled men were stationed at high points near the shore where they could see strategic harbors or wide expanses of the sea along major shipping lanes.

In 1944, SACO started building a nearly unbroken chain of observation posts stretching eight hundred miles from Shanghai to Guangzhou with additional coverage on the shores of the Yellow Sea to the north and Southeast Asia to the south. The coast was divided into five sections, or "nets." Each net contained five to twelve stations reporting to a command and support center. Net Four covered the hottest section, about one hundred fifty miles of coastline in the south, including the key city of Xiamen. The net's command center in Zhangzhou, a ten-day walk from its most distant post, was in a former foreign mission landscaped beautifully within an eight-foot wall.

Keeping track of sea vessels was crucial in this busy section for several reasons. Xiamen was a Japanese stronghold and home to one of China's finest harbors.

Net Four covered the Formosa Strait, through which most freight traffic bound for Japan's holdings in Southeast Asia and Indonesia passed, offering rich targets for the Allies if they could be identified. After the United States lost vital airfields in central China in late 1944, the burden for these attacks fell on American submarines and air power out of Kunming and the Philippines. Given the risks taken by the former working in shallow water and great distances traversed by the latter, quality intelligence that would lead to successful missions became even more important.

The coast watch stations were all in enemy territory, and Dai Li resisted allowing American SACOs to man them. Americans stood out for their size alone; any report of a tall man was certain to arouse suspicion. But as with the weather stations, the first attempt to use Chinese coast watchers on their own failed to yield good results. The Chinese had no training in ship identification and had trouble distinguishing relative sizes of vessels. According to an oft-repeated story, one Chinese coast watcher once reported an aircraft carrier with incoming planes and an escort destroyer that turned out to be a tugboat pulling a barge surrounded by seagulls. While this tale smacks of urban myth, perhaps like other fables, it reveals a broader truth.

To solve the problem, SACO set up another training program specifically for coast watching in June 1944. They rented a temple on a tiny island in the Min River ten miles upstream from Fuzhou. Its high visibility made the island seem like an illogical choice for a spy school, but that was considered an advantage, because the enemy would probably not scrutinize such a conspicuous location. And though unhidden, it was isolated. The Chinese coast watchers learned a simple, accurate system of ship identification and reporting and became much more effective. Capitalizing on the first success, a school for American coast watchers using the same techniques opened a month later in Jianyang.

COAST WATCHING WAS THE LONELIEST and most dangerous job in SACO, earning those who performed it the awe and accolades of their colleagues. Americans were deployed in the two southernmost nets, but they were too exposed to work safely in the north where the Japanese had held territory since 1931. A typical station in the south had one or two Americans looking out over the sea and

SACO aerologists launch a radiosonde weather balloon in China during World War II as a soldier stands guard. The balloon carries weather instruments and a radio transmitter to take upper air readings and relay the data to a receiving station. (National Archives)

A U.S. Navy officer instructs a SACO class of Chinese soldiers with the help of a translator at an unknown location. The house construction is consistent with the buildings at Happy Valley and other camps: rammed earth walls coated with plaster and a tile roof. (National Archives)

General Dai Li addresses Nationalist Chinese troops in Suzhou, Jiangsu Province, March 1946.
The uniformed American sailors are from the ships in Shanghai, visiting Suzhou as Dai Li's guests.
(Roger Moore)

Chinese recruits receive instruction on radio use from American instructors at Happy Valley.
(National Archives)

SACO Headquarters staff at Happy Valley outside Chongqing, spring 1945. Rear Admiral (then Captain) Milton Miles is in the front row near the center in dark trousers. (Roger Moore)

General Dai Li and Rear Admiral (then Commander) Milton Miles, Chongqing, 1942. (U.S. Navy)

Two nurses in Fuzhou, fall 1945. They escorted Motor Machinist's Mate Salvatore Ciaccio by sampan from his post in Fuzhou to a floating hospital. Ciaccio was stricken with paralysis due to multiple neuritis, a complication of beriberi. He recovered. (Courtesy of Sal Ciaccio)

A Chinese prisoner about to be executed for stealing a rifle. The American looking on is not a participant in the execution. The brutal Chinese justice system was agonizing for American SACOs, who were forbidden to intervene. (Courtesy of Sal Ciaccio)

Americans and Chinese load a jeep onto a sampan. Vehicles crossed rivers by sampan ferry. SACOs also traveled by river, vehicles and all, whenever possible due to the prohibitive cost of gasoline. (Courtesy of the Moore Family)

SACO sampan sailors with their Chinese guard. (Courtesy of the Moore Family)

Students receive pistol-shooting instruction at Happy Valley outside Chongqing, summer 1945.
(Roger Moore)

*Motor Machinist's Mate Second Class David A.
Baker, Gunner's Mate First Class William Keith
Barratt, Lieutenant Livingston Swentzel Jr., and
Gunner's Mate First Class James E. Reid,
heroes of the last naval battle of World War II.
Two small fishing junks with American–Chinese
crews defeated a much larger, heavily armed
Japanese junk. Shanghai, September 1945.*
(Roger Moore)

*Unidentified SACOs hike the paths above Happy
Valley with children from Dai Li's orphanage.*
(Courtesy of Don Kochi)

Three winners of the pistol marksmanship competition with their winning targets and their instructors at Happy Valley outside Chongqing, summer 1945. (Roger Moore)

Rear Admiral Milton Miles and Chinese Navy Commander Charles Lee aboard the USS Rocky Mount welcome the 7th Fleet into Shanghai, September 1945. (U.S. Navy)

Rear Admiral Milton E. Miles, 1945. (U.S. Navy)

SACO sleeve patch. Miles's "What the Hell?" pennant is in the center, flanked by the flags of the Republic of China and the United States. This is one of five known designs produced in China.

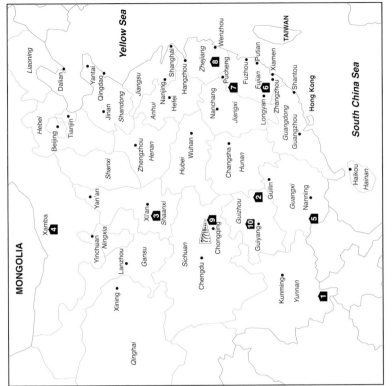

SACO established fourteen main camps in China. Not pictured are Camps 11, 12, and 13, which came online toward the end of the war (and are not mentioned in the text) and Camp 14, which was in Kunming.

Chiang Kai-shek, Madame Chiang, and General Joseph Stilwell in Burma, 1942.

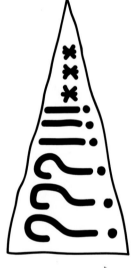

A sketch of the "What the Hell?" pennant.

recording weather conditions, a Chinese radioman, and a small group of Chinese soldiers as guards, housekeepers, and runners. A coast watcher, American or Chinese, might be a radio operator, a weather reporter, and an observer all rolled into one.

Here more than anywhere else, Americans worked to blend in with the scenery, wearing Chinese clothes and imitating Chinese body language in gait and posture. Their most important accessory, however, was not a disguise but rather the primary tool of their trade: a pair of binoculars that dangled from their necks every waking hour.

A typical day for a coast watcher began before dawn and ended when it grew too dark to see. He sat at his perch, looking and taking notes, with occasional forays to docks and shallows below to confer with Dai Li's agents. Every vessel and its movement, whether exciting or mundane, was recorded.

The Japanese constantly scoured the shore for these lookout posts, forcing SACO men to move frequently, sometimes with only minutes' notice. One SACO was working in a hut surrounded by a four-foot wall topped with broken glass to repel intruders when a guard ran up and warned him of a Japanese patrol closing in. Rushing to escape, he tried to leap over the wall but got caught straddling it, ripping gashes in his thighs and testicles. He walked eighteen miles to headquarters at Zhangzhou with blood streaming down his legs. After field surgery, he slowly recovered and continued to serve in China for another year.

Sergeant William M. Stewart, USMC, the first lone American working with two Chinese radio operators and a Chinese aerologist, established a prime post at Sungsue Point with a commanding view of Xiamen Harbor and the Formosa Strait in September 1944. The station became a legendary site of inspiring success, tragedy, and betrayal.

Stewart scored early bragging rights for the coast watch program two weeks after he began monitoring the harbor. The Pacific fleet sent three bombers in to Xiamen with instructions to radio Stewart for targets upon arrival. He guided them to direct hits on an airfield, a freighter, and a fuel depot. Last, he steered them to a clump of trees that had sprung up overnight along the shore. "You see those trees by the water? They don't grow there," he said. The planes bombed the spontaneous grove and sunk what turned out to be a camouflaged destroyer.[33]

Radiomen Second Class Alfred Parsons and J. H. Lively relieved Stewart in December and collaborated daily with Chinese Army Captain Lin Shih Fong, who kept watch on Elephant Mountain, about a mile southwest of Sungsue Point. Beginning in mid-December, the three lookouts noticed a Japanese patrol boat poking around near tiny Whale Island, where Parsons and Lively often ventured, about one hundred fifty yards from the boat pier at the Sungsue Point. On December 14, the boat came within a hundred yards of the point, drawing fire from SACO's Chinese guards. Six days later, a gunboat anchored beside the island for ten minutes and then left.

Lin, Parsons, and Lively grew suspicious of these vessels and decided to investigate. On the morning of December 21, Lin and Parsons headed for Whale Island in a rowboat with two Chinese boatmen at the oars. In addition to his ubiquitous binoculars, Parsons packed a camera, a hand grenade, and a pistol. The plan was for Parsons and Lin to take a trail to the highest point on the island for a better view of the waters on the far side. Meanwhile, Lively would cover them with a high-powered rifle from the pier.

After landing on the island, Lin and Parsons had begun their ascent when gunshots rang out, and a dozen Japanese soldiers came charging along the beach toward the path. Lively squeezed off four shots and saw three soldiers fall, but the others kept going as a second group dashed out from the other side of the island. They all converged on the path and overtook the two SACOs. The soldiers dragged the pair to a gunboat waiting on the far side of the island, and it hightailed for Xiamen.

Powerless to help them, Lively moved to a higher lookout to watch the outcome before retreating to safer ground, radioing headquarters, and receiving instructions to withdraw to Zhangzhou. SACO abandoned Sungsue Point immediately.

Parsons and Lin were packed off to Xiamen but never saw each other again. The Japanese released Lin in October 1945. Parsons was imprisoned briefly on Formosa and transferred blindfolded to Ofana Prison Camp thirty miles from Yokahama, Japan, where he was held until the end of the war. During his captivity, he suffered beatings, torture, lice, and near starvation and was often chained hand and foot. Frequently interrogated, Parsons invented a story about being part of air-to-ground communications for the Allied Air Forces. He knew enough about the subject to spin a plausible yarn, elaborating on it gradually over time and perhaps keeping himself alive as his questioners anticipated the next tidbit.

For SACO, the capture was an emotional as well as a tactical blow. Dai Li's MBIS agents had heretofore been able to rescue or negotiate the release of prisoners Japan had taken, but not this time. Parsons was the first American seized by the Japanese under Dai's watch. They were offering cash rewards of up to $25,000 for the capture or killing of an American SACO, making Parsons a jealously guarded prize. Moreover, SACO's ambushes, sabotage, and espionage plagued the occupation like so many biting flies swarming a warhorse, and the Japanese relished this single opportunity to get in a punishing swat.

With the abrupt closing of Sungsue Point, a favorite middle-aged cook, Wang Chou, a refugee from Xiamen, was out of a job, the latest chapter in his sad story. His city had been set on a tragic downward course immediately after Japan captured it in 1938. Rumors of plump Chinese children being snatched from the streets and roasted in the butcher shops gratified the residents' hatred of their occupiers, but in fact, Xiamen suffered few atrocities. Instead, cut off from the rest of China by land and from the outside world by sea, the trading port began to die of economic starvation. Residents fled inland. With ninety percent of the houses boarded up, criminals and vandals took over the streets, which reeked of garbage.

Wang arrived at Sungsue Point desperate for work in October 1944, and Stewart hired him. The MBIS typically ran background checks on all new employees, which included a hearing before the local magistrate. Wang's hearing was weeks away, and in the meantime, he was to be detained in the local jail. But Stewart had become friendly with the cook and convinced the MBIS to let him stay on during the investigation instead.

When the Sungsue Point staff retreated to headquarters in Zhangzhou after Parsons was captured, Wang came along and was given a job in the headquarters kitchen. In February 1945, an MBIS investigator discovered that Wang had attended a Japanese spy school on Formosa. Alarmed that he could potentially poison the entire staff, MBIS agents immediately had him sent into town on the pretext of buying food, and as soon as he was outside the compound walls, they jumped him.

A search of his room uncovered 31,000 yuan in large bills, six vials of poison, and a stash of American cigarettes, perhaps used to win small favors from unsuspecting Chinese. His exposure led to the arrest of a spy ringleader in the city of Zhangzhou. The MBIS never absolutely proved a connection between Wang and the captures of Parsons and Lin, but they believed he had facilitated them. It was a chilling lesson to the Americans who were susceptible to sob stories and friendly faces. They came to appreciate the seemingly hard-nosed policies of Dai's security staff.

Despite the danger, SACO could not afford to forgo monitoring Japanese naval traffic in this crucial location. A replacement coast watch station had to move five times over three weeks before finally settling on a mountain farther from the coast but high enough for a clear view. A crumbling mountaintop pagoda there made for an excellent observation post—until the Japanese shot the top off.

JANUARY 1945 PROVED EXTREMELY PRODUCTIVE for SACO's coast watchers. Nets Four and Five alone spotted and identified sixty-one Japanese ships in the coastal South China Sea, and other SACO intelligence contributed to major scores by the U.S. Navy.

Early in the month, Admiral Halsey asked Miles to supply target information for a planned attack in coastal Southeast Asia. Two years earlier, French submarine Commander Robert Meynier and his wife, a Vietnamese princess, had enlisted lighthouse keepers, customs agents, harbormasters, and fishermen along the Indochinese coast to keep an eye out for Japanese activity on behalf of SACO. The Meyniers had been recruited for SACO by the OSS, and Donovan's frustration with the lack of results from the Meynier group had contributed to his conflict with Miles.

But even if the OSS had given up on SACO, SACO still had faith in Madame Meynier's friends, and Miles called them to action through his contact in Saigon. A lighthouse keeper near Cam Ranh Bay came back with a report of a twenty-six-ship Japanese convoy plus a list of more ships anchored in the harbor. On January 12, Halsey's bombers swooped in and sunk forty enemy ships, including twelve Japanese Navy vessels, for a total of one hundred twenty thousand tons. A few days later, Miles sent the admiral photos of the havoc wrought by his pilots. Meynier's observers had snapped the pictures with simple box cameras supplied by SACO.

Still basking in the Cam Ranh Bay success, Miles got a message on January 20 from Rear Admiral Eugene Fluckey, commander of the submarine USS *Barb*, nicknamed the "Galloping Ghost" for its stealth and unprecedented speed. The commander was puzzled; every Japanese convoy he was tracking kept disappearing at a certain point along the southern Chinese coast south of Fuzhou. The only possible explanation was a channel dredged in the Haitan Strait. Did Miles know of one? The next morning, Miles replied that indeed the strait must have been dredged because his coast watchers regularly observed battleships passing through.

Fluckey, previously unaware that the navy had coast watchers in China, delighted in this new intelligence bonanza and kept in touch with Miles over the next critical forty-eight hours as he hunted for enemy targets. On January 22, the *Barb* spotted a plume of smoke on the horizon, which betrayed a convoy of eleven Japanese ships steaming south. When the convoy disappeared at a channel entrance and failed to emerge on the other side, Fluckey reasoned that it must have anchored somewhere near Namkwan Harbor, but to seek it out, he would have to venture into waters that may have been mined. Miles reported that his crew knew of no mines in that area. While no guarantee of safe waters, it was enough for Fluckey to risk it. The *Barb* bravely crept ahead in a mere thirty feet of water in the wee hours of January 23.

Meanwhile, Stewart from his new, nearby perch saw the convoy hunkered down in the harbor and asked SACO's local pirate spies to find out what its plans were. Six pirates posing as fishermen selling their wares boarded the ships and learned that the convoy intended to leave at 6:00 a.m. on January 23 and would be sailing at only eight knots due to a damaged ship in the group. An officer at Happy Valley used the data to calculate precisely where and when the *Barb* could best attack the convoy en route at sub-friendly depths. Miles sent this information to Fluckey and Stewart late on January 22. But when Stewart assumed his post before dawn the next morning to watch the ships cast off, they were already in flames.

Fluckey had entered the harbor at 3:00 a.m. and seen the sleeping convoy plus at least a dozen other ships stretched out before him. He closed in and launched his torpedoes at 4:05 a.m. By the time Stewart saw the damage, the *Barb* was galloping out to sea toward safe waters with beer in the cooler for the crew to celebrate their tremendous hit.

At 11:30 a.m., Fluckey sent Miles this message:

> YOUR LATEST INFO RESULTED IN EIGHT HITS IN POT OF GOLD X FOUND YOUR CONVOY PLUS OTHERS AND POSSIBLE LARGE WARSHIPS ANCHORED AT NAMKWAN HARBOR LAST NIGHT X THREE SHIPS KNOWN SUNK X TERRIFIC EXPLOSION X CAN YOU GIVE US TYPES AND EXTENT OF OTHER DAMAGE X MANY THANKS FROM BARB[34]

SACO coast watchers working with the pirates received conflicting reports that three or four destroyers had been sunk and four other ships seriously damaged, possibly including one or more troop ships. Three of the pirates had been killed in the attack. Over the next several days, many bodies of uniformed Japanese soldiers washed ashore, confirming that the damaged vessels must have indeed included a troop ship. Dai Li sent the pirates to search their pockets for information and other agents to comb the wreckage. Residents of a nearby walled fishing village salvaged flotsam from the sunken ships but steered clear of the dead bodies.

In June 1991, Fluckey and Robert Sinks, a SACO coast watcher who had helped track the convoy, paid an emotional visit to Huang Qi, the fishing village whose residents had witnessed the *Barb*'s attack. The isolated village was accessible only by sea and had never had white visitors before. Fluckey was disappointed that there were no written records of the incident but grateful and honored to discover that the story was deeply ingrained in local oral history. The entire community of just a hundred residents crowded around the hut, where Sinks and Fluckey listened to two elderly fishermen recount what they had witnessed that night as teenagers. Four ships were sunk, they said, and three seriously damaged. These four men from two utterly different worlds formed a deep bond through the grave experience they had shared more than four decades earlier.

COORDINATED EFFORTS BETWEEN COAST WATCHERS, radio monitors, and Chinese agents reaped other benefits for the Allies. Dramatic rescues punctuated the monotony of staring at the sea and listening to hours of workaday radio traffic. SACO found and brought to safety thirty airplane pilots and forty-six crewmembers and passengers shot down during the course of the war. Key resources in these rescues were SACO's triangulating direction finders that located distress signals and vigilant, courageous Chinese.

Residents all across China and especially in the southeast recognized these airmen as their allies and risked their own lives to deliver them to safety. Dai Li's ubiquitous network played an important role. In addition, the OSS, the navy, and the army air force distributed illustrated handbills depicting Chinese carrying an American pilot and explaining that the Americans were their friends. American officers even visited small towns near areas where they expected losses and enlisted local leaders to assist downed airmen.

One of the most famous rescued pilots was Colonel Edward Rector, an original member of the Flying Tigers. His P-51 was shot down by antiaircraft fire on December 19, 1944, in the vicinity of Jinmen Island not far from Xiamen, and it crashed ten miles from where he had been spotted bailing out. A pair of coast watchers, Sinks and Radioman E. J. Newell, got the word from Chinese intelligence and hired a motor launch to search for him. They found him slightly injured and took him to Zhangzhou headquarters, where he rested for several days until he was strong enough to walk. A Chinese soldier and an interpreter accompanied him on the three-day trek along back trails to an airstrip at Longyan, where a plane from the 14th Air Force picked him up and returned him to the base at Kunming.

Three months later, another member of the 14th, Captain Eugene McGuire, was hit while making a run against a Japanese Xiamen airfield. Three SACO coast watchers found him unharmed near his crashed plane and sent him with Chinese escorts to Zhangzhou. A few days after he was safe in Kunming, two P-51s, piloted by McGuire and Rector, buzzed the Zhangzhou headquarters compound in salute.

SACO and friendly Chinese fishermen also helped in the rescue of five men who survived the *Arisan Maru*, a Japanese prison ship that was hit by a torpedo from an

American submarine in the Bashi Strait west of the Philippines on October 24, 1944. Nearly eighteen hundred American and Allied prisoners drowned, but five Americans, four soldiers and a civilian, miraculously found a lifeboat, a sail, and two kegs of water and sailed to China wearing nothing but their prison G-strings. Three Chinese families fishing together on a junk picked them up, fed them, shared their own warm clothes, and brought them safely to shore.

The next day, an American navy officer showed up out of nowhere and escorted them on a two-week odyssey to a SACO camp. The refugees were feted as heroes with banquets, fireworks, and marching bands as they made their way from town to town in typical Chinese fashion, on foot, by sedan chair, two-man bicycle, and charcoal-fueled truck. They spent two weeks at the camp doing nothing but eating and sleeping before flying on to Kunming and then Washington, D.C. One of the survivors, Anton Cichy, estimated that he put on forty pounds during his month in China.

With all the joy of restoring battered survivors to health, the men of SACO also performed the grave office of laying their compatriots to rest. After a U.S. Army Air Force plane was shot down off the coast in April 1945, four bodies of American airmen washed ashore. A solemn porter train carried them in simple wooden coffins to Camp Six, where the medical staff examined them for identification and the men ceremoniously buried them in a hastily created cemetery. Clayton Mishler was moved to compose a poem in their honor titled, "Disturb Them Not," a plea to "Let them sleep where sleep is good."

CHAPTER 13

Life as a SACO

LIKE THOSE THRUST INTO WAR the world over, the men of SACO were very young. Though some were married, many had never even lived away from their parents, let alone traveled far from home. But though young and green, each had an independent streak and a craving for adventure to go with it, spurring him to step forward voluntarily for prolonged and hazardous duty overseas without knowing what lay in store. And nearly every one thrilled upon learning that he was destined for a top-secret mission in China.

From the beginning, this was not a typical military experience. SACO recruits were trained in small groups in secluded places stateside. Many a SACO waited for transport in a secret apartment in Washington, D.C., Cairo, or Kolkata and only learned it was time to move when someone woke him in the dead of night and whispered, "Get your gear."

Like the training, the journey to China was mostly a small-group, or even solitary, patchwork affair. Ensign Cecil D. Johnson, traveling on his own, caught flights from New York to the Azores to Morocco to Tripoli, to Abadan, Iran, and finally to Kolkata. He served as a courier during the trip, carrying classified documents in three separate bags, delivering them to recipients en route, and picking up others to deliver as he progressed. He never knew anything about their contents. In Kolkata, he waited several weeks for a flight to Kunming. He came close to being drafted to drive there over the Ledo-Stilwell Road, but he got out of it by finally convincing someone that he had never before driven a truck.

Storekeeper Clayton Mishler also had to make a delivery on his way to China, but in his case, it was a fighter plane. He sailed from San Francisco to Cochin, India, aboard a British Royal Navy aircraft carrier with nineteen other SACO storekeepers, each responsible for one of twenty U.S. Air Force P-40 planes strapped to the flight deck. The SACOs knew not where the aircraft were bound or for what purpose, but nevertheless it was their duty to watch over them. Twice a day for the entire voyage, the men examined the planes for corrosion and checked to be sure the lashing stayed fast. When they docked in Cochin, the British announced over the ship's loudspeakers that all Americans and their planes were to disembark. Mishler intended to stick around and watch the offloading of the planes, but the crew shooed the storekeepers away. The SACOs never heard another word about the planes, and the plunge into the exotic jumble of India soon erased the aircraft from their minds.

Volunteers took many routes and conveyances to India, but for much of the war, while the Japanese held the Burma Road, the final leg into China was always "over the Hump." For most SACOs, this unnerving flight over the Himalayas was the most frightening experience of their service, even compared to night demolition missions and Japanese air raids.

The cargo planes had rickety canvas seats with only subway-style canvas straps to cling to for restraint during turbulence. Below loomed the world's highest peaks, jagged, desolate, and gray. At twenty-eight thousand feet, the temperature dropped below zero in the plane. Mishler was still cold even after putting on every piece of clothing he owned and wrapping himself in two navy-issue blankets. In the thin atmosphere, everyone had to use oxygen masks. But on some flights, there was only enough oxygen for the crew, and the passengers passed out, regaining consciousness when the plane descended to more oxygen-rich air.

Weather created its own dangers, a can't-win-for-losing state of affairs. Snow, rain, and fog posed greater risk of a plane crash, while clear skies made it easier for Japanese fighter planes to attack.

Along with clandestine movements, the men who volunteered for SACO learned to look inconspicuous. Gone were the crisp, head-turning Navy whites with bell-bottom trousers and square collars. SACOs, from officers of the highest rank to third-class specialists, wore plain khaki army fatigues with no insignia of any kind. Milton Miles had two reasons for this policy. First, the Japanese offered bounties for dead American SACOs, and the reward increased by rank. The plain uniforms made the men less attractive targets. Second, it promoted the unique brand of teamwork necessary in a place where every man had to be ready to do everything from cooking to erecting radio towers.

One lieutenant did not get the word about the dress code and showed up at Happy Valley fully decorated and beribboned, inexplicably oblivious to everyone else's unadorned shirt. Rather than correcting him, Miles had all the men wear their insignia to dinner, where he announced that they would no longer be worn. The next day, the lieutenant looked like everyone else.

Many men abandoned military garb altogether when they took to the field. They donned the baggy peasant clothes fastened with thread-loop buttons and circular straw hats favored by Chinese farmers, completing the look with bundles suspended on the ends of yo-yo poles balanced on their shoulders. Some even practiced imitating the nimble gait of the Chinese and took regular doses of Atabrine, a malaria medication containing a colorant that yellowed the skin. They never expected to fool anyone face to face, but the disguises helped them blend into the landscape, at least from a distance.

During cold winters in northern and central China, most Americans, Miles included, adopted Chinese quilted jackets and trousers for warmth without bulk. They were far superior to heavy wool coats for working indoors in buildings without central heat.

Out in remote field stations where men lived and worked in small groups, dress was even more independent. SACO men trimmed their collars with leopard skins taken from animals they had shot themselves and walked around in red silk pajamas made from surplus, weather-instrument parachutes.

SACO MEN NOT ONLY dressed like their Chinese counterparts and neighbors, but they also ate like them. The SACO diet came from local sources. They augmented staples like rice, eggs, sweet potatoes, chicken, and pork with fish, mangos, pineapples, and an occasional pheasant or deer shot in the wild. Cargo space over the Hump was too precious to transport food, although now and then a windfall of flavors from home such as instant coffee, mustard, and canned meat would arrive. They had to "live off the land," but that did not mean pilfering or commandeering farmers' crops. SACO's success depended entirely on friendly relationships with local residents, and to preserve goodwill, the men purchased everything they ate.

As a health precaution, the Americans were prohibited from eating fresh vegetables unless they washed and cooked them thoroughly. Local farmers used human excrement as fertilizer, making raw produce unsafe. SACO's First Lieutenant Robert Barrow, walking between rice paddies with Chinese troops one winter night, slipped and fell into a vat where this fertilizer, called night soil, was stored. Disgusted almost to the point of madness, he stripped off his clothes and ran to a small farmhouse for help. The couple took him in, gave him a hot bath, washed his clothes, and dried them by the fire.

Beyond eating, even drinking carried risk. Every beverage, including water, was served hot, even in summer. Experiments with boiling water and then letting it cool had resulted in attacks of dysentery, perhaps due to microbes growing quickly in the drinking vessels. The beverage of choice, however, was hot tea sipped from individual pots right from the spout.

Milton Miles took advantage of mealtime to foster the cooperation and friendship between Americans and Chinese that were essential to SACO's success. At the camps, the men from both countries sat together to eat Chinese food with chopsticks. This simple act taught the Americans respect for Chinese culture and demonstrated that respect to the Chinese. But a bountiful meal for the Chinese felt meager to the Americans, who were much bigger and accustomed to heartier fare. They were always hungry, and most of them lost weight during their tours.

Radioman First Class Dean Spaulding got a taste of what lay ahead as soon as he got to Happy Valley. Hungry and exhausted after a grueling journey, he arrived after the mess hall was closed for the night. The kitchen staff served him a light meal of fried eggs and rice, which he ate eagerly, if clumsily, with chopsticks.

But Happy Valley also treated everyone to a weekly American dinner, and they all looked forward to it. A plate of southern-style fried chicken and mashed potatoes could work wonders to fend off homesickness.

Dai Li valued the American effort to adopt the Chinese diet, and he reciprocated with a gesture of his own, throwing an elaborate banquet for the Americans on their first Christmas in China, in 1942. At the crowning moment, the navy men practically drooled over a huge cake covered with white icing and topped with an enormous American Beauty Rose made of red frosting. Miles took a generous mouthful and struggled to retain his composure; the icing was nothing but colored lard.

For one SACO, the hospitality he received after a hungry month in the field stayed with him forever. A Chinese Catholic priest treated him to sweet and sour pork, the most delicious thing he had ever eaten. Back in Chicago after the war, the man tried the dish in dozens of Chinese restaurants and even cooked up several batches himself, but he never managed to duplicate it. He finally realized that he would have to starve himself for a month before anything could taste that good, and even then, he could not replicate the unexpected kindness that made that meal unforgettable.

Food was usually plentiful at the camps, but near enemy lines, supplies could be cut off suddenly. When the Japanese began to edge close to Camp Six near the coast in the spring of 1945, no one could venture out to the markets for eggs and chicken, and the camp lived on nothing but rice and sweet potatoes for two weeks.

The Chinese repeatedly impressed the Americans with their resourcefulness in every way, including scaring up meals. A navy instructor on a guerrilla mission wondered how he would survive on his ration of one cup of rice a day, but the three cooks in the company fed everyone seemingly out of nothing, harvesting wild grasses, bark, and game along the way. Like all navy personnel, the instructor carried his field rations of dehydrated cooked rice in a canvas tube around his neck.

A camp cook near China's southern coast picked wild loquats, or Chinese plums, small, sweet, yellow fruits that taste like a blend of apples and apricots and grow in clusters on glossy-leafed trees. He turned them into jelly and American-style "apple" pie.

The Christmas banquet Dai hosted in 1942 was one of many that Chinese army officers held in honor of their American partners. They served exotic fare like shark fin soup and thousand-year-old eggs, interspersed with multiple compulsory *gambei* ("bottoms up") toasts, encouraging guests to drain their glasses of hot, strong wine. Many a night, Americans staggered drunkenly home from parties to the delight of their Chinese hosts.

SACO camps soon appropriated the tradition, giving *gambei* parties of their own to celebrate success or give a buddy a proper send-off. The men could usually find something that resembled vodka from local sources, but cocktail mixers were nonexistent. Radioman First Class Richard Rutan wrote home asking for Kool-Aid drink mix, which his mother dutifully sent along not knowing its purpose.

Where they couldn't buy spirits, they could make their own. Bishop Thomas Megan, a khaki-wearing, carbine-toting Catholic missionary who had lived in China for a dozen years before taking up with SACO, produced his own moonshine and shared it liberally.

SACO MEN, FEW IN NUMBER while working in fluid conditions in the vast country, had to travel far and often to wherever their special skills were needed. Air transport was a luxury; most of the time, they went by truck, sampan, rickshaw, and on foot, taking weeks or months to reach an assignment.

The Chinese Army's trucking fleet consisted of Dodge trucks more than a decade old, kept running with improvised spare parts. Gaskets were fashioned out of paper, and bits of wire substituted for screws. With gasoline scarce and expensive, the Chinese retrofitted the vehicles to burn alcohol, tung oil, or pine root oil.

Some trucks could even run on charcoal, supplemented by precious gasoline only when needed for an extra boost up a steep grade. Charcoal burned in a large metal tank such as an old hot water heater mounted on the truck bed. The fire released a gas that moved through tubing to feed the engine, although the power it provided was often inadequate. To negotiate hills, an ever-present mechanic would get out and place chocks behind the wheels to keep the truck from rolling backward, then turn a crank that fanned the charcoal fire to build up the gas pressure. The driver would then start the engine and ease the truck forward as the mechanic snatched the chocks away, tossed them into the back, and leaped into the front seat of the moving vehicle. If the truck still needed more power, the driver would open a valve to release gasoline, but it was tantamount to burning gold and was used only when absolutely necessary.

A journey by truck could be harrowing in the mountainous landscape over unpaved roads with dozens of hairpin turns but no guardrails. When conditions became too unnerving, passengers elected to walk behind a slow-lumbering vehicle rather than risk the consequences of a mishap. The ride down a mountain was even worse than the climb because a driver would turn off the engine and coast down to save fuel, leaving a truck with substandard brakes at the mercy of gravity. But when winter brought freezing rain and snow, it was too dangerous even for a dare-devil driver, and the truck might have to stop for days waiting for the roads to clear.

No truck ever hit the road without taking a mechanic along. Makeshift repairs without proper spare parts forced a vicious cycle of constant breakdowns and more makeshift repairs. But, like the cooks, the mechanics found ingenious ways to keep trucks moving, and when they couldn't, another truck magically materialized, thanks to Dai Li's network.

In addition to primitive roads and balky vehicles, travelers faced dangers from human predators, both foreign and local. Thus, every trucking party included at least two armed soldiers as guards on board.

After decades of warlord rule, bandits still flourished in the countryside in spite of Chiang Kai-shek's security improvements. When one truck broke down after dark on a remote stretch of road, the party suddenly found itself surrounded by fifteen bandits brandishing rifles, and the soldiers raised their ready tommy guns in turn. The gun-barrel-to-gun-barrel standoff was brief. The leader of the expedition shouted at the bandits, invoking the name Dai Li, and they melted silently into the night.

The Japanese occupation was also an ever-present danger because SACO was a prized target. But the Chinese kept close watch on enemy movements, and trucks could usually find routes around and through them, and when they couldn't, they would lay low until the troops passed, sometimes within yards of where they were hiding.

Trucks could break down or run out of fuel, but sampans depended only on wind, currents, and human muscle at the oars to ply China's network of rivers.

Expert boatmen used poles to guide these small, flat-bottomed workhorses of China's river transport system through rapids, rocks, and sandbars. Traveling SACOs took steam ferries or hired sampans whenever they could to link segments of long overland treks.

In parts of central and northern China, the best way to get around was on horseback. A pair of radio operators rode sturdy Mongolian ponies twenty miles from their remote station into Baoji in Shaanxi Province once a week to pick up a few supplies and have a little fun. SACO chaplain Captain William LaSor, a Presbyterian minister, rode more than seven hundred miles with a Chinese cavalry unit en route to visiting weather and radio stations scattered in the country's interior.

But the most reliable form of transportation, and at times the only option, was on foot. As Milton Miles discovered during that first journey to the coast with Dai Li, it also was the safest way to get around behind enemy lines.

A network of narrow footpaths crisscrossed the countryside linking villages and boat landings. Distances were measured in *li*, a unit of measure that today is fixed at five hundred meters, but during the 1940s, its length was fluid, measuring time and effort more than linear distance. For example, climbing a mountain might be 10 li, whereas descending the same path would be only 6 li.

Marine Major Ed Dupras, a veteran of Guadalcanal, scoffed at the suggestion that he'd better toughen his feet before joining SACO. After what he had been through, he assumed he could handle anything the navy threw at him. But after three months in China, he declared that Marines knew nothing about walking.

The men walked hundreds of miles to reach their assignments or carry out missions. They suffered battered feet and exhaustion and occasionally had to resort to riding in sedan chairs suspended between two poles hoisted on the shoulders of two coolies. It made for a bumpy and humiliating ride; the Americans hated to waste manpower on something they felt they should have been able to do themselves.

At night as the SACOs took off their sturdy boots and nursed their raw and bloody feet, they were awed by the capacity of their undernourished Chinese partners to cover the same distance with seemingly little discomfort despite carrying heavy loads and wearing only straw sandals.

Lieutenant Commander Stanley McCaffrey, who served a year and a half at Happy Valley and in Kunming, summed it up this way:

You probably laughed at the coolie as he rhythmically went hopping along carrying a couple of loads at either end of his yo-yo pole, but you soon had a lot of respect for that little joker when he walked you into the ground, you carrying nothing and him carrying between eighty and a hundred pounds.[35]

To move supplies, pack trains of Chinese porters carried everything from rice and gasoline to radio generators and torpedoes and even a baby grand piano over rocky trails and muddy tracks. What appeared on the surface to be unskilled labor required tremendous stamina, balance, and devotion that every American grew to admire, especially after having to negotiate the same goat path himself. Anything too large for yo-yo bundles was suspended among a team of men using an ingenious system of ropes and bamboo poles. It took fifty-six men using this system to transport a radio transmission and receiver set. To synchronize their footsteps, the porters spoke in a sing-song cadence of short phrases that the Americans imagined could be translated as "I'm tired ... Me too." On long treks, new teams of fresh porters always showed up each morning, another miracle of human infrastructure in a seemingly broken country.

As THEY MADE THEIR TREKS, American SACOs marveled at the exotic, sometimes magical scenes around them. Here a file of pack ponies walked by with bells tinkling around their necks, there a big black pig gently nuzzled diners in a tiny café. Terraced hillsides of rice paddies looked like shimmering staircases, soybean fields in bloom perfumed the air, and dragonflies by the hundreds formed iridescent rainbows.

Lonely tea stands stood on remote stretches of roadsides, sometimes nothing more than a thatched roof atop four poles with a small table and a single kettle suspended over a charcoal fire on the ground. A wayfarer could sometimes buy a snack to go with his tea, perhaps a soft, doughy bun or a handful of walnuts.

Overnight lodging ran the gamut from western-style hotels to traditional inns where the pillows were blocks of dense, varnished wood worn smooth by thousands of heads. One night after a meal of savory pheasant dumplings at an ancient Buddhist monastery, Mishler went to bed and woke to a gentle, distant gong calling the monks to prayer deep in the night. And everywhere from bustling cities to tiny villages, members of Dai Li's vast network whisked weary sailors to their homes for a meal and a warm bed. When night fell miles from the next town, they slept in trucks and sampans with the guards keeping watch in shifts.

CENTRAL CHINA WAS THICK with voracious mosquitos, supplying fodder for wry humor that rivaled tales told in Maine and Wisconsin. Before settling on the "What the Hell?" pennant in SACO's early days, the outfit's first symbol was a cartoon mosquito named Socko. Someone fretted that a confused mosquito could crash into a large mirror at Miles's house and shatter it, bringing the navy seven years of bad luck. A sailor observing an airfield through binoculars claimed that a few of the planes without markings were actually mosquitos.

But the pests were no joke. They carried malaria and dengue fever, a disease that causes high fever and severe pain in the joints and bones, earning it the nickname "breakbone fever." Cases of both illnesses were widespread among the Americans who were exposed to them for the first time.

SACO's ninety doctors and pharmacist mates had their hands full and trained Chinese soldiers as paramedics to help administer to twenty-five hundred Americans and eighty thousand Chinese. They set up a medical center and a field hospital for guerrillas close to the fighting in Hunan Province in addition to the clinics at or near every camp.

Though they suffered few combat injuries, the Americans were plagued with rashes and insect bites, especially fleas. Motor Machinist's Mate Matthew Komorowski-Kaye slept on a dirt floor one night and woke up covered with red welts from sand fleas. After that, he made a rule that the only parts of his body that would touch the ground for more than a few minutes were his shod feet. And for Mishler, one of the greatest treasures he received from home was a can of flea powder.

Motor Machinist's Mate Sal Ciaccio, who shared a house with a small SACO work group near Fuzhou, went through a frightening medical emergency. He started feeling feverish one afternoon, and by nightfall, his face and extremities were paralyzed. Porters carried him on a stretcher to the Min River and loaded him into a sampan in the care of a pair of Chinese nurses. As the boat slipped down the river, his friends knew it was the last they would ever see of him. Ciaccio was admitted to an enormous floating hospital on the river. The ship resembled a small city with amenities that predicted today's cruise ships, including a barbershop, library, and white-clothed dining room with handsome menus. Ciaccio was diagnosed with multiple neuritis, a complication of beriberi, caused by a vitamin B deficiency. He never returned to duty, and his SACO friends assumed that he had died until nearly fifty years later when the Fuzhou roommates got back together at a SACO veterans' reunion.

Ciaccio's illness struck after the war was over, but during its first few months, SACO was ill prepared for medical emergencies. Radioman First Class Earl Randolph had a life-threatening appendicitis attack at Camp One in coastal China, a thousand miles from Happy Valley. Dr. Victor Goorchenko, born in China of Russian parents, ran a clinic several miles from the camp. He came to the rescue, carrying borrowed surgical equipment on a bicycle he pedaled over the rugged footpaths. Assisted by the untrained camp crew, he performed an appendectomy, his first ever, on a mess hall table in a monastery bell tower. Before beginning surgery, he read instructions for the procedure in a French medical textbook. The team boiled the instruments in an ammunition tin, and he used two lengths of rubber tubing sterilized with rice wine to drain the wound. Randolph fully recovered and served SACO another six months.

IN CHINA, SACOS LIVED in fourteen main camps and in scores of small weather and radio stations scattered from the Indochina border to Mongolia. Camp life was more convenient than the open road, complete with mess halls, latrines, and showers, but the men still contended with mosquitos, spiders, fleas, heat, cold, rats, and mud.

The typical camp building was made of earth hand-compacted in wooden forms and then covered inside and out with plaster and topped with a tightly thatched or tile roof. The structures were fast and easy to build using local materials. This ancient "rammed earth" construction method was employed for western sections of the Great Wall of China fifteen centuries ago and is still in use today.

Several camps moved into ancient temples and monasteries that had been abandoned or were so underused that the handful of monks and lamas remaining were happy to find other quarters in exchange for the rental income. The religious trappings left behind made for some odd juxtapositions. At Camp Three, the men in a cave radio station worked under the watchful protection of seventeen three-foot-high statues of the Buddha.

In some cases, camp transients were put up in tents fitted with cots, which kept the men off the ground and away from mud and fleas but offered little warmth during central China's bitter winters, which rivaled those of the American Midwest. Mishler rigged up a charcoal fireplace in the tent he shared with three other men at Happy Valley. He punched holes in a wok and placed it on a bed of stones in the center of the tent. Burning charcoal in the wok, he opened a slit in the tent roof to allow smoke and gas to escape.

Those working at remote weather and radio stations had to set up their own housekeeping in groups of two to six and pay their living expenses with a navy per-diem stipend. Housing ranged from splendid apartments in palaces to makeshift accommodations in caves and chicken coops, but with the help of General Dai's agents and western missionaries, they found ways to live in reasonable comfort.

Foraging, cooking, and tending fires could have consumed much of their time were it not for local servants. Houseboys as young as twelve years old prepared meals, washed clothes, and swept away the spiders for a few coins a day, often eager to serve Americans so they could practice their mission-school English. Ciaccio and friends each had a houseboy and a rickshaw driver, unimaginable luxuries back home in Massachusetts, but they really needed them in China, where hot water came from a kettle instead of a faucet, and shopping for one meal might require haggling with three vendors.

When the Americans had a little cash, they actually liked to shop, especially for the exotic. They were always on the lookout for presents for loved ones and for colorful pieces to spice up their bachelor quarters back home.

In India, Rutan bought several yards of pale blue silk embroidered with silver flowers for his mother. She made it into a smashing evening gown that she wore to the Academy Awards with her son in 1950. Rutan, who lived in southern California, treated his mother to the ceremony, which in those days was open to spectators for the price of a ticket. As they wove through the crowd, whispering onlookers wondered if she was a movie star.

Two navy men browsing through an open-air market in China could not resist tiger and leopard skins for sale, and each bought one. But a few days later aboard a riverboat, they unrolled the skins to find them stinking of rotting flesh and covered with maggots. Gagging, they threw them overboard. Clearly, the hides had not been properly dressed.

Mishler spent leisure hours poking around in bric-a-brac shops, picking up decorative pieces here and there. His best find, though, did not come from a store. While he was browsing through an antique shop in Xi'an, a farmer came in offering to sell a small, dirt-covered object he had found in his field, but the shopkeeper wasn't interested. Mishler bought it for about six dollars. It turned out to be a two-thousand-year-old bronze tiger, now in the collection of the Cleveland Art Museum.

Shopping for pleasure took up only some of the time for SACO men. Free time was spent in time-honored ways with cards and outdoor sports like baseball, basketball, and volleyball, each modified to accommodate the number and skill of available players. They hunted pheasant, deer, wild boar, and tigers. They swam in rivers and ponds and climbed mountains around Happy Valley for stunning views of the landscape. Occasionally there was a movie or a live Chinese show to entertain them, but many an evening was spent sipping hot wine, chatting, and rereading letters from home that came a dozen at a time.

LaSor was one of two chaplains who joined SACO in November 1944. Before that, the men fended for themselves spiritually, attending religious services in Chinese Christian churches and foreign missions. The second chaplain, Lieutenant Chaplain Philip Shannon, was a Catholic priest. He served the camps and watch stations of the coast, while LaSor made the rounds of China's interior.

WHETHER AT HOME, on missions, in training, or on the road, the Chinese repeatedly astonished the Americans with their ability to achieve so much with so little.

On a SACO journey across country, a truck's radiator sprung a leak on a foggy night miles from the nearest town, leaving the party stranded. The next morning before the fog lifted, a young girl and a decrepit woman with a baby on her back emerged as if by magic from the mist. The girl produced a tiny, clay stove from her pack and built a fire while the woman examined the radiator. The woman melted bits of metal on the stove and applied the molten substance to the radiator. After receiving payment from the driver for her services, she led the girl away into the fog, and the trip resumed.

Decades of turmoil had taught the people to tend to business despite profound challenges, always finding novel ways to adapt to changing conditions. After the Japanese invasion, the owner of a Manchurian textile mill moved his operation to a cluster of caves in northwest China. Workers operated looms and packed bolts of cloth in the caverns as diligently as they had in their modern, brick factory.

Conditions were only marginally better for the Americans, who also learned to improvise. For example, to fuel generators, they often had to resort to impure, black-market gasoline that had to be strained. A particular brand of socks produced in Kolkata made excellent filters for this purpose. At Camp Six, a mechanic accidentally broke the stud bolts of a generator, and the only replacements he could get were too large, so he ground them down to size with an eggbeater. When the same camp ran out of mineral spirits to clean firearms, they had to resort to using vegetable oil, but that required extra cleaning to keep mold from growing.

SOME ASPECTS OF CHINESE CULTURE were more difficult for the Americans to accept, despite their genuine affection for the people and their training to respect their partners' differences.

For example, criticizing, arguing, or refusing a request constituted unseemly and insulting behavior in Chinese society. On the face of it, this may seem like a virtue, but in practice, it thwarted communication and created administrative bottlenecks. For example, Americans might meet with Chinese officials to make a proposal about improving radio transmission, and the officials would smile and respond, "We'll take that under consideration." The Americans would leave the meeting naïvely waiting for the Chinese to come to a decision, not realizing that they had been told, "absolutely not."

Worse, the Chinese might make promises they never intended to fulfill. The prohibition on criticism made it even harder to resolve these problems. If a man said to someone, "You assured me that you would sign the documents, and you still haven't done it," it was tantamount to slapping him in the face.

Even Miles, who emphasized getting along above all else, found this maddening. But he did not tolerate anyone who behaved gruffly or displayed a patronizing attitude toward the Chinese. Such men were sent home.

On the flip side, Chinese discipline was positively brutal by western standards, but the SACO men were ordered never to intervene. At times, it took all their willpower to remain silent. Many SACOs witnessed civilians shot or beheaded in the streets for comparatively minor infractions while wailing relatives looked on.

At Happy Valley, a Chinese soldier stole an American's eyeglasses. An officer administered a hundred lashes with a whip to the man's hands every morning in front of the entire camp for two weeks, and by the time the punishment was complete, there was no skin left on them.

A similar but even worse punishment was meted out to a Nationalist soldier in southeast China who had been convicted of treason. In front of the entire company, an officer pulverized his hands with the butt of a rifle until every bone must have been broken, and he was forced to march away, destined to starve to death in the open air because no one would dare to help a traitor.

Americans struggled to accept this seemingly cruel side of Chinese society. Everywhere they went, they met courageous people who went about the business of life under dreadful conditions with dignity and yet seemed callous toward the sick, the dying, and the dead bodies in the streets. But keeping these people at arm's length was truly a matter of survival. Anyone who touched a dead body or a sick person automatically became responsible for it, and no one could afford that. These problems had to be left to the overextended local authorities. The SACOs were warned of this even before they got to China, but turning away from all the suffering was distressing to the end.

CHAPTER 14

Secret Adventures Revealed

AFTER HOSTILITIES ENDED in the summer of 1945, millions of American soldiers, sailors, and flyers began streaming home bursting with tales of war to tell. The men of SACO had been through remarkable experiences in a corner of the world still veiled in mystery, but they had been sworn to secrecy from the start, and most would not utter a syllable about their China days for decades. Little by little, though, their stories began to come out, revealing adventures unique in the American annals of World War II.

Within six months of his appointment to the Friendship Project, Milton Miles received a rude awakening to the unseen dangers of his job when a knife-wielding man tried to kill him on a railroad platform in India.[36] Until then, he had dwelled little on his personal safety despite Dai Li's warnings, but he soon realized he was a marked man. At least three more attempts were made on his life in China, and a flyer posted throughout Asia during the war years promised a bounty of a million dollars for the death or capture of Miles or Dai. Miles initially assumed it was the work of the Japanese, but later attacks gave him reason to suspect that the Chinese Communists also were involved.

After the assault in India, Dai Li counseled Miles to have a security guard with him at all times and to keep a low profile. Dai was therefore disturbed when Miles treated himself to a new Plymouth sedan for a November 1944 road trip from Kunming to Chongqing with planned stops at SACO camps along the way. With so few new American cars in China, the flashy sedan would make Miles an easy target; Dai advised him to travel inconspicuously by truck instead. But Miles had needed this working vacation and was enjoying the fine autumn days driving his new car. War and danger seemed remote until he reached the city of Guiyang to meet Dai. As Miles drove past a row of shops, gunfire shattered his windshield, and his guide slumped over dead in the passenger seat. Miles stomped on the gas and careened through the cobblestone streets all the way to Dai's house like some Hollywood stunt driver. Miles had likely escaped the sniper's bullet because the Plymouth was one of just a handful of vehicles in China with the steering wheel on the left, so that the gunman aimed at the wrong side.

The following month, Dai and Miles were traveling together and warming themselves in front of a charcoal brazier when a man dressed as a servant dumped a handful of live ammunition into the fire. A cook noticed in time to fling Miles and Dai to the ground as bullets flew in all directions. No one was injured. The saboteur was captured and identified as a Communist agent.

The last assassination attempt occurred just before the end of the war in late July 1945. Miles and Dai were on the road again, sharing a bedroom at a Chinese Army headquarters about fifty miles south of Shanghai. Around midnight, Miles was jerked out of bed by a loud clamor of shouts, thumps, and stomping feet outside the door. Instinctively leaping out the bedroom window for safety, he saw that Dai had done the same. Miles crept along the side of the building and peered around the corner to discover his guard holding two men around their necks in choke holds, one in each of his muscular arms, with another lying unconscious at his feet. A fourth man was held at gunpoint by another guard. Miles had nicknamed his usually slow-moving guard "Speed." Now he knew that the man had plenty of vigor but merely preserved it for when it was needed. The intruders, three Japanese and a Communist Chinese carrying grenades and side arms, had tried to enter the bedroom. They were executed.

CHINESE CIVILIANS AS WELL AS FRIENDS OF SACO repeatedly risked their lives to save those of their American allies, as journalist Don Bell discovered when he was shot down while a passenger in a U.S. Navy plane over Xiamen.

Bell, whose real name was Clarence Beliel, was a popular radio personality in Manila when the Japanese captured the city on December 8, 1941, and placed Bell, his wife, and their two sons in Santo Tomas prison camp. The camp was liberated in February 1945, and Bell, who was long presumed dead, immediately returned to work as a war correspondent.

Six weeks later, navy pilot Jim Evans offered Bell an irresistible opportunity to get back into the action. He invited the reporter to join a fourteen-hour patrol flight along the China coast aboard a navy PB4Y2 Privateer out of Clark Field in the Philippines. Bell and the twelve-man crew were flying at five hundred feet over Xiamen Harbor on March 22 when the plane was rocked by antiaircraft fire. Bell, thrown against the gun turret, passed out as the plane's tail section broke off and what was left of the aircraft crashed into the water. The fuselage broke in two and caught fire. As a dazed Bell bobbed in the flaming water, Evans grabbed him by the coveralls and dragged him away from the wreckage, then went back into the inferno for a life raft.

By the time seven survivors had crawled into the raft and cleared the wreck, Japanese artillery opened fire on them from a nearby garrison. A pair of sampans started toward them from a small island, but the Japanese turned their guns on them, forcing them to retreat. The gunfire told Evans that the boats had to be friendly Chinese, and he directed the raft in their direction. With three paddles, one of which was broken, and four pairs of bare hands, they paddled like mad toward the island as the Japanese launched motorboats to chase them. They could see the Chinese wildly gesturing for them to hurry. When the raft reached a muddy shoal, the Chinese rushed up, pulled the men out, and ran with them through knee-deep mud toward a small flotilla of sampans along the island shore. The survivors, bruised and exhausted, kept falling face first in the mud, only to be yanked upright and urged on by their rescuers. They finally reached the sampans, and the Chinese stuffed them in, two men to a boat, and covered them with clam baskets and fishing nets. The boats ducked into a shoreline cave and waited until the Japanese search planes and motorboats had given up. Then it was a terrifying dash across the open water to the safety of the shore.

Not a sound or gesture had passed among Bell, his boatmate, copilot Ensign Kirby Lindsley, and their rescuers throughout the two-hour ordeal. Now that they stood safely on the mainland, Bell and Lindsley in tattered clothes and covered with mud, the Chinese pointed at their ragged new friends and burst out laughing. The group walked to a stone house in a fishing village nearby where the rest of the crew greeted them with joy. As they nibbled cakes and sipped tea, a crowd of Chinese villagers gathered for a boisterous telling and retelling of the crash and rescue. Everyone fell abruptly silent as the sound of a Japanese bomber approached, but after it passed, the party cranked up again.

The Americans were enormously grateful, but solemn thoughts mingled with their joy. Six of the crew were missing and would never be found. Bell had injured his back, and Radioman First Class J. A. Warr had a serious gash in his shoulder.

Out of the blue, an English-speaking Chinese man, Mr. Huang, arrived. He claimed to be a businessman passing through, but he was likely an agent of Dai Li. The sampan rescuers certainly were. Though Bell referred to them as "fishermen," they were actually pirates Dai and Miles had recruited for SACO.

The Americans were surprised to learn from Mr. Huang that they were only seventeen miles from a U.S. Navy camp. He offered to take them there and advised that they leave the village immediately before the Japanese came looking for them. Huang and the survivors boarded a junk and slipped along the shore a few miles, then walked for an hour to a larger town where members of the local militia were waiting for them. By now it was nightfall. The town threw a banquet for them, a Chinese doctor treated Warr's wound, and seven soldiers gave up their beds for the night for the survivors.

The next morning, the group took to the road with Warr in a sedan chair. They had not gone far when they spotted an American striding toward them. He introduced himself as Tucker from the navy.* He was the sweetest sight Bell had ever seen, with his tommy gun, sack of welcome rations, and broad smile. The boatswain's mate was a SACO coast watcher who had seen the crash and had been out looking for the crew ever since. The airwaves had bristled with reports of the crash all night. He led the crew to Zhangzhou headquarters.

---

* "Tucker" is presumed to be Boatswain's Mate Howard Tucker, but the navy was never able to confirm it, despite much effort to do so.

"That night we slept in American sacks, ate American food, smoked American cigarettes, listened to American servicemen swapping their experiences for ours; boy it was Heaven," wrote Bell.[37]

The survivors were transferred to Camp Six to recuperate. The camp's stores of personal supplies were empty, but the SACOs scrounged through their own duffel bags to provide changes of clothes and toiletries for their guests. Six of them left within a week with SACO escorts for the first leg of the journey to Kunming. Warr stayed another couple of weeks and was finally taken to the nearest airfield at Longyan in a sedan chair.

Two months later, an American plane came in low over the camp and dropped a parcel by parachute. The SACOs were delighted to find toiletries and other goodies inside, along with a note of thanks from Warr, who was flying his final mission.

THE CLARK PRIVATEER PARTY'S RESCUE was one of several in which Camp Six played a part. The camp was near the Japanese stronghold Xiamen, a ripe target for Allied air attacks and consequent lost aircraft. The camp's storekeeper, Clayton Mishler, must have felt like a plane crash expert by the end of his tour. The first he encountered was in the summer of 1944 near Xi'an where he was stationed on his own as a SACO courier. Xi'an was a large but remote city in north-central China.

The houseboy from Mishler's hotel came charging up to him in the street one afternoon and implored him to come to the barbershop immediately to help some strangers. Mishler found a pair of U.S. Army Air Force officers getting haircuts. After introductions and the obligatory chorus of "What the hell is the navy doing here?" Mishler learned that they were pilots of a B-29. It had been badly damaged by enemy fire and had made an emergency landing near a rail line forty miles north of the city. The officers had left their crew with the plane and walked all the way to Xi'an, desperate for help because the plane was fully exposed. With heavy Japanese air activity in the area, it was in danger of being captured.

Over the next few days, the Nationalist Army, the U.S. Army Air Force, and the people of Xi'an joined forces to save the plane with a sprinkling of help from SACO.

Mishler first took the officers to a freelance radio service run by an American in Xi'an. They contacted the nearest American air base at Chengdu for aid and replacement parts. Meanwhile, Mishler went to the local military authority, Nationalist Chinese General Huang, for help with security. Huang (not the man who had assisted Don Bell and his party) deployed a thousand soldiers to the site. Half of them surrounded the craft while the other half dismantled a rail spur and turned the rails into a makeshift runway, spacing them exactly to match the landing gear of the B-29.

Chengdu did its part to protect the aircraft with a queue of P-40 fighter planes circling the site in shifts twenty-four hours a day.

The air force airlifted a new engine, aviation fuel, and three mechanics into Xi'an airport. The men and cargo were transported as close to the landing site as they could get by rail and made the rest of the trip by horse-drawn wagon. Two days later, the plane was flight ready.

The crippled B-29 captured the hearts of Xi'an's residents. Updates on its progress buzzed through the streets, and the story filled the front pages of the newspapers. Hundreds of people turned out to help the soldiers drag the plane onto the extraordinary runway with ropes.

When all was ready, Mishler drove the two pilots out to the plane in a jeep and watched as the B-29 taxied down the singular runway and miraculously lifted off. Before heading to Chengdu Air Field, the Superfortress made two low "thank you" circuits over Xi'an as the streets reverberated with hundreds of thousands of cheering voices.

But not every plane crash had a happy ending for Mishler. A presumed Japanese spy plane that SACO nicknamed "Photo Joe" used to fly over Camp Six frequently, and one night it somehow became disoriented after buzzing the camp and crashed into a mountainside. Mishler and three other SACOs rushed up the mountain hoping to secure the wreck before local looters got there. They were eager to secure the aircraft because plane crashes could yield valuable intelligence about enemy technological capabilities and military plans. Such sites, however, were like archaeological digs; if they were disturbed by untrained hands before the experts arrived, information was lost that could never be recovered.

On this night, the four SACOs were indeed too late. As they walked up the steep path, they met a party of Chinese soldiers coming down. The group brandished a freshly severed head on a pike, blood flowing down from it onto the arms of its bearer. The Americans pushed past the grisly procession to the crumpled Japanese plane. The pilot's headless body was still in the cockpit; it appeared he had been flying solo.

American SACOs had strict instructions not to project their own standards onto Chinese practices, even in matters of justice and human rights. But this barbarous display went beyond cultural differences. Such behavior violated international codes of engagement and exposed the Allies to bestial acts of revenge and world condemnation. Nevertheless, the SACOs knew that nothing good would come of confronting the offending soldiers themselves. Instead, they immediately called on General Liu, the local Chinese military authority. He gave his word that the pilot's body would be properly buried that day, head included.

While culture clashes of this magnitude were rare, most of the Chinese soldiers harbored more passionate, personal hatred for the Japanese than their American partners did, a result of years of foreign occupation. When the Japanese bombed Pearl Harbor, the American public experienced a mere taste of what the Chinese must have felt having the enemy in their cities and fields every day for years. Dai Li turned to occupied territories for his best recruits because their emotions established a foundation on which to build dedicated, effective combatants.

Over time, the Americans and Chinese overcame differences in the service of common purpose and enjoyed successes to celebrate together. Ensign John Mattmiller from Kellogg, Idaho, demonstrated this with a mission he designed as a sort of graduation present for the best four students in his swimming and underwater demolition classes, and it was one of Miles's favorite stories. After weeks of practice, they waited until dark aboard a junk across the harbor from a Japanese freighter docked at Xiamen. With packs of explosives strapped to their backs, they swam to the freighter and set five time-delayed charges beneath the water line, and then high-tailed it back toward the junk. As they were hauled aboard, four huge explosions boomed across the harbor, and while the freighter sank, the confused Japanese hastened to defend themselves against the attack they thought had come from the sea.

Explosives were the best weapons SACO had when up against more numerous Japanese forces. China had ample supplies of TNT, but the sophisticated plastic explosives and detonator fuses the Americans imported were more compact, less volatile, and easier to use. A favorite was a white, powdery substance resembling flour that the men nicknamed "Aunt Jemima" because of its appearance and because it could be baked into "pancakes" without losing its explosive properties. It also could be consumed in small quantities if necessary, but SACO had learned its lesson with the first class of guerrillas at Camp Two and did not test this property needlessly.[38] They transported the powder in Chinese flour sacks that had to be scrounged up locally. Eventually, Miles had several hundred replicas of the sack produced in the United States, and the supply lasted for the rest of the war.

After graduation, the soldiers were eager to try out their new skills and American explosives. In early 1944, one Chinese group came up with an ingenious device that they placed in the arm of a sedan chair slated for a visiting Japanese government official. Its detonator, designed to be tripped by a magnetic field, was expected to go off while he was inspecting some tanks, but it failed. Despite the saboteurs' disappointment, it was merely a case of delayed gratification. At the end of the visit, the chair was loaded onto a cargo plane that proved too heavy for takeoff. As gasoline drums were being offloaded to reduce the weight of the plane, the chair bomb went off and destroyed the plane with fifteen Japanese soldiers and crew inside.

The officers at Camp One near Shanghai integrated explosives into their work with Chinese troops. More than any other SACOs, they were anxious to get out into the field and wreak some havoc on the Japanese, who were right at their doorstep. But even after the Americans had won Dai Li's approval to let them see some action in spring 1944, General Ma, commander of the Loyal Patriotic Army that Camp One had trained, kept putting them off. When the American SACOs finally were included in missions in September, the result was disappointing because the plans were too complicated and the Americans were still forced into safe, background roles.

They finally hit the right formula with a demolition attack on the railroad in Zhejiang Province, southwest of Shanghai, in late November 1944. Three American navy officers and one hundred thirty-one LPA guerrillas and their officers set out to destroy a length of track between the provincial capital and another key city using small packets of plastic explosives called clams. The plan was to strategically lay the clams on the tracks at night and detonate them. As LPA

Major Ho and SACO First Lieutenant Milton Hull surveyed the track and selected explosion sites, Ho said the mission would have even greater impact if they could blow up a Japanese train. Hull and Ho had become friends and discovered that they shared a number of ideas about making simple, targeted strikes.

Hull had a new, navy-developed detonator for railroad demolitions that was vibration- and weight-sensitive so that it would go off under a heavy car to cause maximum damage. He had not yet trained the Chinese to use it, but it was a simple job for two men, and he suggested he do it himself with the help of his translator, a highly capable officer in his own right. Ho readily agreed, and they planned the mission for the next day at Anhua Station. After dark on November 26, Hull and the translator set a twenty-pound, plastic explosive charge under each rail and met up with Ho and seventeen soldiers at a civilian's home close to the tracks near the target site. They sent for the mayor of Anhua to find out when the next Japanese military train was expected.

The mayor arrived eager to share information. He said, "I will tell you when the train is coming and will be killed tomorrow for doing it, but after I am dead the mayor that takes my place will help you in any way he can."[39]

Hull was stunned. He knew the Japanese exacted punishment on the local civilian population for Chinese acts of sabotage. Guerrilla successes led to burned villages and random executions. These atrocities posed a gut-wrenching dilemma for the Allies, who knew that even as they uprooted the enemy, innocent civilians suffered. Yet there was no winning without fighting, and the mayor was willing to take up the battle.

A troop train, he said, was due at 10:30 p.m.

Hull positioned eight snipers at the station and beside the rails near the explosive packs. When the train came by, an explosion ignited the locomotive in great plumes of fire and steam. Several cars derailed, and as troops poured from the first three cars, the snipers opened fire, killing eight Japanese. Within minutes, the Japanese turned artillery guns on the guerrillas, who ran off into the night with Hull.

They all escaped with no injuries. Rather than heading west to safety as the Japanese might have expected, they ran east into occupied territory and kept running for eight days, ducking Japanese, Chinese puppet troops, and Chinese Communists. But these were chance encounters. If the Japanese were hunting for them, they had probably set off in the opposite direction.

Ho meanwhile divided his eighty men, each with a clam, into small companies of five or six. They crept up to different sections of the railroad over the next several nights, blowing up eighteen rails, then thirty, then eighteen more.

In contrast to Hull's feat, two other navy personnel on the mission ended up frustrated by their Chinese commander's reluctance to place them in danger or, as Camp One commander Horton suspected, to let them see how American equipment was put to use. LPA Colonel Shu designated them "observers" but refused to let them near the tracks as fifty Chinese guerrillas set their clams. Horton had asked the two Americans to measure the distance between the rails, but Shu would not even let them do that. Although they heard some explosions, they could not honestly report whether Shu had used sixty clams as he reported or what damage had been done.

The November success prompted more. Camp One worked with small bands of Chinese guerrillas for the next several months pulling off similar demolition missions. The fate of the mayor of Anhua is unknown, but Hull's encounter with him was the first lieutenant's first glimpse of local enthusiasm for the American presence. He was welcomed everywhere and believed that the sight of an American told the besieged people that the world cared about them and their struggle.

BY EARLY SUMMER 1945, the navy men had become less tethered. Dai Li's approval had led to successful joint operations, making American participation in the field routine. A SACO-led mission again demonstrated the power of well-placed explosives. For weeks, about three hundred soldiers and plain-clothes spies in central China plagued a force of six thousand Japanese holding a town. Their coleader was an American SACO from Camp Two who had put them through training with heavy emphasis on demolition. Sequestered in the hills above the town, the guerrillas kept their eyes on the Japanese in the valley below and made it increasingly difficult for them to get food. The spies went into the occupied town every day to gather intelligence while begging on the streets, relaxing in teahouses, and selling vegetables. Armed with the information from the spies, guerrillas slipped in at night and blew up stockpiles of food and arms and ambushed foraging parties by day. They set off strategically placed and timed explosives to create the illusion that the town was surrounded. In the face of being starved out, the Japanese commander surrendered and was shocked to hand over his sword to an American leading a small Chinese force.

"You should have seen the looks on their faces when I came down from the hills with my rag-tag bunch," the American SACO recalled years later through tears of laughter.[40]

The SACO managed to keep his trophy sword at his side for the rest of his tour until he fell asleep on a train on the way home and woke up to find it had disappeared. At first he was crushed, but years later, he considered the loss a stroke of luck. He had nine children after the war, and the sword would have been a dangerous souvenir to have around the house.

THE MEN OF CAMP TWO were the most integrated with the troops they had trained, and they spent less and less time at the camp. When Miles stopped there on his camp tour in late 1944, he found it deserted except for a few desk clerks and the camp commander. Determined to observe his men in action, he walked two days through the snow-covered hills to the field camp of Guerrilla Column Four near the town of Paoching. The camp roasted a few pigs in his honor, giving the ranks a welcome break from their winter diet of unhusked rice.

That night, Gunnery Sergeant Earl McCalmon roused Miles from his bed after midnight and invited him along on an ambush. Miles had wanted action, and this was it. Intelligence reports had just come in that the Japanese, after holing up in their garrisons for weeks, had sent a supply detail to pick up rice at their Paoching warehouse. It was a chance the Chinese had been waiting for.

Miles, McCalmon, twenty-five Chinese guerrillas, and a Chinese colonel slipped quietly from the sleeping camp and hit the trail with McCalmon at the head, the colonel at the rear, and Miles mixed in with the foot soldiers. They walked four miles in the dark, dodging ice patches along the path, until a hand signal traveled man by man down the line, and the party stopped. They climbed a thirty-foot ridge and lay on their bellies side by side looking down at the path with the colonel and the sergeant as bookends. The Japanese would pass McCalmon first, and everyone was to wait for the colonel to shoot before opening fire.

Shivering in the dark in utter silence with his gun ready, Miles felt old and a bit reckless. An hour passed. He heard muffled footsteps and rustling canvas.

The stars faintly illuminated the blanket of snow as a backdrop to the black shapes of the Japanese human pack train. Waiting, waiting, the first report at last rang out, followed by a shower of gunfire. Two figures dropped to the ground and then more as the Japanese turned and ran back down the trail, leaving ten dead in the snow.

Miles had witnessed a signature SACO guerrilla mission the likes of which was repeated hundreds of times, inflicting ten times more casualties on the Japanese than on the Chinese with no Americans lost. These simple operations worked thanks to SACO marksmanship and stealth training, quality weapons, and effective intelligence. The attacks truly hampered the Japanese, who were loath to leave the safety of their garrisons for fear of the "short guns," their term for the carbine-toting guerrillas as opposed to the longer rifles issued to the regular army.

The people living near Camp Two were well aware of the American presence among their countrymen. After a SACO group liberated one town, grateful residents presented a hand-embroidered silk wall hanging featuring the flags of Nationalist China and the United States to U.S. Marine Corps Major Ed Dupras, commander of Camp Two, and Colonel Lin of Column Four. No one in the town had ever seen an American flag. They relied entirely on a written description and rendered it perfectly.

MILES'S TWO-DAY WALK from Camp Two to the guerrilla field was typical for SACOs. Whether due to no trucks, no roads, or too many Japanese, walking was a universal component of SACO duty.

Motorist Machinist's Mate Second Class Matthew Komorowski-Kaye did not know at the time that his march halfway across China would be his last mission. A member of Scouts and Raiders, he was teaching special combat skills and assisting the weather forecasters at Camp Three north of Xi'an in June 1945 when the camp received orders to pack up all its weapons, ammunition, and equipment for Guerrilla Column Five, which had not been resupplied in nearly two years. The desperate troops were a thousand miles to the east, and most of the distance traveled would be through Japanese territory.

A party of Chinese and Americans loaded everything into five trucks and drove east for three uneventful days before relentless rain turned roads in to impassible rivers of mud. They waited out the deluge at an isolated farmhouse for five monotonous, hungry days and then took to the road again.

One of the trucks soon began to spew steam from a cracked cylinder head. From the perspective of a fellow mechanic, Komorowski-Kaye watched in awe as the Chinese repairman shaved slivers of rubber from the tires and stuffed them into the crack. As they melted and conformed to the opening, he added more until it was sealed. Onward they went over the still-treacherous road. A truck lost traction, perhaps having sacrificed too much tread for engine repairs, and slid down an embankment, breaking apart as it came to a stop. Even this did not deter the repair crew. They took the body apart and reassembled it screw by screw, and on they went again, hours later.

But no mechanic could fix the next obstacle. By now they were deep in enemy territory, and the roads were too dangerous. They were forced to retreat to the cover of the mountain trails and continue on foot. A pack train of one hundred twenty-five coolies replaced the five trucks, each man half Komorowski-Kaye's size but carrying a load on a yo-yo pole, which Komorowski-Kaye could barely lift. He admired their professionalism and good cheer, hoisting their burdens and walking hour after hour without complaint. A fresh crew arrived each morning. Though hired behind the scenes by Dai's agents, in American eyes, they seemed to materialize on cue as if by magic. In one region where the people looked especially malnourished, the crews were larger so that each man carried a lighter load.

A few days into the march, one of the Americans had an attack of appendicitis. They radioed Happy Valley, which dispatched a plane to pick up the stricken man. By the time it arrived, Pharmacist's Mate P. J. Morris had decided to accompany the patient. Before boarding the plane, he turned his medical bag over to Komorowski-Kaye. Morris was worried about leaving the men to fend for themselves, but at least they would have medication and first aid supplies if someone else took ill or got hurt.

After the plane disappeared and the march continued, the bag with its prominent red cross made Komorowski-Kaye a marked man. At each overnight stop, local Chinese with abscessed teeth, broken bones, and hacking coughs lined up at his door. He dispensed aspirin and Atabrine tablets willy-nilly. Word of his healing powers must have spread because the lines grew longer each night. Finally, when faced with a pair of seriously wounded soldiers on stretchers, he blurted out, "I'm not a doctor; I'm just carrying the bag!" The nightly visits from the sick and injured ended.

After thirty straight days of walking, the caravan from Camp Three piled the long-anticipated equipment in a heap at Column Five headquarters. It was nearly August. Komorowski-Kaye was thirty pounds lighter, and the bones and ligaments in his feet and ankles did not seem to mesh properly.

A few weeks later, a column of Japanese walked sullenly past him. Reflexively, he grabbed for the gun that was not at his side.

A Japanese officer greeted him politely, if coolly.

The war was over, but it would be months before Komorowski-Kaye and the men of SACO really believed it.

PART 6

Amazing Groups Among Remarkable Men

CHAPTER 15

The Yangtze River Raiders

IN LATE MAY 1943, Joseph Champe, a thirty-one-year-old lieutenant in the U.S. Navy Reserves from West Virginia, arrived in Chongqing. Like Miles, he was a U.S. Naval Academy graduate turned engineer with an interest in demolition devices. He stayed at Happy Valley long enough to suck down a few pots of tea straight from the spout before being packed off with SACO explosives expert Lieutenant Commander Ed Gilfillan for the Chinese Navy's mine-making depot at Chenki on the Yuan River.

During Champe's three-month duty at the mine factory, a stretch of the Yangtze to the north in the heart of China began to capture his imagination. The twin cities of Hankou and Wuchang straddled the mighty river, the third longest in the world, at the point where a major north-south rail line connecting Beijing in the north and Ganzhou in the south met. The cities also marked the midpoint between China's two large inland lakes, Dongting and Poyang. The lakes and the three-hundred-mile section of the Yangtze extending between them formed a major fluvial highway for Japan's supply chain to its holdings in Burma, the most fertile ground in the country for inland underwater demolition attacks. The railroad formed a lifeline from Manchuria to the southeast.

Champe had the idea that a handful of SACOs could inflict almost unlimited damage on Japanese ships in the region with nothing but a couple of sampans, perhaps a small steamer, and a steady supply of the mines and sophisticated demolition packs Gilfillan was turning out in Chenki. Over the next year, his brainchild developed into the Yangtze River Raiders, a specialized unit of guerrilla and sabotage teams whose mission was to obstruct Japanese shipping routes on land and river, destroy supplies, and impede communication. The Raiders were based in the heart of the lakes region near the point where Hunan, Hubei, and Jiangxi Provinces meet.

Miles supported Champe's concept from the start, but nothing could be done without Dai Li's seal of approval. As was his wont, the general immediately grew the idea into an extensive plan with multiple teams operating out of multiple bases. This tendency was one of the main gripes most of the American SACOs had with the Chinese. Simple ideas expanded into elaborate schemes, overdeveloped on paper to the point that they could never be executed. Fortunately, though, Champe and Miles succeeded in keeping the plan sufficiently grounded to become reality.

IN FEBRUARY 1944, Champe joined Camp Two, which had been established in the summer of 1943 near what would become the Yangtze River Raiders' target area. Within weeks, he became something of a celebrity among his Chinese partners, who were as impressed with his devotion to their cause as with his innovative ideas. He created a new method for minesweeping that improved safety while leaving the enemy mines intact. As a bonus, SACO redeployed these mines against the Japanese so that they suffered losses from their own arsenal, an incendiary, proto-recycling program.

He also designed mines that were precursors to the improvised explosive device of the twenty-first century, made cheaply and simply with ordinary materials. He filled glass candy jars with debris such as broken glass and scrap metal and a small explosive charge. The mines were buried along roadsides and detonated by hand as an enemy vehicle passed. The Chinese Navy was so impressed with Champe that they asked him to teach a special demolition class in the city of Changsha not far from Camp Two. The class was a hit with the standing-room-only crowd of officers in attendance.

In April, Miles and Dai came to Camp Two for a conference that officially launched the new unit. Although it took a year from Champe's initial idea to the first field mission, the unit ultimately became everything he had originally conceived and more. By the end of the war, the Yangtze River Raiders went on to train and deploy four teams of twelve to twenty saboteurs and some eight hundred fifty guerrillas deployed in three operation groups.

Champe's cocommander was Colonel Tong Shien, a thoughtful, diligent officer and former newspaper reporter whose cautious approach was at first a foil and later a balance to Champe's go-get-'em style. Champe's initial task was to secure supplies, and Tong's was to provide the men. They often struggled to resolve disagreements because they both dug in their heels. Tong believed the training camp site should be chosen primarily for safety, while Champe wanted proximity to the action so the newly trained forces could jump right in while they were still pumped up and without having to walk for days.

After some haggling, Champe concluded that the time had come to back off and conceded the point. They chose Manjiang, Jiangxi Province, a three-hundred-mile trip from Camp Two, which they expected to cover in fourteen days. Six Americans and a hundred Chinese left on May 24, 1944, headed north to the new headquarters of the Yangtze River Raiders under the joint leadership of Champe and Tong and with sufficient supplies to set up headquarters and begin training.

As they moved north, however, the Japanese were pushing south, their largest offensive in two years, deploying some four hundred thousand soldiers from Manchuria to establish a land corridor through the middle of the continent. Tong and Champe were barely underway when they ran into Japan's advance troops. By the time the SACO men got to Changsha, the capital of Hunan Province, four days later, the city was frantic, the streets jammed with civilians rushing they knew not where in search of safety. Japan's advance plainclothesmen had arrived, and the aerial bombing attacks had begun.

Champe immediately threw himself and SACO's materiel into defending the city. Working with engineers of the regular Chinese Army, he again pulled his candy jar trick, filling every glass jar and ceramic jug they could scare up with junk projectiles and granular TNT and burying them across the approach routes into Changsha. They also put together some underwater mines by stuffing large tubes of bamboo and sealing the ends. The Chinese would detonate these weeks later after Champe was gone, slowing the Japanese advance and inflicting some five thousand enemy casualties, a mere dent in the torrent of hundreds of thousands flowing into the city.

Next, Champe canvassed house to house in search of stranded civilians and herded nine British and American missionaries—including women and children—to SACO's new island medical camp in the Xiang River. SACO had barely taken over an old Standard Oil facility on the island when the Japanese push began. The unsuspecting Commander Dr. Cecil Coggins, the last man there, was busy burning every shred of paper and cigarette butt to obliterate any evidence of American presence when Champe arrived with the refugees and turned them over to the doctor. Coggins and the missionaries crowded onto a pair of sampans under the protection of one of Champe's men, Pharmacist's Mate First Class C. E. Richardson. As panicked Changsha residents tried to push their way onto the boats, Richardson fended them off at gunpoint for fear of being swamped and escorted the group as their sampan poled upstream along with thousands of other fleeing craft. After Richardson saw the party safely onto a railroad car to continue their journey, he returned to the others at Changsha.

Camp Two, meanwhile, found itself in the direct path of the Japanese push. It pulled up stakes and moved to the relative safety of Honkiang, about one hundred twenty miles west of its original base in Nanyo.

In Changsha, the Yangtze River Raiders, now reduced to a mere thirty men, hunkered down at the abandoned island camp. In the confusion, they had lost about seventy-five Chinese guerrillas. Whether these men had been killed or captured or simply walked away is unknown. The remaining Raiders still held vain hopes of commandeering some SACO motorboats stored in the region to harass the advance by water, but they never got the chance. In a stroke of luck that seemed to hover over Champe, Lieutenant Ted Cathey of Camp Two came up the river on a steamer and took the Raiders aboard just as Japanese troops were about to mount the wall around the SACO island facility.

It was now June 12, and the Raiders headed back to where they had started, the city falling to the Japanese on the heels of their departure. At the abandoned site of Camp Two, they picked up three trucks as battered as the usual specimens, along with six more Chinese soldiers to form the core of the guerrilla team. Now a party of thirty-six, they limped ahead along a roundabout route to their destination, stopping often for improvised repairs and loading the trucks onto flatbed rail cars to save fuel whenever the opportunity arose. They eventually exchanged the trucks for sampans down the Kan River. Coming upon Japanese patrols, they abandoned the boats and took to mountain trails for two hundred miles, spending the last of their money on porters to carry what remained of their supplies.

It was mid-July when they finally arrived flat broke and worn out at Manjiang on the Wuning River in Jiangxi Province after a nine-hundred-mile journey. They settled in an empty schoolhouse, an apt headquarters, since their first order of business was to open a school. Their first students were sixteen experienced Chinese saboteurs, who learned new techniques and how to use American explosives and arms. They immediately split into five teams and, after winning crucial support from local residents, began stinging the enemy, blowing a hole in a factory here, uprooting a railroad track there.

By then, Champe had convinced Tong that they would be much more effective if they moved closer to the Yangtze River before starting their guerrilla training program. Thus, in September, they relocated thirty-five miles north to Xiushui and set up a new camp in a temple tucked in the mountains fifty miles south of the great river and half that distance west of Poyang Lake.

SACOs had become accustomed by this time to taking over empty temples, but compared to some of the ancient monuments they had found, this one was nearly new, only about a hundred years old. It featured elaborately carved woodwork, great heaps of trash in every room, and a leaking roof that seemed enchanted by repair-resistant sprites, as every patch job merely moved a stopped leak somewhere else. The Americans and Chinese each took a separate wing of the building; another building on the grounds was already home to several farm families.

In the interest of cleanliness, the Americans installed floors and window screens, replaced wall coverings, and added a new kitchen and restroom. The Raiders made these changes over time as materials were scrounged locally or received from Chongqing, and the neighbors found the new-fangled improvements fascinating. They would come over unannounced with friends to show what the crazy foreigners were up to, sometimes barging in on a SACO using the restroom.

The Raiders had barely settled when, on October 16, word from Chinese intelligence reached the camp that Japanese patrols were on the way to eliminate any pockets of Chinese resistance and were expected to occupy Xiushui in a matter of days. The conservative Tong wanted to begin immediate evacuation preparations, but Champe advised waiting until the Japanese actually got to Xiushui before doing anything. Tong reluctantly agreed, the Japanese never came, and they faced future alarming reports with less urgency.

The new camp was primarily a training and planning center, and as each class of Tong's recruits was deemed field ready, they moved out to remote, primitive camps for operations. When the Raiders first arrived at Xiushui, however, the training was put on hold because of limited supplies and lack of "graduation" weapons. New supplies were expected in September but did not arrive until mid-November. The story of how these men got the equipment and arms they needed offers a window into American military snafus that frustrated the men of SACO and have plagued military operations throughout history.

Long before the Yangtze River Raiders became a reality, Miles had sent Champe to Kolkata to select the supplies such a unit might need from navy warehouses. Materials had been in the queue for Hump flights since the Raiders became official in April, and by September, they were in Kunming and Chongqing.

Champe received word from Chongqing shortly after they got to Xiushiu that Master Sergeant B. A. Paglia, a new communications officer, was on the way to join the Raiders and was bringing their long-awaited weapons and materiel. Knowing how difficult it would be for him to find the temple hideaway, Champe dispatched Aviation Machinists Mate First Class Joseph S. Shragal to meet him at Changsha and escort him to the camp. Although the Japanese occupied the city, their presence was porous throughout China, and SACOs routinely moved with caution through their territory.

But either someone in SACO considered Changsha too risky or instructions somewhere along the communication chain were misconstrued. Whatever the reason, it took Shragal and Paglia a month to finally connect. Shragal waited around in Changsha, fully expecting Paglia every day, until at last he went to Ganzhou, site of a U.S. hostel and airfield, to see if anyone knew what the holdup was. There he found Paglia and six other Americans assigned to the Yangtze River Raiders. They had been waiting for Shragal for four weeks. Had no one made a move, they might have been stuck in limbo until August 1945.

Shragal now had the personnel he needed, but not the supplies. The SACO shipment had arrived before Paglia got there, and for some inexplicable reason, the storekeeper at Ganzhou had sent it on to Jianyang, more than a hundred miles in the opposite direction. Paglia went there to get the equipment, but by that time, the Painter coastal survey expedition had been through and commandeered some of it under full authorization of the navy.[41]

Shragal turned out to be the right man for the job. For days, he relentlessly sent messages, pulled strings, and cut through red tape until the remaining SACO materials were assembled and the missing supplies replaced from stores in Kunming. Everything was finally shipped to Ganzhou. At last men and materiel were packed onto a flotilla of four large sampans and began the trip on October 24 to Changsha.

Once in Changsha, though, the most trying leg of the journey lay ahead. They now had to transport the goods overland one hundred thirty miles to headquarters at Xiushui by porter train. A human convoy of four hundred fifty men carried everything from firearm magazines to huge drums of fuel alcohol, eight men to a drum, along narrow, perilous paths through the mountains. Throughout the war, every American who witnessed the work of these porters found them truly heroic, but to those who performed it, it was simply how they earned their living. Carrying an average of seventy pounds each and weighing perhaps only one hundred thirty pounds themselves, they scaled stone steps carved into mountainsides and descended muddy paths. The Americans kept well ahead of or behind this three-mile train of men to make sure they did not disrupt the synchronized pace.

The supplies and reinforcements arrived at last at the camp sometime around November 17, but as a result of being opened by the Painter team and then shuttled all over central China, many items were broken, lost, or packed illogically, making assembly difficult. For reasons lost to history, Shragal remained in Ganzhou through January, and Champe joined him there briefly in December.[42] Perhaps they were scrounging up items they needed for a particularly hard winter. Unseasonable cold had already descended by November, and the Raiders were to suffer through the coldest, snowiest winter that region had seen in more than twenty years. With cash in short supply, they limited how much they spent on firewood, only keeping the kitchen, dining room, and sick bay warm.

As weeks had passed at Xiushui without receipt of the promised supplies, training of the First Guerrilla Field Unit had gone on nevertheless, and on November 26, they were fully armed and ready to move out for their operation phase.

But now there was a new holdup. Colonel Tong refused to let the two Americans whom Champe had assigned, Paglia and Gunnery Sergeant Thomas A. Petrosky, go along because he had no orders to do so. Dai Li's general order to include Americans in all missions was only a month old, and perhaps at Tong's isolated post, he had not received it. Regardless of the reason, Champe was beside himself. His brainchild seemed to be washing out from under him. In his mind, this was a joint mission from start to finish, and the presence of the American teachers in the field was crucial to its success.

Facing the most serious conflict of their joint command, Champe threatened to inform the navy that his mission could not be accomplished, take his toys, and go home. Tong knew that without American supplies, leadership, and teachers, there could be no Yangtze River Raiders. Tong and Champe finally agreed to separately ask their commanders for instructions and to abide by their answers. Dai and Miles responded swiftly that the Americans were to be included in all missions. The crisis taught Tong and Champe that they shared the same goal and could find solutions to any conflict. From then on, they leaned on each other and voiced their opinions with confidence that any disagreements would be resolved in the way that would best serve to thwart the Japanese occupation.

On December 3, the two hundred fifty members of First Guerrilla Field Unit at last left the camp bound for an operating base to the east at a town then called Tai Tse Miow on a lake that drained into the Yangtze.* It was a brutal, frost-bitten trek, creeping along at night and sleeping through the day outside in the elements or occasionally in houses, where they would take the doors off their hinges and lay them across pairs of logs to make beds. For nearly three months, they walked along snow-covered mountain paths, engaging the enemy in small skirmishes along the way.

But when in February 1945 they reached their destination to set up a field headquarters, an enemy force of ten thousand—two thousand Japanese marines

---

* Most place names in China have been changed since World War II. In this case, the current name has not been identified.

199

and eight thousand Chinese puppet troops—was waiting for them. The guerrillas were surrounded. The Chinese commander of the guerrilla force sent a small squad north to create a diversion, and when the Japanese moved to attack, the Chinese unit stole through the gap to safety, withdrawing to near the city of Juichang. It turned out to be a better place for their field camp. As a major highway crossroads, it proved to be fruitful because the Japanese had begun shifting their troop and supply transportation to trucks in response to new 14th Air Force attacks on the Yangtze and the railroads. The SACOs then began disrupting their convoys.

On March 28, 1945, the guerrillas aborted a planned predawn attack on an enemy armory when they encountered an unexpected artillery force guarding the facility. The Japanese must have been tipped off. The guerrillas slipped back into the darkness without being detected and instead split into two groups to launch simultaneous raids on two nearby targets the following morning. As two Americans sprayed guards with machine gun fire and took out two blockhouses and a mortar gun, the Chinese burned a warehouse containing about fifty tons of rice and thirty-five tons of salt, plus oil and clothing. They ripped out the phone lines and chopped down the telephone poles. One Chinese SACO was killed in the operation.

The work of these two days illustrates the purpose of the guerrilla teams. Unlike regular army units, SACO guerrillas never engaged large Japanese forces. They had neither the numbers nor the equipment. Their role was instead one of harassment. With handfuls of men making quick, precision strikes, they hindered the enemy's ability to move freely and supply troops, forcing them to take costly security measures. In training, instructors emphasized that there was nothing heroic about challenging a superior force needlessly. When confronted with overwhelming opposition, a guerrilla could best serve his country by withdrawing to fight another day, and the raids were designed to make that possible.

Nevertheless, heroes arose from unexpected quarters. One longhaired, perpetually sleepy trainee who did not seem to have the makings of a guerrilla went on another warehouse raid with Colonel Tong and was assigned to cover the rear while the bulk of the force broke their way in through the front. But the Japanese were now wise to these attacks, and the SACOs met formidable guards inside. The Chinese would have been wiped out if not for the sleepy soldier who saw what was happening and sprayed the guards with tommy gun fire. They turned to him, allowing everyone else to escape. Mortally wounded, the lone guerrilla made it out the back and flung himself down a hill, drawing the guards' attention while the others ran off.

Throughout the spring of 1945, the First Guerrilla Field Unit preyed on the Japanese in the area, attacking convoys, destroying bridges, and raiding a distillery. The Second and Third Units were deployed in April and June and covered different sections of the lakes region.

MEANWHILE, THE YANGTZE RIVER RAIDER sabotage teams were derailing trains, sinking steamers, and blowing up a few bridges of their own, not to mention military radio stations. The Chinese saboteurs were well seasoned even before joining the Raiders and adding American tools and techniques to their arsenal.

It was no easy matter to penetrate the Beijing–Hankou–Guanzhou railroad line, Japan's link to the southern provinces. The Japanese protected it ferociously with armed sentries, attack dogs, and electric, barbed-wire fences. In addition, they sent scout trains to clear the tracks ahead of troop and supply trains, which always had four or more empty cars in front of locomotives to bear the brunt of any explosion. But undeterred, a Raider sabotage team overcame all these defenses and scored a spectacular hit for SACO on April 20, 1945, near the Wuchang rail crossroads. The saboteurs waited for the advance train to pass, slipped through the fence past the guards and dogs, and quickly planted fifty pounds of TNT under the track. Their highly dangerous detonation method was to lie in wait and simply pull a trip wire when the middle of the train was over the charge, sending the locomotive and five cars of ammunition plummeting down a thirty-foot cliff. They relied on the postexplosion uproar for cover, and on the way out, they snipped phone lines for good measure, adding a bit of chaos to catastrophe.

Another sabotage team combined one of Champe's ingenious inventions with nuts-and-bolts intelligence work to sink a Japanese steamship at Jiujian, a Yangtze River town. To set up the mission, two Raider saboteurs got jobs as stevedores on the Jiujian docks, giving them access to information about the ships' cargos and schedules. They chose a Japanese steamer loaded with a hundred tons of iron ore, a perfect target for Champe's latest underwater mine system, another device singularly suited to China for its use of plentiful materials and simple technology.

Three and a half pounds of plastic explosives were suspended from each of two bamboo floats that hovered about two feet below the surface of the water. The devices were fitted with pencil detonators, which use acid reservoirs in fragile vials to eat through a wire that trips the explosion. The operatives connected the floats with a line of thin cable slightly less than the length of the target ship. Disguised as fishermen plying the river in a sampan, they dropped the floats well apart so that the cable lay under the water in the steamer's path. The bow of the ship caught the cable and dragged the two charges along. Natural fluid dynamics drew them inward toward the ship, and they eventually hit it amidships on both sides with enough force to crush the detonator reservoirs. The sampan glided off to safety before the acid broke the tripwire and triggered the explosion that ripped gashes in the sides of the steamer and sunk it. A month later, the Raiders used the same technique with larger explosive packs to sink a shipment of ammunition and salt.

The loss of salt stores was a serious setback for the Japanese, who counted on it for preserving vegetables and fish and as a key ingredient in pickles, a Japanese staple. A precious commodity worldwide, salt played a role in economics, politics, and international relations in Asia. In 1905, Japan launched a program to free itself from foreign salt, much as the United States is working to reduce dependence on foreign oil in the twenty-first century. The Japanese government took over salt production and distribution through twenty-two Japan Salt Monopoly Offices.[43] Although the occupation of China likely provided new sources for the seasoning, it was as essential to the war effort as the ammunition lost with it.

LIKE MANY SACO OPERATIONS, the Raiders also found themselves in the pilot rescue business. Two U.S. Army Air Force pilots came through the camp at Xiushui after being shot down during the bitter winter of 1944–45. On December 18, a guerrilla team saw John Wheeler's P-51 descend into the mountains in flames and found him with only minor injuries. By the time they got him to the camp on Christmas Eve, his feet were so swollen that he couldn't walk. After a few days of SACO nursing, they took him to the air force group in Ganzhou. Three weeks later, the Raiders rescued a second pilot who had parachuted into enemy territory and was found in good condition.

Raiders also contributed to SACO's growing weather net. Aerologists Mate First Class L. E. Williams arrived at camp with Paglia's group in November 1944 and immediately began sending weather readings to Happy Valley. He could not calibrate the barometer correctly for several days because the instrument needed adjustment according to altitude, which took some time to determine with help from Chongqing. The Raiders built him a wooden shack to serve as the camp weather station, from which he faithfully sent the standard three reports a day. In January, SACO Weather Central asked him to add a fourth, suggesting that he train a Chinese assistant to help him, but without any teaching materials, he decided to just take the fourth observation reading himself, making for a long day. A month later, however, four new field weather sets arrived with a supply delivery. Williams selected the ten Chinese guerrilla trainees with the best English skills and turned them into aerology assistants. Two stayed in Xiushui with him, and the others joined field sabotage and guerrilla camps to set up three remote weather stations. After a tentative beginning, including a report that it was seventy degrees Fahrenheit and snowing, the Chinese provided excellent data.

A Philadelphia urologist, Lieutenant Junior Grade Dr. Vincent Balkus, also arrived with Paglia to serve the thirty-six Yangtze River Raiders who would grow to nearly a thousand scattered over twenty-five thousand square miles by June 1945. Although he was spread very thin with only two pharmacists mates to assist him, he took preemptive actions to save precious time when casualties were expected. He established a tiny field hospital at Wuning, a central location the men could reach within two days in much of the operating area. Though the hospital stood empty most of the time, there were instances when doctor and patient could meet there more quickly than Balkus could get to a camp. Balkus also had guerrilla unit commanders inform him when major strikes were planned, and he would often go out to the field camp beforehand, just in case.

Miraculously, no American Raider was ever seriously wounded, but tending to the Chinese guerrillas kept Balkus and his assistants, Chief Pharmacist C. E. Richardson and Pharmacists Mate First Class Charles Franklin, constantly on the move. SACO could spare no additional pharmacists mates, so Balkus trained several Chinese as medics. But due to their inexperience, they were sent out on their own only as a last resort.

The doctor performed many surgeries under primitive conditions. The first time he operated in Xiushui, three American SACOs trained flashlights on the incision and had to be relieved at frequent intervals to dash from the room and vomit. None had ever witnessed surgery before.

In addition to his medical skills, Balkus rivaled Champe for mechanical ingenuity. He built his own water and alcohol distiller out of copper tubing savaged from airplane wreckage, an oxygen tank, and a wooden box. He also made a precise set of scales from odd bits such as a pistol cleaning rod and a silver chain purchased in Xiushui. In addition to all this, he brought his culinary hobby to the River Raiders kitchen. He figured out how to make American-style cakes and breads using Chinese ingredients and shared his recipes with the Chinese cook, who added them to the house menu.

PUPPET TROOPS ALL OVER CHINA had been secretly collaborating with Dai Li throughout the war while on the Japanese payroll, and those in the lakes region were no exception. As the spring wore on, they began to sense that they were in danger of being on the wrong side at war's end. A group approached now-General Tong about surrendering. On May 25, a thousand puppets surrendered to the Chinese commander of the First Guerrilla Field Unit and joined the Raiders, followed by three thousand more at Xiushui three weeks later. Tong accepted them on condition that they bring their own arms and supplies. With these additional men, the Raiders began taking small towns from the exhausted and undersupplied Japanese.

Meanwhile, Miles had enlisted the 14th Air Force to supply the Raiders, who delighted in the spectacle and bounty of five tons of supplies falling by parachute into a field rimmed with signal fires.

The grueling pace and exposure to the elements were tough on the American SACOs and on their footwear. In April 1945, Richardson and Petrosky had to return from the First Guerrillas to Xiushui because their boots had completely disintegrated after five months, and the Chinese straw sandals they wore did not help the infected, bleeding sores on their feet. When they got back to the main camp, Balkus diagnosed them both with malaria to boot. After recovering, Richardson returned to the guerrillas but then nearly died of small pox contracted while nursing a sick Chinese soldier.

In February 1945, Miles had decided that it was time for Lieutenant Joseph Champe to return to Happy Valley after more than a year and a half without relief. Champe reluctantly agreed. He had been hankering for amenities of the real world like movies, hot showers, and electricity. The new commander, U.S. Marines Captain Donald B. Otterson, did not get to Raider headquarters until May 8, and even then, Champe declined to leave until the graduation of a new class of guerrillas just a few days off.

On May 16, he finally bade an emotional farewell to Tong, who had become a deeply respected partner and beloved friend, and started down the mountain trail with Thomas Petrosky and Joseph Shragal, also overdue for return to the mother ship. For a mile and a half, Chinese guerrillas who had learned from Champe and proudly served under him formed ranks on both sides of the path. The pop-pop-pop of celebratory firecrackers tossed into the air marked the progress of the three Americans.

When Champe left, the Yangtze River Raiders had grown to twenty-one Americans and nearly a thousand Chinese, to be later augmented by the puppet troops who rejoined their countrymen. Tong estimated that the Raiders had destroyed some five billion yuan worth of Japanese ships, locomotives, radio stations, factories, warehouses, and other property. They had killed two hundred thirteen Japanese and one hundred three puppets, while their own losses numbered fourteen lives.

IT IS THE FATE OF THE SOLDIER to suffer a kind of culture shock when shifting from a constant state of high adrenaline to a world of typed reports and poker games. At Happy Valley, the banquets and clean bunks left Champe cold. Isolated in the lakes district, he had been sheltered from the baroque political maneuvers and army–navy power plays that had spilled over from Washington to Chongqing. But now it was all right in his face. He had even heard talk in Kunming that Communist guerrillas were fighting the Japanese in the Yangtze region. As far as he could tell, the Communists and Japanese were working together.

CHAPTER 16

The Crown Jewel on the Gobi Desert

FEW PARENTS WILL ADMIT to having a favorite child, but in time their intimate friends will discover their preference despite their best efforts to conceal it even from themselves. For Milton Miles, that secret favorite had to be Camp Four, a dozen Americans stationed in an old Catholic mission a month's truck ride north of Xi'an on the edge of the Gobi Desert near the small town of Xamba, Inner Mongolia. Like many a specially loved child, Camp Four was independent enough to be charming without being troublesome. Miles never mentioned the unit without inserting an adjective like "colorful" or "offbeat." More than at any other camp, these isolated men had to make do and create their own universe.

Their primary mission was to gather weather information. The camp stood in meteorologically uncharted territory, and its position was particularly useful for tracking Asian weather patterns headed toward the sea between Japan and the Philippines. In addition, like every other SACO camp, it trained recruits for the Generalissimo's army, gathered radio intelligence, and fought Japanese forces.

SACO WEATHER CHIEF IRWIN BEYERLY had selected the site near the upper bend of the Yellow River, the northernmost reach of the pan-China weather net, in August 1943. Dai Li resisted the idea at first. His influence was spotty in the region where kinship and tribal loyalty far outweighed any vague connections the people felt to the remote powers to the south. But Miles insisted and finally won. The opportunities to collect weather data and enemy radio messages were of great importance to the navy. He convinced Dai that the station would be useful to the Nationalists as well, opening the door to new alliances with the insular people of the steppes.

Ilya Tolstoy, the OSS officer who had undertaken the eponymous mission to Tibet, was to command the camp, and SACO had even taken to calling it Pact Tolstoy, but he arrived in Chongqing with orders for the army, and they would not give him up.

Instead, Miles appointed Marine Major Victor R. Bisceglia. The Happy Valley crew dubbed him and the eleven men he chose for the camp the Twelve Disciples. Their combined skills covered just about everything the camp would need to get started: weather monitoring, radio communication, carpentry, plumbing, firefighting, photography, and medicine. The last was especially important because no other medical treatment would be available for hundreds of miles. After the near tragedy at Camp One when a local doctor had to perform an emergency appendectomy on a SACO under makeshift conditions,[44] Miles had made it a rule that every camp would have medical service on site or prearranged nearby. Dr. Robert Goodwin, an obstetrician in civilian life, served as physician and elder statesman for the team.

On November 18, 1943, the Twelve Disciples and eighty Chinese guards, drivers, mechanics, and interpreters departed from Happy Valley in twelve charcoal-burning trucks for Xamba. The Mongolian town was eight hundred miles due north, but the convoy would have to add hundreds of miles to the journey to skirt around the Communist Chinese stronghold in Yan'an. They feared not being attacked but rather being looted. Always desperate for supplies, the Communists were known to stop vehicles and help themselves to their contents before letting them proceed.

After encountering the familiar delays due to broken-down trucks and crumbling roads, a new kind of obstacle stopped the travelers in Ningxia Province on December 13. The Yellow River had frozen, ending ferry service for the season, but the ice was not thick enough for vehicles to safely drive across it. The SACOs were stranded for nearly a month along with dozens of other parties waiting for officials to give the go-ahead. One family grew too impatient and started their truck across unauthorized. The ice gave way in the middle of the river, and the truck disappeared into the black torrent below. No one survived.

Frustration aside, the delay turned out to be to the men's advantage. They made friends with the local governor, who grew concerned that the Americans' navy-issued winter gear was not warm enough for the region where temperatures routinely reached thirty degrees below zero Fahrenheit. He presented them with quilted suits; wool blankets from a local mill; long, goatskin coats, hats, and trousers sewn fur side in for extra warmth; and thick, felt boots. In their new outfits, the men blended in with the Mongolian herdsmen, and they were ready for winter in the steppes.

After celebrating Christmas in the warmth of a bathhouse and smothering their innkeeper's bewildered four-year-old daughter with presents from Santa Claus, they finally received safe ice clearance on January 8, 1944. After another ten days of driving, they arrived at last at Xamba on January 18.

The modest town on a vast plain with purple mountains rising at the northwest horizon was two miles from the Gobi Desert's easternmost dunes. The lone outpost had swelled recently with Beijing refugees fleeing west to escape the occupation. Its neat row of adobe stores reminded the Americans of the desert southwest in the United States. There were a few restaurants, a busy outdoor marketplace full of textiles, food, and housewares, and a handful of large, elegant houses.

The local Nationalist military authority, General Gao, upon word from Dai Li, reserved several rooms at his officers training facility as SACO's permanent home, but the space was inadequately furnished and much too small. The narrow bunks were a foot too short and were arranged head to foot so that a man could not even make do by hanging his feet over the edge.

A Belgian Catholic mission with about a dozen small buildings clustered within a high wall stood nearly empty just outside town. General Gao offered the mission to SACO, and Bisceglia readily accepted it. It had the space and security they needed as well as a good site for the weather station. When the group arrived to move in, however, a priest and two nuns preparing to leave looked bitter and angry. Bisceglia was disturbed to learn that Gao had summarily kicked them out of their own mission and commandeered it for SACO. The major went to the Belgians and arranged to pay rent, and it turned out to be an excellent investment. The missionaries no longer needed such a large facility and were able to rent smaller quarters in town for a fraction of the income they received from SACO. Instead of resenting the newcomers, the Belgians became their friends, sharing meals, books, and advice.

Ensign Theodore Wildman, the camp's radio expert who had helped crack a spy network in Kunming[45] and one of the original SACO pioneers, enlisted the entire group to help erect a radio tower and then sent a message to Happy Valley on the first day. After that, his first order of business was to construct a direction finder that looked like a small water tank with probes protruding from it. Once it was operational, it dramatically improved SACO's ability to pinpoint the origin of intercepted radio signals all over China. Xamba, about five hundred miles due west of Beijing, was the best location SACO had to monitor radio traffic coming out of Japan's northern holdings, and the radio operators reaped enough code to send seven reports to Happy Valley every day.

Aerographer Robert Sizemore had been making a daily weather report to Happy Valley throughout the journey and delivered his first from Camp Four on January 30. The men built a platform for the weather station, which also gave a commanding view of the compound and the plains beyond. It gave Sizemore better readings from his rudimentary ground instruments, which was all Happy Valley could give him when the convoy had set off. But even this limited data, reported on schedule three times a day, significantly expanded the Weather Central's scope. More sophisticated equipment started arriving at Happy Valley that winter and made it to Camp Four in June 1944, and Miles personally delivered the first radiosonde when he visited in February 1945. The data collected from the upper atmosphere helped Beyerly at headquarters compile longer-range forecasts and produce more complete maps.

Slowly, the compound was transformed from religious mission to military camp. The Chinese SACOs decorated the compound's plain mud outer wall with large plaster insets painted with Nationalist slogans, weapons and ammunition filled the storage rooms, and armed guards stopped anyone attempting to enter the gate.

ARRIVING IN XAMBA in mid-January gave the team a rude introduction to the brutality of winter in this exotic yet bleak corner of the world. The men had to acclimate themselves quickly during the most challenging days of their duty; every detail of work and living had to be arranged, and nothing was routine. The only heating system they had at first was their own body heat, captured in the heavy winter clothing they had received in Ningxia. They never removed their Chinese suits, even when they went to bed, and they often wore their long parkas indoors. Growing beards provided extra insulation and conserved razor blades.

Chief Shipfitter William Shelley crafted a stove out of an oil drum for the mess hall and added stove pipes that wound through the living space like octopus tentacles, heating the quarters to a relatively tropical forty degrees Fahrenheit. They ate hot, hearty, but monotonous food. Rice did not grow at that latitude; the dominant staple crops were millet and tiny potatoes, and they always had plenty of cabbage, pork, mutton, and beef.

They could have had unlimited wild game, too. Pheasants and rabbits were utterly unafraid of human presence and often stood staring curiously at a raised gun barrel. Even the sound of the shot did not spook them. But since the SACOs had other plentiful food sources available, they chose not to waste precious ammunition, especially since there was no sport in it.

Next to the cold, the remoteness from their supply source troubled them most. With six months between supply deliveries, they were careful to conserve every strip of gauze and tablespoon of coffee.

Servants brought water from a well in large jars suspended on their yo-yo poles. The water was the color and consistency of hot chocolate and left a layer of sediment in the bottom of each canteen. If a man failed to rinse it out daily, he would soon be carrying a canteen full of mud. For batteries and medical use, they needed pure, distilled water. They constructed a distiller out of aircraft parts using plastic explosives molded into the crevices in place of gaskets. The choice of materials gave them some unnerving moments during the distilling process, especially when the contraption glowed red-hot, but it never blew up.

Running the camp under these circumstances was a daily battle, but one well worth fighting. The work of the Twelve Disciples gave the navy precious information that could not be gathered any other way. No one recognized this more than William Donovan, chief of the OSS. For reasons Miles never understood, Donovan was determined to commandeer Camp Four for the OSS. Like a disgruntled spouse in a bitter divorce settlement, he practically demanded that it be turned over to him in January 1944 when Miles was called to Washington over the OSS–SACO rupture.[46] King and Purnell fended off this unaccountable request then and repeatedly until the end of the war. After everything their men had been through to get there and put the stakes in the ground, they were not about to give it up.

THE AMERICANS AND CHINESE of Camp Four were fortunate to have a physician all to themselves, even if Dr. Goodwin's specialty made for an absurd match in an all-male outfit. Goodwin had few other duties beyond giving the men advice for staying healthy and the physical labor all hands contributed as needed. Thus, he cheerfully offered his medical services to any local resident who asked. His favors soon grew into a medical clinic in Xamba, where he kept a full schedule of appointments, doling out SACO's limited medical supplies with caution. Camp patients automatically went to the head of the line. During his yearlong tenure in Xamba, Goodwin had five thousand appointments and performed twenty-five surgeries, in addition to soothing the minor injuries and ailments of Camp Four.

Goodwin performed a cesarean section, the first ever in Inner Mongolia, on a nineteen-year-old dwarf mother who had been in labor for several days and would have died without the procedure. Mother and baby came through the operation in full health. Shortly thereafter, the wife of a lieutenant in General Gao's army also needed a cesarean. But when General Gao's own wife approached the end of her pregnancy, the general was insulted that Goodwin intended to deliver the baby the old-fashioned way, denying her the special treatment that a mere lieutenant's wife had received. After the Gaos' child was born, the general was pleased to see that his wife's procedure was in fact superior; her large belly incision was closed with an elegant "hem stitch." In his wisdom, the good doctor had decided that it was better to dupe the general with a few dozen diplomatic sutures than to risk unnecessary surgery.

But not everyone in Xamba was taken in by the foreign doctor. General Fu Zuoyi, governor of the region and a former warlord's lieutenant turned Nationalist, opted for traditional acupuncture after dislocating his shoulder in a bicycle accident. Still in agony after several days, he turned at last to Goodwin. Fu's guards stood vigilant in the examining room with their eyes fixed on the doctor as he gently eased the general's shoulder into place. Fu's relief was immediate, and his response was generous. He presented SACO with twenty-four fine Mongolian ponies along with three horse handlers to care for them. Far and away the best of these handlers was an elderly Chinese named Lao Zai who would purr softly to an agitated horse and gently run his fingers along its back while stealthily attaching a bridle.

The animals were perfect for Mongolians, but for Americans, they were a bit small. From atop his mount, Shelley's feet nearly touched the ground. Nevertheless, the Twelve Disciples really took to the ponies. Horsemanship became their exercise, transportation, recreation, and competitive outlet. Like something out of the Old West, they rode through dusty, Big Sky country into town for liberty and errands. They had horse races and learned rodeo tricks. Even men who had never ridden before became masters of their ponies.

Camp Four's finest horseman was Lieutenant Donald Wilcox, a veteran mounted police officer who came to Xamba with the notion of teaching the locals to ride and forming a cavalry. He quickly discovered, however, that every person in the area, from toddler to decrepit old lady, could ride circles around him and do tricks on horseback that he had never seen before. Moreover, the locals had no interest in practicing dull cavalry maneuvers. It was clear that they could ride bareback shooting with both hands without any instructions from him.

But Camp Four still had other skills to teach, and like all SACO camps, training recruits for Chiang Kai-shek's forces was an integral part of their mission. They were charged with training men for the area's Column Eight under Fu's command. These tribal, nomadic people, however, were reluctant to come to the camp. They were even more insular and suspicious of foreigners than the Chinese whom SACO had previously encountered, and most had never seen a white person. Moreover, they did not have Dai Li close at hand pressuring them to attend.

Consequently, only thirty-five men showed up for the first class, and they were a scruffy, bungling lot. But with patience and respect, the SACOs turned them into marksmen. They had no previous firearms experience, yet thirty-one qualified for their weapons thanks in part to one-on-one coaching by Chinese teachers during rifle range practice. During the ten-week course, the students gained confidence and learned skills such as scouting, camouflage, map reading, and ambushes.

While the classes progressed, Goodwin's medical diplomacy was winning many friends for Camp Four. Word got around that the SACOs were men of worth. Fu, a respected governor and military leader, talked up the "teachers" to his troops.

The positive reports brought sixty-five students to the next course, who were healthier, brighter, and better educated than the first group, and results were commensurately superior. The third group was even bigger. In all, Camp Four taught five hundred sixty-nine guerrillas in four sessions.

Sizemore also gave special instructions in an effort to expand the weather net even farther north. He taught a small group of northern Mongolian nomads to take weather readings using the simple, concealable kits that had been used on the coast. SACO hoped these men would deliver weather reports from across Mongolia to the Siberian border. As in the previous experiment, the radios impeded their ability to make regular reports, but some data came through.

SUMMER ARRIVED. Bitter cold gave way to scorching heat, with temperatures often soaring to a hundred degrees Fahrenheit. Ripe melons and fresh vegetables perked up the menu. The Twelve Disciples rode bareback to the Yellow River and dipped naked into the water, still astride their ponies. Closer to camp was a swimming hole filled with water that tasted of alkali and was ice cold even on hot days.

They slowly built relationships with residents of Xamba. A local basketball club challenged the Americans to a few games. Camp Four organized a team and enjoyed playing, but the competition was a tad lopsided. Camp Four beat Xamba in nine out of ten contests. The style of play must have been aggressive, though, since Lieutenant Dr. Jean Neighbor, who had relieved Goodwin, had to return to Chongqing after his front teeth were knocked out during a game. Neighbor was replaced by Dr. Henry Heimlich, who later won fame for his life-saving, antichoking maneuver.

A tragic experience at Camp Four in 1945 later inspired Heimlich to create another life-saving procedure. A Chinese soldier shot in the chest suffocated from accumulating air and blood in his chest cavity while Heimlich was performing surgery to save his life. The soldier was the first person ever to die in the care of the twenty-five-year-old doctor. The memory of the soldier gasping for breath haunted Heimlich for nearly two decades. In 1964, he invented a simple valve inserted through the skin that allows gas and fluid to drain, relieving pressure on the lungs.

LIKE THE FIRSTBORN MALE in a royal house, the care and feeding of the radio set was the focus of the camp even for those with other responsibilities. It was the key instrument for their weather and intelligence missions as well as their lifeline to the outside world. Keeping it running was a team effort fraught with challenges in their remote station.

The radio and weather instruments depended on a generator to run. Repairs fell to Chief Photography Specialist Robert Eastman who had a real talent for working with gasoline engines and had tinkered with speedboat motors much of his life. He did his best to keep the delicate machine going, but months of punishing use on poor-quality, forty-octane fuel bled the life out of it. The generator finally conked out in December 1944. For months afterward, it ran on human fuel: the men took shifts turning the hand crank day and night. Miles even took a turn when he visited in February 1945.

One of SACO's crack generator mechanics, Motor Machinists Mate First Class Irvin Sheffer, came to the rescue in early summer. During his long trek from Chongqing to Camp Four in the company of a Chinese guide, he glided by sampan on the Yellow River and rode a pony down the path along its banks.

AS RESOURCEFUL AS THE MEN OF CAMP FOUR were in work and play, their isolation was a true hardship. They received no mail for nine months after they first arrived. During this interval, they got word to pick up some mail sacks in Xamba. One of the company rode into town and came back with a treasure of precious mailbags. When he opened them surrounded by his eager comrades and spilled out the contents, though, all hearts were dashed to pieces. It was only money, deemed worthless compared to precious words from home. After the camp got its first real mail delivery, Miles realized that it was even more important to this group's morale. SACO arranged regular mail service thereafter about every ten days. It was carried by air from Chongqing to Lanzhou and then by horse and cart for the remaining four hundred miles.

After months of no word from home, Storekeeper First Class James McGrail finally got an oversized envelope in the mail containing a phonograph record. Record players were nonexistent and perhaps unknown in Xamba, and there was no use ordering one. His tour would probably be over by the time it arrived. One of his colleagues saved the day with a homemade contraption that needed two pairs of hands to operate and involved a hand drill, a filed sewing needle, and a paper cup. It was well worth the trouble. Though the sound was wobbly and obscure, McGrail heard the voices of his girlfriend and family sharing town gossip and espousing their love and affection. The exact words, however, were subject to interpretation, requiring the entire camp to pitch in and help decipher them, listening over and over to the homemade record.

Like the mail, supplies also were a long time coming, and batteries had to be carefully conserved. The crew therefore listened to the radio for entertainment on a very limited schedule, indulging in a precious hour now and then when they were together at mealtime. Someone in SACO must have been wise to the schedule, for one morning when Camp Four tuned in at breakfast, the announcer dedicated the next song to "the Twelve Disciples." That was it. No mention of Camp Four, Mongolia, or even the navy. Three words telling them that someone out beyond the steppe and the Yellow River remembered their existence buoyed them for days.

Though these hardy souls were chosen for their resilience, resourcefulness, and good nature as much as for their skills, the challenging conditions of Camp Four were enough to wear any man down. Three months was an adventure; six months was a burden; nine months was intolerable. And Goodwin could see it. Under his advice, Miles shortened the relief rotation for Camp Four to six months, as opposed to the usual stint of a year at other posts.

Aerologist Sizemore was the exception due to his irreplaceable knowledge of that rare spot on the globe. He stayed eighteen months through June 1945. He grew the weather station from little more than a thermometer and barometer nailed to a wooden plank to a Class 1 station with the most sophisticated equipment known to meteorology in his day. During the course of his service, he rose in rank from Aerologist's Mate Second Class to Chief, one of the largest advancements in SACO.

A TRUCKLOAD OF RELIEF PERSONNEL in late May 1945 brought one of SACO's two chaplains, Rev. William S. LaSor, who remained with the camp for a month. Had he been inclined toward a missionary career, Camp Four would have made an excellent testing ground. In a single church service, he preached to a congregation of American and Chinese Christians, Buddhists, Daoists, Muslims, and tribal Shamanists. It would be fascinating to know his sermon topic for this eclectic group, but alas, it is lost to history.

A month was all the time LaSor could spare as he made the rounds of SACO camps and weather stations throughout China's vast interior, but he left Camp Four in good spiritual hands. The Belgians had use of a beautiful mansion for Sunday Masses, peculiar, multicultural affairs catering to Americans as well as Chinese. The priest conducted the service in Latin while the Chinese chanted prayers in unison in their native tongue with no apparent relationship to what was going on at the altar. A beautiful Chinese banquet table with tapered ends served as an altar with a Belgian crucifix hanging above it, while a red-lacquered cabinet decorated with Daoist imagery held European candlesticks and glass cruets.

The previous February, the first aircraft ever to land at Xamba brought then-Commodore Miles and General Dai for a visit. Dai, concerned about the loyalty of a new local army commander, wanted a face-to-face meeting with him. Miles took the opportunity to visit the men of Camp Four and deliver new weather and radio equipment.

It took some finagling to arrange transportation. Making the trip by truck would have taken two or three months in the best of circumstances, more time than either man could spare. With no landing strip available, the army could not justify risking a plane crash at the edge of the Gobi Desert for little more than a social call, but the Chinese National Air Corporation had no such scruples and agreed to provide a plane and crew.

Camp Four had an easy time of preparing an airstrip on the flat, featureless landscape. It was merely a matter of removing stones, debris, and scattered vegetation and smoothing the earth to create an unbroken surface. However, the pilot would have no means of finding the strip in the vast yellow plain from the air so that he could actually land on it.

With signature Camp Four ingenuity, the team created temporary visual markers that could be seen from the air but required no construction in the bitter cold. Wildman contacted the pilot by radio when the plane was in the vicinity and instructed him where to direct his attention. The SACOs then detonated four explosive charges buried at the corners of the airfield, issuing four dust columns that delineated the area. As the plane drew closer, a second explosion sent rows of dust plumes into the air so the pilot could clearly distinguish the exact edges of the field.

The visit lifted camp spirits, and for Miles, it was an eye-opener. It was one thing to read reports that the camp had no supplies, but it was quite another to see it firsthand. Before departure, he gave the men his fleece-lined jacket, all his toiletries, and the plane's entire supply of toilet paper.

THOUGH AT TIMES LIFE AT CAMP FOUR may have felt like some strange desert fantasy from another age, there was indeed a war on, and the SACOs never forgot it. Manchuria, Japan's longest-held stronghold, lay hundreds of miles away across the empty expanse to the east, and the enemy pressed incrementally west with the occasional excursion coming within a hundred miles of the camp.

The men maintained a twenty-four hour watch and knew the Japanese were monitoring them as well. In between cranking their generator, sending their reports, and riding their ponies, they managed to inflict a bit of mayhem on the enemy, demolishing a few railroad bridges and track sections to impede their movements.

Wilcox organized some of Camp Four's Chinese graduates into what Miles later liked to call the only navy cavalry unit of the war and joined Column Eight in an engagement with a Japanese armored force one hundred thirty miles east of Xamba on May 14, 1945. The cavalry augmented their attack with horse-mounted bazookas, another World War II first. The Chinese column destroyed two tanks, including one that Wilcox knocked out personally with submachine gunfire. The three-hour battle in which the Chinese outnumbered their enemy a thousand to six hundred cost the Japanese sixty men and the Chinese two.

Camp Four's final battle played out like a theater stunt. As Wilcox accompanied a small Chinese company on a reconnaissance mission, they came across a large Japanese force only twenty-six miles from camp. Wilcox launched a camel-backed bazooka charge in the dead of night, visiting upon the enemy the terrible spectacle of what looked like fire-breathing monsters descending on them, but inflicting no damage. After their midnight skirmish, both sides went their separate ways having suffered no losses other than rattled nerves.

By the time the war ended, all the original Twelve Disciples had moved on, and Camp Four now had thirty-six Americans. Everyone crowded into the radio room the day the news broke that the Japanese had surrendered. Awed Chinese officers asked whether it was true that the Americans had flattened an entire city with a single bomb, but the Americans at Camp Four knew no more than the Chinese.

While the Americans were jubilant, the Chinese were wary. They suspected that a tougher, lonelier conflict lay ahead. The Russians, they feared, would now maneuver to take the northern provinces previously occupied by the Japanese. General Fu threw a victory banquet in town, but while the food and trappings were festive, his mood was not. Perhaps his mind was on the impending civil war.

THE AMERICANS WERE NOW FLUSH with desire to go home and expected orders to return every day, but with no army or navy planes available to pick them up, they were stuck. Lieutenant Schyler Cammann and a couple of friends took advantage of the two-month wait to ride horses through the mountains, visit nomads, farmers, and lamas, and camp under the stars.

Though the party had been warned that the Mongols out in the wilderness were likely to run away from them, the first one they met, an elderly woman, grinned warmly at them. She treated them to goat's milk, and Cammann gave her a package of American sewing needles amid earnest nods and smiles. As the three SACOs were received as guests in a Mongolian family's felt-walled yurt home, a spirited young teen showed off to the strangers using an inflated goat scrotum to make a flatulent sound, a sort of Mongolian whoopee cushion, proving that raging hormones produced similar results the world over. For Cammann, who held degrees from Yale and Harvard, these excursions laid the groundwork for a lifelong study of Asian culture, and he was to become an expert in Tibetan art.

On October 11, Cammann and four other navy men were the first of the remaining thirty-six Americans to head south for Chongqing and eventually home. They set out in a truck full of equipment to be dropped off in Xi'an, the first leg of a long odyssey. After a problematic, four-hour ordeal crossing the Yellow River by ferry, they heard a sickening "pop" under the hood of the truck. The water pump had cracked. They did a patch job with a leather washer Cammann carved out of a pistol holster and limped ahead, overheating up hills and coasting down.

With night falling and a desert crossing ahead of them, it was too dangerous to continue with a patched-up water pump. They stopped at a temple and rented lodgings from the lamas for the night. Planning a way out of their predicament, they decided that Cammann and Chief Radioman John Pike would go to the SACO weather station in Ningxia some fifty miles away and radio Happy Valley for help. With no other available transportation, they rented a pair of camels from the lamas of the temple, but their hosts were initially reluctant to turn the precious animals over to strange westerners. It took Cammann four days to convince the holy men to release the camels. After a three-day ride on the loping beasts, camping under the stars each night, Cammann and Pike at last reached the city. Luckily, the SACO station was still open, and Happy Valley made arrangements to send spare truck parts by plane and truck.

In Ningxia, the pair met three more trucks from Camp Four that had broken down on the road. The men were staying with the same governor who had given clothes to the original Twelve Disciples in December 1943. When Cammann and Pike got back to the temple to reunite with their friends and return the camels, two more trucks had arrived, the last of Camp Four sent to rescue everyone else.

A few days later, all the repairs were complete. The six trucks formed a caravan and made it to Xi'an in mid-November. Most of the party took a Chinese National Air Corporation flight to Chongqing. Two Americans and a Chinese interpreter loaded the equipment into a new Studebaker truck and departed for Happy Valley on Thanksgiving Day. By then, the Communists had already taken over territory not far from Xamba, and northern Mongolians allied with Russians were preparing to fight the Chinese.

CHAPTER 17

The Sailors and the Flyboys

MILTON "MARY" MILES alternately characterized his experience in China as the highlight of his life or its most frustrating. Starting with nothing but verbal orders and a small canvas bag containing a few shirts and a water mine, he had built the Sino–American Cooperative Organization, supplying the U.S. Navy with priceless weather information and intelligence while giving the Japanese many a bad day. The process itself and the wonderful relationships he built with his men and his Chinese partners brought tremendous satisfaction and pride. But at the same time, he had to fight the U.S. Army, the State Department, and the Washington, D.C., bureaucracy every inch of the way. With few exceptions, every interaction he had with an American official outside his own branch of the armed forces, be it government or military, eventually degenerated into a head-butting contest.

One notable exception was Major General Claire Lee Chennault, a darling of the American public but, like Miles, a thorn in the side of the U.S. Army. Miles took an immediate liking to the founder of the legendary Flying Tigers, American volunteer pilots who fought the Japanese over China's skies in the earliest days of the war. The two men had much in common. Both were viewed by their peers as mavericks in the positive and the pejorative senses. They had begun their singular careers in China as confident veterans while entirely dependent on the Nationalist Chinese and had worked with them to achieve difficult goals. Both had definite ideas about how their jobs should be done and stuck to them at great professional cost. And as the war drew to a close, both felt manhandled and rejected by a theater commander, General Albert Wedemeyer, who seemed to neither respect either of them nor understand their missions.

But before their separate political problems peaked at war's end, Miles and Chennault worked together in a harmonious, mission-focused way that brought benefits to SACO as well as the 14th Army Air Force.

CLAIRE LEE CHENNAULT was seven years older than Miles, a product of the Deep South. Born in Texas in 1893,* he grew up a carefree boy in the backwoods of Louisiana hunting, fishing, and selling skunk pelts for pocket money. His middle name came from the family of his mother, Jessie Lee, who was distantly related to Robert E. Lee. Jessie died when Claire was eight years old, and two years later, his father, a cotton farmer named John Stonewall Jackson Chennault, married Claire's beloved teacher, Lottie Barnes.

After attending Louisiana State University, where he served as an ROTC cadet, Claire's first job was teaching in a one-room schoolhouse in Athens, Louisiana, while he was still in his teens. He got married in 1911, and for the next six years, he moved his growing family around the South in search of higher-paying teaching jobs to feed what would eventually be eight children.

Like Miles, he was inspired to join the military when the United States entered World War I in the spring of 1917. He first applied for army flight training school but was rejected. He ended up in officer training school and emerged a fresh new infantry lieutenant. He was then assigned to Fort Travis in San Antonio, Texas. During off-duty hours, he hung around Kelly Field, an Army Signal Corps base across town, and received casual flying lessons in a Curtiss Jenny. After another unsuccessful application, he finally got into flight training school on the third try in 1918, but the war was over before he could be deployed.

---

* Chennault played fast and loose with his date of birth all his life. In his memoir, he says he was born in 1890, the date he gave the U.S. Army when he enlisted. The consensus among historians is that he was born September 6, 1893, in Commerce, Texas. See Byrd, p. 5.

His capabilities as a teacher, leader, and pilot earned him a command of the 19th Pursuit Squadron in Hawaii before landing back in San Antonio as the head of primary and basic training in 1926. He developed a passion for aerial acrobatics and taught his pilots tight formation flight, for which he won high praise even as he was criticized for his men's lack of polish on the ground.

His next assignment was with the Air Corps Tactical School in Alabama, where he stayed until 1937. During his tenure there, he formed and led a flashy aircraft performance corps, the Three Musketeers. He also threw himself into a debate about the very nature of the U.S. Army Air Corps of the future.

Conventional wisdom among military experts in the United States and Europe favored the theories of Italian General Giulio Douhet, who posited that wave after wave of heavy saturation bombing over enemy territory would pummel a country into submission in short order. Thus the focus in the U.S. Army began to shift from the small, swift pursuit planes of the early days of military aviation to large, less agile bombers that flew at high altitudes and could cover great distances.

The so-called Douhet Doctrine was poppycock in the gospel according to Chennault. He insisted that if an army favored bombers at the expense of fighters, it did so at its peril. Fighters flying in formation as a team with a heavy dose of ground intelligence could hit changing, rich targets in the air, on land, and on sea in a way that bombers could not. His own experiments and research convinced him that fighters even got an exponential advantage when deployed in teams. He was relentless in arguing his case and finally put it in writing in an eight-page document that directly contradicted then Lieutenant Colonel Henry H. "Hap" Arnold, his future boss. Chennault's abrasive style perpetually drowned out the content of his arguments, and in 1937, he got tired of arguing. Suffering from bronchitis and other ailments thanks to a two-pack-a-day smoking habit, he retired at age forty-four.

But his retirement was brief. Although he would not return to the U.S. Army for five years, he was soon back in action, this time as a private U.S. citizen in the service of Nationalist China. Madame Chiang Kai-shek recruited him to train and reorganize the fledgling Chinese Air Force. He stood to earn a hefty fee for a three-month assignment, and as soon as he was feeling better, he found himself at sea aboard the *President Garfield* bound for Shanghai.

Upon arrival, Chennault faced a daunting task. China's supposed air force of three thousand planes in fact consisted of only ninety-one functioning aircraft, and the pilots knew little except how to take off and land. Chennault succeeded in making dramatic improvements in the face of scanty resources as well as some of the cultural obstacles that Miles would later encounter. For example, he constantly had to remind pilots that actions sure to get them killed were wasteful, not heroic.

In 1940, Chiang Kai-shek saw that China's air-power problem could not be solved without more American help. He asked Chennault to recruit five hundred American pilots and procure that number of American planes for China, which was suffering punishing air attacks from Japan. Chennault managed to get a hundred Curtiss P-40s intended for the British by offering them a later, more advanced production run instead. And much to the chagrin of the Army Air Force, he recruited about a hundred American pilots and two hundred ground personnel by offering them salaries significantly higher than they were receiving in the United States. These men formed the American Volunteer Group known as the Flying Tigers.

When the United States formally entered the war after Pearl Harbor, the Flying Tigers took to the air in direct combat against the Japanese. In July 1942, Chennault was recommissioned into the U.S. Army as a colonel, and the AVG became the 14th Army Air Force based in Kunming.

UP-TO-THE-MINUTE GROUND INTELLIGENCE continued to play a primary role in Chennault's vision of effective air power featuring pursuit aircraft, moving him to constantly seek ways to expand and improve it. Dai Li knew of Chennault's goal and had reached out to him in 1938 with an offer to supply information through his MBIS agents. The relationship failed to develop as Dai had hoped, however, because Chennault was reluctant to get too cozy with Dai, not because of the spymaster's sinister reputation with Americans, but because of his caustic relationship with the Communists. Despite the 1937 truce between the Nationalists and Communists, there was still a lot of bad blood, particularly with Dai. The Communists were already working with Chennault supplying intelligence from previously opaque regions of China, and he feared they would cut him off if they saw him as Dai's partner.

Although Chennault was well aware of SACO's intimate ties with Dai, the aviator did not hesitate to work with Miles. He even let a SACO contingent move into office space at the 14th Army Air Force base in Kunming.

The arrangement started out informally. In late 1942, Miles stopped in at Chennault's Kunming office to take a look at some photos of a recent bombing mission to Hong Kong he had heard about. Miles could not help pointing out that, while the bombers had done excellent work turning a warehouse complex into rubble, they had missed some ripe opportunities. Several Japanese navy ships, including a cruiser in drydock, had gone unmolested. What Chennault needed was a pair of crack navy photo interpreters whom Miles knew were on their way to China. Miles suggested they could look over aerial photos in advance and make sure the pilots did not miss any targets, and Chennault jumped on the offer.

The United States had barely dipped its toe into the waters of the growing aerial photo intelligence field by the time World War II began, but the armed forces soon jumped in. The first six-week navy photo-interpretation classes began in January 1942 in Washington, D.C. The interpreters were trained to distinguish features such as buildings and roads in aerial photos based on texture, shade, and shape and to identify subtle changes over time that indicated enemy activity. The interpreters could also identify specific ships, land vehicles, and aircraft. After the sixth class graduated in October 1942, seven members volunteered for SACO.

Two of these graduates, Lieutenant Charles Cook and Ensign William Emmons, arrived at Happy Valley in January and February 1943 and reported to Kunming that spring. Miles, ever alert to tricky personal dynamics, advised them to tread lightly at first to avoid coming off as a pair of navy know-it-alls trying to tell the airmen how to do their jobs. The navy officers proved useful as well as accommodating, pointing out targets in photos, organizing the base's photo files, and building ship models to help the pilots practice identification. Soon, Chennault was asking for more. A combined Chinese and American SACO team rooted out an enemy spy network around his airfields.[47] After that success, he asked Miles if SACO guerrillas could provide security for a new remote fueling base that was in the works. Miles had to turn him down because at that time, mid-1943, SACO's supply chain had not developed. They did not have enough weapons in China to arm such a force.

Chennault invited Miles to install SACO radio and weather equipment in Kunming. At the same time, SACO weather stations in other parts of China began reporting weather conditions directly to Kunming, while SACO Weather Central in Chongqing sent Chennault some of its first forecasts. With so much going on between Happy Valley and Kunming, Miles offered Lieutenant Ray Kotrla, the high-energy, multitalented officer who had taken over Miles's bathroom darkroom in the early days of Happy Valley, as SACO liaison to the 14th. Shortly after reporting, Kotlra was in the air on reconnaissance missions snapping photos. In January 1944, the SACO group at Chennault's headquarters officially became Naval Unit Fourteen, and by May, it was a beehive of ninety-eight personnel.

The photo unit kept track of Japanese shipping, including the merchant fleet, in Xiamen, Fuzhou, Hong Kong, and other key ports. The SACOs of Kunming compiled photo intelligence, reports from SACO coast watchers, enemy radio transmissions, and information from Dai Li's agents into a daily mimeographed sheet the pilots dubbed "the Morning News," and none of the pilots wanted to take off without it. Soon, they were racking up big hits on Japan's merchant fleet along the south China coast. These SACO contributions helped the 14th Army Air Force sink eighty-three thousand tons of Japanese shipping between October 1943 and May 1944.[48] SACO further consolidated the Morning News into weekly and monthly digests called the "Enemy Shipping News" to help big-picture people in Kunming, Chongqing, and Washington spot trends for long-range planning.

MILES PLACED GREAT FAITH in the potential of land and sea mines in China as a low-cost means in terms of both money and personnel to inflict tremendous damage on the enemy. Chennault agreed, and the two began working on plans for a joint mining and reconnaissance project along the south China and northern Indochina coasts in early 1943. Admiral King had been pushing for it for months with support from fleet commanders Admiral Halsey and Admiral Nimitz. General Marshall, however, saw the idea as just another avenue for the navy to supplant the army in China. He discouraged the plan, and therefore, so did Stilwell, who kept coming up with vague reasons to put them off: too difficult, insufficient, too risky. But in October 1943, Chennault and Miles at last received approval for a mission that proved to be exemplary for coordination between services and intelligence sources.

Haiphong Harbor, a well-sheltered port with a bottleneck entrance in present-day Vietnam near its border with China, was the chosen target. It was on Miles's ongoing hit list of places the Pacific Fleet wanted mined and was near the limit of the 14th Air Force's range from Kunming. Lieutenant Joseph Champe personally escorted a shipment of sea mines for the mission from SACO's preparation and storage facility in Assam, India, over the Hump to Kunming while on his own supply mission for his planned raider unit.

On October 26, 1943, SACO aerial intelligence officers Kotrla, Lieutenant Ralph DuBois, and Lieutenant Commander Duane McCann were on board the 14th's squadron of B-24 bombers as they headed for Haiphong. SACO coast watchers simultaneously reported a convoy of nine or ten Japanese ships heading for the harbor. The SACO observers helped the pilots and bombardiers zero in on the precise altitude and location to release the mines at the harbor entrance. Seeing the planes overhead, a Japanese freighter heading out to sea rushed through the narrow exit seeking safety, but instead, the ship hit a mine and sunk. The convoy got wind of the disaster and turned around in a panic short of the entrance, stopping at a port in the nearby Hainan Strait.

SACO radio interception experts picked up the convoy's ill-advised radio conversations and forwarded its location to 14th AAF command, which immediately sent B-24s out again, this time armed with bombs, and sunk six of the ships in the strait.[49] The previously sunken freighter forced the closure of Haiphong Harbor for the rest of the war.

As the campaign continued over the next eighteen months, its effects on the Japanese grew exponentially. Working together, SACO, the Pacific Fleet, and the AAF prosecuted a multipoint assault in which each played a distinct role. SACO identified targets and provided mines and onboard navy reconnaissance personnel to get the most out of the ordnance. In addition to launching missions and doing its own damage, the AAF ran reconnaissance missions to identify Japanese ship movements for the navy, often with SACO photographers on hand. The mines and aerial attacks forced Japan to alter shipping routes, venturing into deeper waters, where American submarines waited with torpedoes at the ready.

DURING A CAMP TOUR in December 1944, Miles personally delivered intelligence to the air force that led to a crippling attack. He had taken part in a guerrilla mission with Column Four, ambushing a Japanese supply group in the wee hours of the morning,[50] but there was even more to the story. The group had been on its way to pick up rice from a hidden warehouse, which turned out to be no ordinary warehouse. Chinese spies described a three-acre storage area in Paoching containing hundreds of horses, tons of rice, and tens of thousands of winter uniforms. Too large for a guerrilla attack, it was an ideal target for the 5th Fighter Group, part of the Chinese American Composite Wing of the 14th AAF. Headquartered at an airfield in Zhijiang about two hundred miles from the warehouse, the pilots were itching for some action, but it was too dangerous to phone or radio the information to them. It had to be relayed in person, the old-fashioned way.

Miles and two other navy officers walked ninety miles in three days and then drove a jeep the rest of the way to the airbase. Within hours of their arrival, the planes were in the air with the SACO officers aboard to help find the storage facility in Paoching, and in short order, it was in flames. A month later, Miles heard that a Japanese advance had been cut short because the soldiers had no winter clothing.

SACO found other ways to share target information with Chennault's fliers. Second Lieutenant William E. Buckley, USMC, who spent months in the field with Column Four, worked out a system with the 5th Fighter Group to point out targets without risking radio communication in the hot enemy territory. He made large arrows out of white fabric that literally pointed the way. It was so successful that he taught the technique to eighteen Chinese soldiers in the column. They split into six groups and spent the rest of the war discovering and flagging targets for the airmen.

SACO also achieved excellent results guiding pilots to objectives via ground-to-air radio. The observer on the ground would wait until he made eye contact with the plane and then begin communication via a prearranged radio frequency. In some cases, they used walkie-talkies.

MILES CALLED SACO AND THE 14TH AAF "a perfect fit,"[51] but some culture clash was inevitable. At the airbase at Guilin, tensions became so serious that the navy built its own quarters separate from the airmen. About twenty-five SACOs were stationed there, providing radio reconnaissance and weather forecasts. The airmen felt insulted that the navy men refused to salute, but it was a navy tradition not to salute "uncovered," that is, when not wearing a hat. The reason goes back to the origin of the gesture. In the distant past, military men removed their hats in deference to their superiors, which evolved into a quick tip of the hat for the sake of convenience and efficiency. Eventually, the act became even more convenient, morphing into a mere touch of the hat with the fingertips to symbolically tip it. It therefore made no sense to symbolically tip one's hat if one was not wearing one.

Even after they learned why the sailors were not saluting, the AAF officers resented this unique navy tradition and insisted that the SACOs start wearing hats so they would be compelled to salute. But the plain army fatigues uniform they wore did not include a hat. The conflict most likely went deeper than hats and salutes, but whatever its cause, the navy decided to minimize contact by constructing a separate building on the base. The battle of the salute finally receded when the real war intruded, and the Americans had to blow up the base in the face of a Japanese takeover.

Another potential problem arose when Miles's old adversary General William Donovan inserted the OSS into the workings of the 14th Army Air Force.

Donovan's alliance with SACO had proven disastrous, and he had been trying to get out from under it ever since he signed the SACO Agreement in early 1943. Technically the agreement barred the OSS from any activities in China outside the SACO organization, and those actions within it were subject to the approval of Dai Li and thus of Chiang Kai-shek. This restriction was intolerable to Donovan, who felt he could not do his job without having free rein to work with Communists, the British, and anyone else he chose using any means necessary to obtain information.

Donovan's staff repeatedly advised him not to remove the OSS from SACO because it could mean being kicked out of China entirely. But he still needed a way to expand the OSS while concealing his activities from Dai and Miles. For this, he turned to the 14th Army Air Force.

Back when Donovan had first tried to implement the Dragon Plan of espionage and special operations in 1942, one of his few supporters in China had been Chennault, who welcomed any effort to improve intelligence for his air force. At that time, however, Donovan could see tensions building between Stilwell and Chennault, and he preferred to keep the OSS clear of the inevitable explosion between them. But once Donovan was sure that Stilwell's days in China were numbered, the crusty old flier's organization became more attractive as a way to sidestep Donovan's commitment to SACO. One big advantage was the location of Chennault's headquarters in Yunan Province where Dai's and Chiang's authority was relatively weak. It would be easier to conceal OSS activities there.

En route to Chongqing to fire Miles in December 1943, Donovan stopped in Kunming and met with Chennault to float the idea of working together to their mutual benefit.[52] For Chennault, the proposal held great promise for more ground intelligence.

They followed up the quick chat with three days of talks held between Christmas and New Year's Day in Kunming. Donovan did not attend himself but sent Colonel John Coughlin, who had replaced Miles as China's OSS chief, and Coughlin's deputy, Captain Carl Hoffman. At Chennault's side were three of his top staffers, including his intelligence chief Colonel Jesse Williams. Both sides were eager to work together. Chennault's group could provide office and equipment space and management in exchange for OSS intelligence, agents, research and analysis, propaganda, and resources, but there was one obstacle, which Coughlin unflinchingly laid out. The OSS, legally prohibited from working outside SACO, had to keep this joint project completely under the radar. Chennault clearly understood, suggesting that placing 14th Army Air Force personnel in command of the group would keep Miles and Dai from discovering what was really going on. Hoffman offered a meaningless and confusing name for the group to further conceal its OSS connection: the Air and Ground Forces Resources and Technical Staff, shortened to the laughable acronym AGFRTS.

Thus the marriage between the 14th Army Air Force and the OSS began very much like that of the OSS and SACO, with a honeymoon during which each partner basked in the good fortune of having secured the other. But as in its previous alliance, the OSS and the 14th quickly became disenchanted with one another, and outsiders contributed to their squabbles. The trajectory of the 14th's experience astonishingly mirrored SACO's.

COLONEL HEPPNER AT OSS'S COMMAND POST in Delhi felt uneasy about the relationship almost from the start, and Coughlin quietly agreed. Heppner worried that the balance of power leaned too much in favor of the 14th with its real estate and officers, and that it threatened to subsume the OSS. Moreover, the secrecy imposed on OSS's role in AGFRTS would let the 14th take credit for the entire operation.

Major Wilfred Smith, assistant to Williams, was placed at the helm of AGFRTS. He soon began complaining that the OSS seemed to have its own agenda and was not delivering what it had promised. Compounding the problem, Heppner and Coughlin squabbled repeatedly over personnel and other matters that should have been settled easily. Finger-pointing and petty turf wars mushroomed both within the OSS and between the OSS and the AAF.

In the eyes of General Stilwell, AGFRTS constituted yet another unorthodox intelligence operation on par with SACO, set up outside his command without his consent and stomping all over the unity of command principle. The army wanted to put AGFRTS under the army intelligence agency G-2, but Chennault, who was already in a perpetual state of war with Stilwell, pushed back. In April 1944, Theater Command finally approved the arrangement as originally conceived after reams of accusatory and cajoling memos circulated for months.

The agents the OSS brought in were the kinds of men who would have made SACO recoil: Major Paul Frillmann was a former missionary, and Captain Charles Stelle was a Harvard professor of oriental studies, born and raised in Beijing. Both were descended from the foreigners of China's recent past now reviled by the Chinese for better or for worse, although Frillmann was an ardent champion of the Chinese peasantry. Unlike Miles, Chennault had no problem with "old China hands" and considered their experience a plus; in fact, Smith, Chennault's chosen chief for AGFRTS, was a missionary's son raised in China. But perhaps the old flying tiger would have disapproved of Frillmann and Stelle on other grounds had he known their backgrounds. They both thoroughly and unabashedly despised the Generalissimo, who was Chennault's friend and avid supporter.[53]

The OSS eventually insisted on having one of its own officers included in AGFRTS command to offset AAF dominance and potentially defuse Smith's complaints. Into this mix of missionaries, academics, professional spies, and military officers of every stripe arrived one Philip K. Crowe, a New York advertising executive fresh from big-game hunting in the bush. He became Smith's new executive officer.

All the resources the OSS was throwing into AGFRTS explained why it had trouble scaring up a few men to work on SACO research projects and had to borrow teachers for its spy school from the navy. Donovan was now contributing as little effort and money as he could get away with into SACO. Dai Li had to deal with it without any help from Miles, who had entirely washed his hands of anything connected with the OSS.

Experience should have told the OSS that they could not hide the true nature of AGFRTS from Dai Li. He was fully aware of it and resented the OSS's perfidy, but perhaps in the interest of retaining what assistance he was still receiving from the agency, he did not protest outright. Instead, he grew increasingly concerned that the OSS would pull out abruptly. He began pressing its officers about their intentions for SACO. His disquiet finally led to the ill-fated conference with the OSS's General Miller in October 1944 that began with an air-clearing conversation but would end in diplomatic disaster at a dinner during which Miller launched into the insulting, racist, two-hour tirade that threatened to completely derail the operation.[54] During their private meeting before the debacle, Miller told Dai outright that the OSS was a partner in AGFRTS, but it was a bit like informing a twelve-year-old that there is no Santa Claus. Dai did not seem ruffled by the news, but he appreciated being told. His main concern was whether he would still get presents, that is, whether the OSS intended to stay in SACO.

Miles could only shake his head at AGFRTS. In a letter to Metzel, he called it more of OSS's "empire building," as the agency appeared to be duplicating SACO's program piece by piece.[55]

The evolution of Donovan's relationship with SACO was repeated with AGFRTS. Donovan had offered Chennault a partnership through AGFRTS to get past obstacles the OSS faced in China just as he had done with SACO. The initial agreement prompted celebration and great expectations, but the era of good feelings was brief. After going with the flow for some months, Donovan tried to take over, and when that failed, he wanted to get out from under it altogether. But unlike his struggle with the Joint Chiefs and the navy in the case of SACO, he got a boost in the separation process with AGFRTS when General Albert Wedemeyer assumed command after Stilwell's recall in October 1944.

UPON WEDEMEYER'S ARRIVAL in Chongqing, the alphabet soup of American intelligence agencies running around helter-skelter and forming and breaking alliances in search of larger slices of the pie left him flabbergasted. In his view, their turf wars, ill-defined command structures, and competition for Hump tonnage frustrated their own missions, were detrimental to the American armed forces as a whole, and were confusing to the Chinese. Wedemeyer was determined to clean up the mess, and that cleanup was sure to fundamentally change SACO, AGFRTS, and the OSS.

Chennault, smelling something foul in the wind, exchanged letters with Wedemeyer to try to maintain the status quo. The air commander's first letter in November stated AGFRTS's vital role in the 14th Army Air Force and asked that it remain under his command. Wedemeyer wrote back January 1 that he intended to remove AGFRTS from the 14th, retaining Major Smith, but in the role of unit leader, reporting to the army. Two weeks later he appointed the OSS's Colonel Richard Heppner chief of all U.S. intelligence in China so that AGFRTS was now under OSS control. On February 4, Chennault wrote again. This time he expressed concern that new command might prevent him from getting the information he needed, and that in any case, he would like to have his officers back.

From that point on, Chennault appears to have written off AGFRTS and turned his attention elsewhere, as Miles had done after he was removed from the OSS. Three months later, AGFRTS no longer existed. It became the OSS Zhijiang Unit Field Command, one of three OSS operating centers under Heppner's command at the behest of Wedemeyer. By then the OSS was setting up SACO-style guerrilla training camps, and Wedemeyer had already begun to push Chennault and Miles out of China.

Wedemeyer took no pleasure in overseeing Chennault's fall, but he had no choice. General George Marshall felt that Chennault had been disloyal to Stilwell and had done a terrible job in east China as the Japanese made their push south in June 1944. He was so disgusted with Chennault that he told Wedemeyer he would never decorate or promote the old airman. Marshall and General "Hap" Arnold, chief of the Army Air Force, shoved Chennault aside by moving the 10th Army Air Force from India into Chennault's base in Kunming and pushing the 14th into a northern corner of China in the summer of 1945. The move made no military sense and was entirely personal, but Wedemeyer could not stop it.[56]

Chennault did not stick around to see the 14th take up its new quarters. He left China on July 31, 1945, and was on a plane between Tel Aviv and Athens when he got word that Japan had surrendered.

CHAPTER 18

Adventures with Pirates, a Princess, and a Priest

A POPULAR PREWAR COMIC STRIP, *Terry and the Pirates*, by Milton Caniff, depicted a young American adventurer in search of a gold mine in China who got mixed up with Chinese pirates and warlords, and Terry's main adversary, the powerful and sensuous Dragon Lady. In the grand tradition of the comics, Terry always avoided disaster with the help of his Chinese cook and translator, Connie, and a lovable Mongolian giant. Shortly after Pearl Harbor, Terry abandoned the treasure hunt and joined in the struggle against the Japanese as a U.S. fighter pilot.

The Sino–American Cooperative Organization has often been compared to the comic strip. Like Terry and his partner, SACOs poked along the Chinese coast and rivers and roamed through an exotic landscape, narrowly escaping danger with the help of gold-hearted, heroic Chinese who became their fast friends.

And like Terry, SACOs mingled with fantastic characters like gun-toting clerics, a princess, and pirates, including their own "Dragon Lady"—a female chief of staff to a pirate commander. In fact, when the comic strip's Dragon Lady, originally a foil to Terry, gave up her pirate activities to join the Nationalist Chinese resistance against Japan, navy leaders in Washington got nervous that she was beginning to resemble SACO's real-life collaborator a bit too much. Captain

Jeffrey Metzel, SACO's backstage manager in Washington, D.C., wrote a friendly letter to Caniff asking him to lay off the pirate queen for a while.

Although Caniff's Dragon Lady had made her grand entrance onto the comic pages eight years before Milton Miles first got to Chongqing, the cartoonist graciously complied. In 1956, he was invited to the SACO Veterans' convention and sent his regrets in the form of a signed poster featuring his famous strip.

Terry and the Pirates, rip-roaring fantasy though it was, had a basis in truth.

Piracy has a rich history in China going back at least to the fourteenth century, with some seventy thousand participants at its peak in the early 1800s. For poor young fishermen, sailors, and petty criminals, working for pirates was often a second job to make ends meet, like a struggling worker in the twenty-first century pulling a few shifts a week flipping burgers. It was one of the few segments in the rigid economy that offered a way to get ahead, and the shadow economy it produced gave vital support to the legitimate one.

In addition, the institution held the promise of rare escape from the ironclad Confucian social order in China. Almost no other lifestyle offered adventure and financial independence to women, who were accepted into Chinese pirate society and judged on their own merits. Unlike Europeans, Chinese women did not pretend to be men in order to join a pirate company, and while in a decided minority, they were not uncommon. Several women even rose to be top leaders within pirate hierarchy, serving as inspiration for Caniff's Dragon Lady. Most active Chinese pirates, however, were single men in their twenties, with very few over forty except those in management positions.

The pirates derived significant income from thievery on the sea, but even more important was their protection racket. Huge pirate leagues employed accountants, managers, and bill collectors like any other business, augmented by enforcers. They exacted payment from foreign and domestic shipping companies and issued passports to those who had paid up, allowing their ships to pass freely through Chinese ports.

In the early 1900s, piracy flourished in the South China Sea north of Hong Kong, as government authorities cheerfully looked the other way in exchange for a share in the pirates' spoils.

Chang Gui Fong and Chang Yizhou, pirate leaders of the World War II era, weathered China's twentieth-century chaos by offering loyal service to anyone who would take their business. Chang Gui Fong, commander of the Brethren of the Green Circle, based on an island at the mouth of the Yangtze, controlled the coast from Wenzhou to Shanghai and points north, while Chang Yizhou plied the waters from Xiamen to Wenchow. Combined, their circles numbered nearly ten thousand men.

Dai worked out a deal with the two leaders, giving them free rein of the lucrative opium trade in their sections of the Chinese coast in exchange for serving as Dai's eyes and ears in their territories and doing occasional jobs for him.[57] In addition, both pirate kings received payment from the Japanese as well as impressive military titles and Japanese "staff" who in truth occupied their headquarters and monitored their activities.

Fiercely independent, the pirates felt no patriotic loyalty to the Nationalists, but they resented the clinging Japanese and wanted their freedom back. In many ways, the pirates were China's Roma, outcasts from the greater society but with a distinct and proud culture, the work of many generations of isolation and tradition.

MILTON MILES DISCOVERED on his first trip to the coast in 1942 that Dai Li had a cooperative relationship with several pirate circles. The navy officer's guide even introduced him to a couple of pirates while in Wenzhou, a coastal city about midway between Shanghai and Xiamen.

This was not the first time Miles had come across Chinese pirates, but his previous encounters had involved not mutual cooperation, but gunshots, including a near-miss while he was serving on a gunboat, the USS *Pampanga*, in the 1920s, when a bullet ripped through the hat of his boat's captain.

Though Miles had not known it at the time, Dai worked with the pirates on SACO's behalf in 1943, purchasing gasoline they salvaged off a Japanese freighter after an American submarine sunk it.

In the spring of 1944, a meeting with the buccaneers became a priority after Admiral King told Miles to be ready for the U.S. Navy to land on the China coast by December. With coast watch stations planned in pirate territory, it was essential that the pirates be informed and perhaps even recruited to work with the SACO observers.

Moreover, Miles hoped to enlist them as guerrilla soldiers. Their piracy methods demonstrated some of the very skills that made for a good guerrilla, combining secrecy, planning, undercover work, sudden attack, and swift get-away. The pirates' typical modus operandi was to preselect a passenger ship and identify a concealed rendezvous point along its route. A group of pirates would board the ship at its departure disguised as passengers and, as it neared the specified location where their partners waited in junks, they would suddenly produce arms, demand the passengers' valuables, and sometimes seize hostages if they were likely to bring a high ransom. They would then scramble onto the waiting junks and speed away.

Dai arranged a secret conference in May 1944 with pirate representatives at a place called Tung Feng.* Miles, Lieutenant Seth "Si" Morris, and Eddie Liu traveled for two weeks from Chongqing by truck, horseback, and on foot to meet Dai and twelve other Chinese generals at a lovely old temple with intricately carved woodwork and rice paper windows that washed out with every rainstorm.

The first pirate to join them, representing Chang Gui Fong, was a taciturn man with a long, drooping moustache, an Ichabod Crane physique, and a battered, brown felt hat. Two days later, two short, stocky men in black, baggy fishermen's suits reported on behalf of Chang Yizhou. "Fishermen" from their circle were to rescue journalist Don Bell's party shot down near Xiamen the following year.[58]

With everyone at last assembled around a conference table in the temple, Dai Li introduced Miles as Brigadier General of the Sea Winter Plum Blossom, invoking a rough equivalent to the English term Commodore along with the Chinese name Dai had given him. All three pirates rose from their seats and bowed in deference to a mighty, fellow seafarer.

The pirates had come to the table hoping to gain legitimacy in the eyes of the "emperor." Completely isolated from mainstream society, they were unaware that China was no longer under imperial rule, but such details did not matter to them. They simply desired to return to the good graces of the national leader, whether emperor, chairman, president, or generalissimo. To achieve this, they asked to be placed on the tax rolls in the belief that paying taxes would automatically anoint them as law-abiding citizens of China. In exchange, they were eager to attack and expel their Japanese handlers and intended to take over all the lighthouse islands along the coast to keep the enemy from returning.

---

* This exact location cannot be identified, either due to a misspelling by Miles, a name change by the Communist government, or some combination of the two.

Dai said the time had not yet come to turn on the Japanese. The pirates would be far more useful if they continued to keep up the pretense of serving them even as they performed as SACO agents. It would allow them to spy on the Japanese up close without arousing suspicion.

The pirates also needed Miles's help to stop American planes from bombing their junks. They had been caught in several attacks against Japanese boats, at a cost of two junks sunk, two damaged, and several lives lost. A radio identification system proved to be impossible because most of the boats lacked the equipment. Instead, Miles worked with the 14th Air Force to establish specific "safe havens" where no junk would be bombed. The pirates knew to head to those areas when an attack was imminent or when anchoring for the night.

Miles and Dai proposed several operations:

- Extend Miles's pet weather net, the mother of all SACO activities. A junk equipped with weather instruments and a radio in the northern seas of Chang Gui Fong's territory could collect and transmit data to fill a blank space in the navy's weather map.
- Enlist an already established crew of teenage girl bicycle couriers in Shanghai who worked for a woman pirate officer in the Brethren of the Green Circle. Each girl, ostensibly an ordinary bicycle messenger, carried a second folding bike so she could smuggle someone out of the city, such as a compromised spy or an escaped prisoner.
- Train and arm pirates as guerrillas at SACO training camps opening in the coming weeks. These guerrillas would operate on land and sea.
- Coordinate spying activities among both pirate groups and SACO's new coast watch stations.

The pirate representatives assented to everything, especially the training camps, because they were still using guns left over from the Russo–Japanese War of 1905 and were most eager to replace these obsolete weapons. They reluctantly conceded to wearing army uniforms in training camp but adamantly insisted that they would don their own clothes upon graduation.

The talks satisfied both sides. In accordance with Dai's policy, the pirates were offered no money in exchange for their services, and these negotiations demonstrated that this policy was right. The pirates never asked to be paid, and yet they were eager to betray the Japanese who were paying them. No doubt Dai's power motivated them, but they also appreciated respect and fairness and the chance to retaliate against the side that had pushed them around.

Before the meeting broke up, the pirates produced vials of garlic water and made slow circuits around the table sprinkling the officers as a priest would administer holy water. In their tradition, garlic sealed bonds between people and had protective powers, even from bullets.

"There will be no bullets between us," they vowed in unison.

THE PIRATES WERE BETTER than their word. Although some of their commitments to SACO never came to fruition, those failings were the result of wartime logistical troubles rather than lack of cooperation. They risked their lives over and over to rescue dozens of American pilots and crew shot down over the Chinese coast, and many died while gathering intelligence and taking up arms against the Japanese.

In the vicinity of Xiamen, they supplied irreplaceable intelligence. It had proven too dangerous for Americans in that area to venture beyond their concealed coast watch stations, but Chang Yizhou's men, dressed and equipped like fisher folk, kept close watch over Japanese activities and developed working relationships with navy coast watchers. Many pirates were fluent in Japanese and could strike up conversations with unwary Japanese sailors under the pretense of selling fish or looking for work.

A perfect system was devised for getting Chinese and American spies out of custody in Shanghai. Speed, above all, was key to such an operation because within ten hours of arrest, the complex bureaucracy buried a detainee under so much paperwork that it became practically impossible to secure his freedom. Whenever an Allied spy, typically an OSS agent, had been captured, the bicycle girls, working with a Shanghai informant, would spring into action. The informant, the Chinese wife of a Japanese magistrate, would quickly get word to Dai Li's network. The MBIS would immediately respond with the offer of a bribe to a Japanese court official, who gladly took the money. The bicycle couriers would deliver the cash in exchange for the prisoner, unfold the second bicycle for the prisoner to ride, and lead him to a waiting agent outside the city. The system was swift, efficient, and remarkably inexpensive—the cash delivered for the bribe was, of course, counterfeit, printed by the finest MBIS craftsmen.

AT CAMP EIGHT, three hundred ninety-nine pirates attended guerrilla training. Hundreds more were trained at Camps Six and Seven.[59]

Eager to get his newly trained men into action, Camp Six's Captain Earl Dane proposed a joint mission. One patrol from his unit and one from Camp Seven would attack near the isolated coastal town of Putian. The town was midway between the two camps and had a small Japanese garrison whose scouting parties would make good targets for beginner guerrillas. The plan was excellent, but its outcome was an utter failure. The pirates belonged to different cadres, and when they met in the field, they adamantly refused to work together. But at least no scuffles broke out between them.

The same could not be said of a French intelligence unit and a contingent of patriotic Thai students from American colleges training at Happy Valley in the summer of 1943. The two groups were working with SACO on entirely different projects; the French were building an intelligence network in French Indochina, and the Thais were training for commando raids in Thailand. They happened to run into each other at the mess hall, and the encounter quickly deteriorated into a brawl.

The fight blindsided the Americans, who had unwittingly placed a powder keg beside an open flame. A tradition of rancor between the French and the Thais went back more than fifty years, ever since the French had swallowed some of Thailand's territory into French Indochina through border disputes during the late nineteenth century. After Germany took over France and Japan muscled into Thailand early in World War II, a brief war between beleaguered France and Thailand erupted in Southeast Asia in 1940 and 1941. Against this bitter backdrop, it probably took little more than a condescending look or an ill-judged adjective to send the mess trays flying at SACO headquarters. The SACO officers made sure the French and Thais never crossed paths thereafter.

Submarine Captain Robert Meynier led the French contingent. He joined SACO to launch an OSS intelligence mission in French Indochina, the region of Southeast Asia that today comprises Vietnam, Cambodia, and Laos. The country was an important Japanese stronghold, and the United States had virtually no presence there, which General Donovan and Miles, who at that time were still working well together, were eager to correct. However, competing factions in France and among its allies were divided as to whom they considered the true leader of the Free French. Some supported General Henri Giraud, an heroic figure who had escaped a German prison early in the war by rappelling down a cliff while wearing a Tyrolean hat and was the top military officer of Free France. Others were in the camp of Charles de Gaulle. This led to an uneasy compromise of the two men becoming copresidents of the French Committee of National Liberation in June 1943. The Meynier mission, which had begun with high hopes, touched off a miniwar among rival factions of the Free French in Chongqing and thus never met Donovan's expectations.

Donovan and Miles had determined that a French connection was imperative to an effective intelligence operation in Indochina. Donovan arranged for Miles to meet with General Giraud in Algiers in spring 1943 on his way back to Chongqing after getting the SACO Agreement signed in Washington.

Giraud offered Miles the services of Captain Meynier for the SACO–OSS mission. Meynier had been virtually idle in Africa since making his own dramatic escape from the Nazis a few months earlier. The Vichy government ordered the French Navy to scuttle to avoid German capture in Toulon, France, in November 1942, but Meynier and two other submarine captains refused to surrender and slipped their vessels out of the harbor as the rest of the fleet was blown up just ahead of the German seizure. Meynier even managed to sink a German and an Italian submarine and capture prisoners before piloting his sub, *Le Glorieux*, into Casablanca. He received the *Croix de Guerre* for his exploits.

Miles and Meynier shared a kind of seagoing simpatico and hit it off from the start. Miles was impressed with the captain's leadership ability and purportedly extensive knowledge of Indochina. For his part, Meynier was eager to get back into action and readily accepted the job. After flying to Washington for a mysterious meeting where he received secret codes for radio transmission, Meynier assembled a cadre of French military officers and native Indochinese French Army soldiers and trained them in Algiers. In July 1943, the new intelligence group left for Chongqing.

It turned out that it was not Meynier himself, but his wife Katiou, an Annamite (Vietnamese) princess and priestess, who had deep knowledge of Indochina. Half European, she was descended from Indochina's former ruling family, and her father and uncle were powerful political figures there. Her experience and connections were crucial to Robert Meynier's plans.

It would be no easy task to bring Mme. Meynier to Chongqing; she was detained in a Nazi prison camp in Europe. But such problems never fazed Donovan, who tapped his connections with the British Special Operations Executive to break her out. The rescue succeeded but at a terrible cost. Three British agents and seven French resistance fighters were killed storming the prison and extracting the princess.[60] She was shuttled from house to house before boarding a British reconnaissance plane in the dead of night for a flight to London, where Commander Junius Morgan of the OSS met her plane and took her to the Chinese embassy.

Though she was now safe, the OSS needed to hide her movements from British notice because the agency had concealed the true purpose of her rescue in the first place. Had the SOE known that she was slated for a Giraud mission to Chongqing, it might not have cooperated. The British government supported the London-based de Gaulle and was sponsoring his French Military Mission, an intelligence operation already established in Indochina. Had they discovered that Mme. Meynier was bound for Chongqing, they could easily have deduced what the Americans were up to and tried to detain her.

In a plot seemingly taken from the storyline of an adventure comic strip, Morgan invented a cover for the princess. She would travel as Paula Martin, a U.S. Army WAC with laryngitis, so she would not have to speak and reveal her limited, heavily accented English. Accompanying her were French and Annamite soldiers. Because Annamites would have aroused British suspicions, the contingent was identified as members of the Army of the Philippines. Apparently it troubled no one that a lone member of the U.S. Army suffering from laryngitis was traveling in a party of French and Filipino soldiers.

By this time, it was late August, and Captain Meynier at Happy Valley was crawling out of his skin with anxiety for her. When Mme. Meynier finally arrived in Kolkata, Miles sent her husband to meet her and accompany her over the Hump. Once at Happy Valley, the former beauty queen's status among the Annamite soldiers astonished Miles. They would bow or kneel before her in the footpaths, and he even witnessed some kind of rite in her honor involving candles and incense.

Robert and Katiou fell with relish into planning and writing reports. They intended to establish a propaganda and intelligence network of French and Annamite Indochinese. The goal was to track the Japanese as well as monitor the attitudes of the population and steer the people toward support of the Allies in advance of a potential invasion. They also planned to sabotage Japanese shipping and to set up smuggling routes for commodities such as rubber and tin needed for the war effort. The captain boasted of a potential network of three hundred thousand agents.

But such aspirations were doomed from the start. Another group, the French Military Mission based in Chongqing, was already working in Indochina at the direction of Charles de Gaulle's government in exile in London and financed by Great Britain. Thus the stage was set for a Giraudist-versus-de-Gaullist rivalry. The FMM's agents operating in cooperation with Dai Li had established a radio intelligence system the previous year with agents in the field. Although Dai Li was leery of their British connection, he tolerated them because they provided valuable information.

In addition, the FMM had the blessing of Chiang Kai-shek, who was friends with de Gaulle's representative in Chongqing, General Zivoni Pechkoff. Pechkoff's charm and intelligence had won over the Generalissimo, who named him French Ambassador to China. In blunt contrast to Pechkoff, his chief of staff and the head of de Gaulle's intelligence service in China, Colonel Louis Emblanc, was pushy and easily annoyed.

P. L. Thyraud de Vosjoli, a French secret agent in Chongqing at the time, wrote in his memoir that Pechkoff's detractors often quipped, "General Pechkoff, French Ambassador to China, who is neither General, nor Pechkoff, nor Ambassador, nor French."[61] Pechkoff was another character who could have stepped directly from a *Terry and the Pirates* panel. He was born Zivoni Sverdlof but was adopted as a young man by the Russian novelist Maxim Gorky and assumed Gorky's original surname Pechkoff. He joined the French Foreign Legion at the beginning of World War I at age twenty-nine, and had reached the rank of Colonel by 1943, but de Gaulle designated him a general for the mission to China. As to the title of ambassador, the Generalissimo gave an honor that was not his to bestow, as a country of origin normally appoints its ambassadors.

Captain Meynier, carrying orders signed by both Giraud and de Gaulle, had gone to see to Pechkoff and Emblanc as soon as he got to Chongqing. Like Miles before him, Meynier had the awkward obligation of reporting to fellow countrymen in the Chinese capital but thereafter having nothing to do with them, leaving only bitterness in his wake.

Members of the Free French intelligence community knew well of Mme. Meynier's rescue and were angry that lives had been sacrificed for what appeared to be the inconsequential purpose of bringing a hero's wife to his side. In addition, they resented Meynier's plans to build a second intelligence network on top of, and potentially at the expense of, their own.

Meynier's appearance on the scene was a total surprise to Pechkoff, who from the beginning attempted to pull rank on the captain. He demanded that Meynier report to himself instead of Giraud, communicate with Chongqing French officials only through him, and turn over the secret codes he had received in Washington, D.C.

Like Miles before him, Meynier ignored these demands and went about his business, unavoidably making enemies because the very nature of his mission placed him square in the crossfire between the political supporters of de Gaulle and those of Giraud. He made the rounds in Chongqing calling on French intelligence officers, most of whom, at Pechkoff's request, refused to see him. Meynier was forced to circumvent the ambassador by sending his translator, SACO's Lieutenant Robert Larson, in his place.

Despite these roadblocks, the Meyniers were able to make some progress. They were not able to enter Indochina, but Mme. Meynier toured along the border, using her influence, charisma, and networking skills to recruit native and French Indochinese to feed intelligence to Miles at Happy Valley. The pair established contacts inside the country through correspondence with associates of Katiou's father and uncle.

Other members of their team got through the border, including Father Bec, a Catholic priest who had served in Indochina before the war. He focused on American pilots shot down in Indochina, where there was no system in place for their recovery or for collecting information about their fate. He also distributed handbills in French and Vietnamese with instructions for how to assist a downed pilot and even got the leaflets into prison camps. He designed an ingenious, nonverbal signal, a bamboo stick with a folded sheet of paper in the cleft, for Indochinese to communicate their good intentions to pilots. He informed pilots and natives about the device so that a pilot could tell that a person carrying such a stick was his friend. Father Bec also organized other priests who enlisted their congregations, creating a Catholic underground to funnel information to Miles.

The activities of Father Bec particularly infuriated Emblanc, who tried unsuccessfully to have the priest deported to North Africa. While Miles thought the French Military Mission wanted to get rid of him because he achieved so much,[62] the true reason is unclear.

It is easier to understand why the French Military Mission worked to minimize Mme. Meynier's work in Indochina. It went beyond resentment over her costly rescue. They feared that she would turn the public against the French, and in fact, she capitalized on anti-French as well as anti-Japanese sentiments to win new agents for the network. There were also unsubstantiated rumors in Chongqing, North Africa, and London that the U.S. Navy planned to reinstate the monarchy after the Japanese were driven out, elevating the beautiful princess to Empress of Annam.[63]

Meanwhile, Dai Li got into the ruckus. Always suspicious of the FMM, he accused them of spying on China, while they accused him of having one of their agents killed. In January 1944, he abruptly ordered them to stop all radio transmissions, effectively shutting down the intelligence network.

Around the same time, Miles returned from Washington newly promoted to Commodore to find a copy of a letter a SACO agent had intercepted. Written by Emblanc, it proudly announced that he had gotten Miles fired from SACO.

But even as Emblanc's false victory made him look ridiculous, the de Gaulle camp had won out over the Giraud side on the international stage, and the Meyniers had lost their guardian angel. Henri Giraud lost the copresidency of the French Committee of National Liberation in November 1943, leaving Charles de Gaulle sole leader of the Free French and in sole command of the Meynier group. Previously, the expenses for the group had been split between SACO and the French, but Miles was notified that the French were taking over a hundred percent of the cost, and thus, a hundred percent of command.

By then, the OSS had lost interest in the Meyniers, and requests for equipment such as radios went unanswered. But the bitterest blow came in the form of a visit by Captain Mullens of the Air Ground Aid Service, the White House-sponsored group charged with saving downed pilots in Asia. He asked that Meynier's people discontinue their pilot rescue program. The Meyniers were baffled; they were the only rescue group active in Indochina. But Mullens said that the AGAS simply did not trust them.[64]

This was the last straw. Charles de Gaulle recalled Robert Meynier in the summer of 1944, but by then, Robert and Katiou were more than ready to get out of China. In contrast to their joyous arrival, their departure was bitter and sad. But the contacts they had established continued to feed information to Miles until the end of the war. Long after the Meyniers were gone, their work contributed directly to a successful U.S. Navy attack on Japanese ships in Cam Ranh Bay.[65]

FATHER BEC WAS NOT THE ONLY CATHOLIC PRIEST to work with SACO and the OSS. Bishop Thomas Megan, an American Catholic missionary, connected with Miles and Donovan through his long-standing relationship with Dai Li. The bishop's career as a devout servant of the Church, spy, and underground organizer could have supplied enough material for an adventure comic strip all his own.

Megan, born in 1899, grew up on a farm in Eldora, Iowa, an intelligent boy constantly in trouble at school for smoking, chewing tobacco, and acting up. After nearly being expelled twice in one year, his father sent him to a Catholic missionary academy in the Chicago suburbs. Visions of exploring the wild streets of the city prompted him to accept his father's decision, but he was surprised to find his vocational calling there, taking a post in China in 1926 soon after his ordination. He would spend the next twenty years in northern China growing a congregation of ten thousand, leading an order of monks who tended the wounded in the battlefield, and spying for the Americans and Nationalist Chinese in the fight against the Japanese and Communists. Missionary work turned out to suit him well. Sporting a goatee, wearing traditional Chinese robes, and fond of painting the town with visitors, he thrived in the freedom that was possible far from the judging eyes of Iowa, Chicago, or Rome.

As Prelate of the Catholic mission in Xinxiang, a city about three hundred miles east of Xi'an in Henan Province, Megan worked in Japanese-occupied territory north of the Yellow River. When the Sino–Japanese war broke out in July 1937, the bishop became a hero to the people of Xinxiang after he negotiated with a Japanese officer in Xinxiang's forced surrender. The residents credited him with saving their lives.

Three years later, he inherited leadership of the Little Brothers of St. John the Baptist from Father Vincent Lebbe, who had come to China from Belgium in 1900. Lebbe founded the Little Brothers as stretcher-bearers during Chiang Kai-shek's campaign against the warlords in the 1920s. Their heroic service came to the attention of Dai Li in 1937 during a terrible battle against the Japanese in Shanxi Province, prompting Dai to help Lebbe expand the mission to nursing and lay activities such as making shoes and uniforms.

Lebbe, a long-standing enemy of Zhou Enlai dating back to a rivalry over the hearts and minds of Chinese students in the 1920s, was captured and tortured by the Chinese Communists in spring 1940. He died less than two weeks after Chiang Kai-shek secured his release, leaving Megan in charge of the Little Brothers. Through this monastic mercy mission, the bishop became good friends with Dai, whom he counted among the most capable Chinese he had ever met.[66] Working with Dai, Megan developed an extensive intelligence network of Catholic laity and monks.

On December 4, 1941, a Japanese military officer paid a surprise visit to the Xinxiang mission. He assured Megan that, should war break out between the United States and Japan, the twelve priests at the mission would still be safe, as they were performing humanitarian work. In addition, three of the priests were Germans and hence Japanese allies.[67]

The visit left Megan uneasy. He immediately began plans to evacuate the Americans to safety south of the Yellow River, leaving the mission in the hands of the Germans. But the other priests wanted to stay. On December 8, Megan and another American priest escaped just as Japanese soldiers burst into the mission compound with guns drawn, demanding, "Where is the bishop?"

The remaining American priests were rounded up as enemy aliens and placed in an internment camp, while a bounty of 10,000 yuan was offered for the capture of Bishop Thomas Megan. The priests endured grueling interrogations as the Japanese tried to find out where the bishop could be hiding. Megan and the other priest slipped into the mountains, where they knew the Japanese would not venture. Some weeks later, disguised as coolies, they boarded a ferry full of laborers and crossed to the south side of the Yellow River.

For the next two years, Megan ran a Catholic mission and continued his clandestine activities at Luoyang about one hundred twenty miles from Xinxiang on the "safe" side of the river. But in 1944, when the Japanese began their big push south, Luoyang was caught directly in their path. Megan had to flee because he still had a price on his head, but the timing could not have been worse. He was needed in Luoyang. His priestly work now included famine relief, as war and weather had destroyed food production, leading to mass starvation in the region. Despairingly, Megan closed the mission and headed west on a bicycle.

When members of SACO in Xi'an first ran into Megan in the summer of 1944, he had once again assumed the tough-guy image of his youth. He spoke fluent Chinese, wore Chinese clothes or SACO-style khakis, carried two guns, and made his own corn whiskey. He raced jeeps through the streets of the ancient city with all the confidence and recklessness of a New York cab driver. With SACO, he found shelter, companionship, and easy communication with Dai. His connections, language skills, superior marksmanship, and natural talent for espionage made him indispensable to SACO and the OSS, although he worked without an official appointment for a year. He exposed eight double agents working for the Japanese in Xi'an and managed an underground network of Catholics across northern China. When a U.S. military plane crashed nearby with the key to army secret codes on board, he came to the rescue as no one else could. He located the wreck through his spy network, commandeered a jeep to get to the site along with a county official to help him find it, and personally recovered the secret code in a bundle of cash hidden by a bewildered farmer.[68]

The OSS officially hired Megan in May 1945. The bishop and his band of holy spies solved the operational dilemma that had hindered the United States since the start of the war. Northern China was rich with Japanese activity worthy of intelligence, but it was also the Communists' stronghold. U.S. intelligence could not operate in the area without cooperating with the Communists and thus antagonizing the Nationalists. Nearly everything the United States attempted to do in that part of China stepped on someone's toes. But Megan, although a Nationalist sympathizer, was able to work entirely under the Communist radar. He continued to deliver until the war ended.

The Japanese had seized the mission in Xinxiang in late 1941. After they withdrew from China, the mission compound bounced between Nationalist and Communist control several times and was looted and severely damaged in the process.

Megan could not go back to the mission as long as the civil war raged, but he fully expected the Nationalists to prevail and planned to rebuild. He went back to the United States in 1947 to raise money for the new mission, but he was never to return to China. He suffered a stroke while serving as a parish priest and died in 1951.

PART 7

The Adventure's End

CHAPTER 19

It's All Over

MILTON MILES GOT HIS FIRST INKLING in May 1945 that the war was soon to end. The MBIS had intercepted a message from Japan's Emperor Hirohito to General Yamashita urging him to find a way to "conclude the war quickly and at little cost."[69] Indeed, Hirohito would repeat that position a month later in a meeting of the Supreme War Council. He said it was time to stop all talk of fighting to the last man and start thinking about how to end the war.[70]

In the months between this revelation and war's end, Miles suffered the death by a thousand cuts of his authority, his respect on the U.S. military stage, and his SACO. General Wedemeyer had won the day with the Joint Chiefs in April. Miles was officially under his command. But Chiang Kai-shek would not sign the document that made it so, and Wedemeyer believed it was due to Miles's conniving. Miles had nothing to do with it, but he had predicted it. And in true Chinese fashion, Chiang never refused outright to sign; he just never did it.

Before being placed under army command, Miles had operated like a sea captain, planning and executing his activities with his team, making independent decisions as they came up, and ordering supplies directly through Jeff Metzel in Washington. But the army way was all about conformity, not independence, an endless stream of forms, reports, and approvals up the chain of command. To contemporary army thinking, these steps prevented waste and ensured the most effective, coordinated effort. For Wedemeyer, who had stepped into a theater in disarray, enforcing the system was most urgent. Among other programs, he set up an administrative team, G-5, to monitor and control the activities, supplies, and expenses of SACO, the OSS, and similar groups conducting clandestine and quasi-military activities.

But in the eyes of Miles, G-5 was an unnecessary babysitter that slowed down every aspect of his program. The very notion that he should reveal plans for, say, blowing up a couple of barges was an intolerable security risk, as well as patently ridiculous. These were missions of opportunity and could not be planned months in advance. G-5 wanted to approve everything SACO did. They asked for mountains of reports on SACO resources, personnel, and plans in duplicate and triplicate with deadlines Miles could not possibly meet with his small staff. They read the "Enemy Shipping News" before it was distributed and changed the distribution list, removing the submarine commanders without consulting anyone. Before Miles could arrange an airdrop of medical supplies to a field hospital, for example, he had to specify the contents, weight, and dimensions of every package and specify whether the materials would be used to treat Americans or Chinese. G-5 would then decide whether it was an appropriate use of materials and flying time. Previously, he had simply called his friends at the 14th Air Force in Kunming, and they made the drop within a few days at their convenience.

These new army people were typical of the "high-hat, red-tape clerks" Miles had banned from SACO from the very start. He was annoyed by their paperwork, their patronizing attitudes toward the Chinese, and their menu choices. He believed G-5's processes existed entirely to keep SACO from doing anything at all, and indeed, after April 1945, SACO achieved nothing that was not already in the works and fully supplied.[71]

Another detail that rankled Miles was Wedemeyer's insistence that SACO was a quasi-military group and thus fell under the auspices of G-5. Miles defined "quasi" as "semi" or "partially." Although SACO conducted secret operations, Miles saw nothing that made it anything less than fully military. Although a purely semantic argument, it symbolized the profoundly different views the men held of the fundamental nature and even legitimacy of SACO.

To the China Theater Command, Miles came off as a hostile renegade gone native, jealously guarding his un-American fiefdom in Happy Valley at the cost of the war effort and the integrity of the United States. Wedemeyer particularly abhorred SACO's intimate connection to Dai Li, who was in Wedemeyer's view the most unsavory, despised figure and ruthless criminal in China. He firmly believed that the navy's association with the man brought shame to the United States and compromised national security.

But the most painful development of all for Miles was the mushrooming OSS. William Donovan had shaken off Miles, SACO, Dai Li, Claire Chennault, and AGFRTS, and was at last building the Dragon Plan of his dreams with full support of Wedemeyer. He seemed to be duplicating everything SACO had done but without Nationalist government involvement. Guerrilla training camps, coast watch stations, and even weather stations were in the works. Miles believed there was a move afoot to simply replace Chinese-American SACO with the all-American OSS. And he felt that the Americans behind the scheme were motivated by a notion of white supremacy, though loath to admit it even to themselves.

In June 1945, Miles saw proof that such a displacement scheme was indeed underway. General Wedemeyer had arranged a meeting with Chiang Kai-shek, Dai Li, and two Chinese army officers: General Chen Kai-ming, who was training Chinese soldiers with the OSS, and General Yi, commander of the SACO guerrillas. Wedemeyer was visibly miffed when he arrived at the Generalissimo's home to find Miles, whom Dai Li had urgently summoned. Wedemeyer had asked for the meeting to make a troop adjustment but had deliberately left Miles out. Now, like it or not, Miles would be in on his request to remove parts of SACO Columns Two and Four from the field and replace them with new OSS-trained troops.

Miles said nothing while the others discussed the plan's merits and drawbacks. Yi expounded on the excellent track record of the SACO troops and advantages of their intimate local knowledge. Chen emphasized the special training the new OSS troops had received. In a rare breach of protocol, Chiang and Dai discussed the issue in their obscure, native dialect, leaving everyone else in the room in the dark, including the translators. Everyone, that is, except for Miles, who had picked up some of the language over three years working closely with the two

Chinese leaders. Finally, Dai, still speaking in his childhood tongue, asked Miles for his opinion.

Miles said "no," and no it was. The decision certainly earned Miles no points with Wedemeyer.

WHEN WAR'S END FINALLY CAME, Miles was in the thick of battle. On a tour of coastal operations in late July, he and Dai Li had escaped death when their guards intercepted four trained assassins trying to get into their bedroom.[72] The next day, they got word that two Japanese columns were closing in on them, and they were clearly after the SACO leaders personally. As Miles, Dai, and their guards literally headed for the hills, they were caught in a developing pincer maneuver. Constantly on the move for days with little sleep, they managed to stay a few hours ahead of the Japanese soldiers, but Miles suffered a debilitating attack of malaria. Dai left him on a hilltop with guards and ran off to direct nearby Loyal Patriotic Army units to engage their pursuers from behind.

Miles lay helpless on the ground under a mountaintop tree, alternately shivering and sweating as the *Enola Gay* released its terrible payload some eight hundred miles away over Hiroshima on August 6. By the time the second bomb was dropped August 9 on Nagasaki, the LPA had routed one Japanese column, and the other was breaking up for lack of food and ammunition.

Throughout the fight, Dai returned at intervals to check on Miles, who was recovering thanks to frequent doses of aspirin and Atabrine. Dai brought vague news he had heard over the radio of a "big bomb," and hours later, foot messengers delivered the staggering story that the United States had wiped out two Japanese cities with atomic bombs. Dai got through by radio to a nearby communication station and found multiple messages for Miles from Chongqing. Japan had sued to end hostilities. Happy Valley wanted instructions, and Wedemeyer wanted Miles back at theater command headquarters in three days for an emergency conference.

With surrender on the near horizon, the Generalissimo ordered all troops to secure major cities, and on August 12, Miles issued an "All SACO" for Naval Group China personnel to go with their guerrilla units carrying weapons and radios and to do so as gentlemen. With the nearest airport three hundred fifty miles away, he sent a request for a plane to pick him up there in two days and scrambled to get a jeep and driver. Miraculously, he got to the airfield on time, but the plane was two days late, having first dropped off an army colonel at another city. Miles missed the conference.

IN THE HEADY DAYS after Japan accepted Allied surrender terms on August 14, local authorities across China treated American SACOs to lavish celebratory banquets featuring such delicacies as shark fin soup and, of course, plenty of *gambei* toasts. In Zhangzhou, elated residents paraded through the streets by torchlight, ending in the walled schoolyard of SACO coast watch headquarters. They cheered, set off firecrackers, and partied with the Americans late into the night.

But tensions remained high between the Japanese and the Allies. No one could be sure what his opponent knew or how he would react. Every encounter was like walking through a minefield.

The men of Camp Eight were ordered to shut down and proceed to Shanghai. After making their way to the coast, eight Americans and twenty Chinese under the command of U.S. Navy Lieutenant Livingston Swentzel appropriated a pair of fishing junks in the vicinity of Wenzhou on August 19 to sail up the coast for Shanghai some three hundred miles to the north. The fishermen piloted the boats with Swentzel commanding one and U.S. Marine Second Lieutenant Stewart Pittman in charge of the other. They divided what arms they had between the junks, each carrying a rocket-launching bazooka, a heavy machine gun, and assorted grenades and rifles.

The next day around 9:30 a.m., a large black junk loomed ahead of them. As Swentzel drew the two boats closer, the black junk turned broadside to reveal a 75-mm howitzer and Japanese crew. The howitzer fired and hit Swentzel's rudder, and the flying splinters injured an American army captain and a Chinese translator. Swentzel took over for the fishermen crew and sent them below for cover. He contacted Pittman by walkie-talkie and hoisted an American flag. The next blast from the howitzer sent Pittman's foremast crashing to the deck. The Japanese meanwhile strafed the small junks with machine gun fire, killing both Chinese machine gunners whose slick blood flowed over the decks.

The first couple of SACO rockets missed their marks, a serious setback with each boat having only five rounds. But Pittman erected a jury mast and maneuvered his junk in position to disable the howitzer and kill its crew. According to differing accounts, either machine gun fire or a perfectly landed bazooka rocket put it out of commission, but in either case, Pittman's shipmates made the score. With the big gun silenced, the little boats closed in, and a rocket hit the black junk square in the side, producing a terrible spray of wood shards and human flesh. Three more rockets hit their marks, and the small junks circled the black giant with guns blazing, ready to fling the grenades onto the deck when the ammunition ran out.

But it never came to that. The Japanese signaled their surrender with a dirty white t-shirt impaled on a bayonet. At 10:15 a.m., Swentzel boarded the Japanese vessel to find forty-four of its eighty-three men dead and thirty-five wounded. On the SACO side, four Chinese had been killed, and four Chinese and one American wounded. The Japanese lieutenant surrendered his sword to his American counterpart. The final naval battle of World War II and the last ever U.S. Navy firefight under sail was over.

All three junks limped back to the nearest port of Haiman, with Americans and Chinese at the helms. The men of Camp Eight turned over their prisoners and captured junk to Chinese authorities and had repairs made to the fishing boats. Getting back underway at last, they entered Shanghai on September 2 to find relations with the Japanese precarious. When they sailed up the Huangpu River and landed in the fashionable district of the Shanghai Bund, a group of Japanese soldiers detained them at gunpoint for hours until some Chinese troops toting machines guns broke up the standoff and took the Americans to the home of a SACO general.

TO THE SOUTH AT ZHANGZHOU, a SACO photographer pulled an audacious stunt that drew cheers from his peers and jeers from his superiors. He helped himself to a SACO sampan specially fitted with an outboard motor and chugged down the river to Xiamen, where a Japanese force still occupied the garrison. Climbing onto the dock, he stood face to face with a Japanese general and some fifty soldiers. He demanded surrender, and the general complied, turning over his sword. The officer was gracious, promising in perfect English to cooperate with the U.S. Navy. One can only imagine what went through his mind as the brazen enlisted man confronted him.

Back at Zhangzhou headquarters, the photographer who brandished his prize was showered with kudos from his friends, but the celebration was brief.

His prank had been a major breach of international military decorum, and the officers in Zhangzhou and Chongqing were furious. Orders went out to all SACO that no one but a Chinese general was to accept the surrender sword of a Japanese officer. The photographer spent the rest of his tour confined to quarters.[73]

THE WAR WAS OVER, but the work of the war machine cranked up several notches. There were endless decisions to be made, logistics to be arranged, bills to be paid, and paperwork to be filed while eight million American service personnel around the globe jockeyed for transportation home.

Miles and Dai discussed the future of SACO. First and foremost, they would maintain the hard-fought weather net under Chinese command and continue to feed its data to the U.S. Navy. Chiang Kai-shek was keen on starting a new school with American instructors to build the foundation for a modern Chinese navy. Dai and Miles also hoped to keep Camps Three and Four open for gathering intelligence on the Soviets, whose long history of supporting the Chinese Communist Party posed a growing threat to the Nationalists. The Soviets had declared war on Japan and entered Manchuria in early August. Though they did so with Allied support, it paved the way for a Communist occupation.

Predictably, Wedemeyer and Miles did not see eye to eye on the postwar fate of SACO. Wedemeyer wanted to shut it down within a week, while Miles favored a slower winding down to allow the Chinese to take over weather and communications operations. Miles also proposed a separate navy command in China going forward, but Wedemeyer lobbied to keep navy and army under joint command, including the weather service. On this last point, Miles strongly objected because the forecast needs of the army and those of the navy were entirely different, and he feared that the navy's priorities would be swamped by those of the army. The two officers submitted their divided opinions in writing by order of the Joint Chiefs.

Meanwhile, the navy had awarded Miles a wartime promotion to rear admiral as the senior naval officer in China on August 13. He flew to Shanghai on September 4 to bring the city under control and begin preparations for the U.S. Navy 7th Fleet to make a triumphal entrance.

At the airport, SACOs and friends greeted him like a conquering hero. SACO pioneer Webb Heagy, combat champions Joe Champe and "Swede" Swentzel, and Camp Six commander Si Morris met the plane, along with a host of LPA troops. A long file of pirates shot off firecrackers indiscriminately like so many school children.

Naval Group China set up shop at the Glen Line Building, an office building on the riverfront. Four flags snapped in the sea air on the rooftop: the Chinese flag, the Stars and Stripes, a two-star flag signifying rear admiral headquarters, and the "What the Hell?" pennant.

The cast of Shanghai characters Dai enlisted to help Rear Admiral Miles must have made Wedemeyer's hair stand on end (if he even knew about it). Du Yue-sheng served as point man, recruiter of work crews, and general problem solver. Miles characterized him as a somewhat shady labor leader, and indeed, he had organized the city's rickshaw drivers, stevedores, and porters. But his reach went far beyond labor unions. He had been the leading crime boss of old Shanghai for three decades, in charge of all manner of criminal activities from the opium trade to slavery, and head of the Green Gang that had done the dirty work in Chiang Kai-shek's purge of the Communists in 1927. Du was an unusually tall, lean man who went around in ankle-length silk robes trimmed with genuine shrunken monkey heads to protect him from enemies. He lived in an absurdly opulent mansion that later was converted to a hotel after he fled the city ahead of the Communist takeover in 1949.

Also at Miles's service was the pirate king Chang Gui Fong and his four thousand followers.

For Miles's personal transportation, Du secured a car once owned by the Shanghai police chief, a former Japanese collaborator who had left the country. It was an American import custom made in 1925 for Al Capone. The protective cocoon on wheels sported a bulletproof gas tank and windows, half-inch-thick steel venetian blinds, and convenient side slots to accommodate tommy gun barrels.

Miles's first priority in Shanghai was to bring neglected and damaged power plants back up to full strength. Strategic use of pirates and military guards had prevented sabotage after the Japanese surrendered, but the plants were cranking out less than thirty percent of capacity. Pirate crews cleaned up the power facilities and then started cleaning the streets. Shanghai utility workers in conjunction with navy electricians made repairs.

THROUGH IT ALL, Miles was still fighting malaria and working twenty hours a day putting the city in order, establishing a communications system, commanding the local Chinese troops, procuring quarters for his team and the throngs of navy personnel to arrive with the fleet, and dealing with attacks on SACO from Wedemeyer and his colleagues.* He was taking liberal doses of aspirin and Atabrine and began supplementing them with uppers and downers to keep up his grueling schedule and then crash when he could grab a few hours of sleep. The pill popping and inadequate rest had a devastating effect on his state of mind.

During World War II, Atabrine was issued to all members of the armed forces working in malaria-infested areas. Many men resisted taking it in light of myths that it caused impotence, but in some cases it in fact had a serious side effect: temporary psychosis.[74] Miles later admitted that he certainly exceeded the recommended dosage because he often lost track of what he had taken and thought a double dose was better than none. Compounding this with Benzedrine and sleeping pills, he descended into a very strange psychological place. When Admiral Thomas Kincaid, commander of the 7th Fleet, saw Miles in Shanghai on September 16, he detected signs of "war shock."

In his impaired mental state, Miles believed he was perfectly rational until he looked back on it. He could not remember certain events in which he had been most active. His professional self-editing function had evaporated, leading him to make foolish comments to his superiors, some, unfortunately, in writing. He wrote to a navy liaison officer that the future of the navy in China depended on getting out from under the army, whose red tape only hindered operations, and those remarks ended up on the desks of Wedemeyer and the Joint Chiefs out of context.

Miles's blurry state continued for weeks. On September 19, the 7th Fleet sailed into Shanghai. Beautiful women greeted the gleaming ships with enormous armloads of flowers. Cheering crowds, bunting, and firecrackers marked the festive moment that confirmed the war was really over. Miles had directed all the arrangements and was on center stage.

---

* Shanghai had become a gathering point for military personnel in China waiting to go home, but Miles didn't know it at the time. He was preoccupied with getting ready for the fleet, a daunting task.

Wedemeyer had flown in from Chongqing for the celebration and pressed Miles for a private conference. After a full day of ceremonies and parties, they finally caught up with each other as Wedemeyer was preparing for bed. Instead of allowing Wedemeyer to steer the conversation, an exhausted and foggy Miles launched into a long harangue about SACO's accomplishments. He said that his group and the 14th Army Air Force were the only Americans who had actually done anything worthwhile in China. They would have done even better if not for the army's roadblocks. Miles must have said more, but he had only a sketchy memory of the night. Wedemeyer was flabbergasted and brusquely refused to take any more.

On September 21, Miles flew back to Happy Valley. His staff sensed that he was coming unhinged, but with no experienced senior officers present, no one stepped up to confront him. The next day, he had lunch at the Press Hostel in Chongqing and, with his mind racing, invited all the reporters to a Happy Valley press conference the next morning where they would learn the real truth about the China Theater. Luckily, he had enough wits about him to cancel the conference before the day was over, but army and navy officers heard about it nevertheless and dispatched a team to Happy Valley to prevent it.

That night after dinner, Miles gathered the SACOs for one of his famous tea talks. The subject was the atomic bomb. He gave a detailed but incoherent description of the technology and its deployment with rambling sidebars on obliquely related topics. He was still talking after everyone had gone to bed and the lights were shut off. Someone finally coaxed him to his room.

Miles woke up the next morning feeling rested and opened the door to find an armed guard outside. He was under house arrest. A physician arrived and confiscated his razor. Next came SACOs Si Morris and Chief Yeoman Ward Smith, who sat with Miles for hours while he continued to babble. This time it was about unpaid bills and cash in a safe in his Shanghai office. Smith scribbled frantically in a notebook to take it all down in case anything Miles said could later be used to help his cause. Dai Li kept his distance, knowing that he was the root of Miles's trouble with Wedemeyer. During the next few days as Miles's body chemistry returned to normal, he began to recover his senses.

Miles was feeling back to normal but still confined to quarters a few days later when Chiang Kai-shek sent a pair of emissaries, General Mao Jen-Feng and monk-turned-general Pan Qiwu, the beloved SACO liaison, on a precious errand.

In a bittersweet ceremony more appropriate to a crowded parade ground than the confines of Miles's bedroom, they bestowed on him China's highest national security award, the Order of the White Cloud and Golden Banner. They festooned him with a broad, red and white sash and two enormous medals and read the Generalissimo's glowing commendation aloud.

By September 29, Miles was feeling like himself again when a plane arrived at Chongqing to take him back to Washington, along with Morris, Ward, and four other SACOs. Beyerly in Shanghai had assumed SACO command. Wedemeyer had brushed aside Kincaid's suggestion of a special navy flight, insisting on making the travel arrangements. If his aim had been to sling a final insult at Miles, he could not have chosen better. Miles was to fly home in an aging C-54 transport plane with canvas seats and no amenities. At a stopover in Shanghai, Dai Li came to the airport to meet the plane. It was the last time Miles and Dai ever saw each other.

A FEW DAYS EARLIER in Washington, D.C., the shutdown of the OSS ended the SACO–OSS rivalry. General William Donovan's hopes for continuing his agency during peacetime died with President Roosevelt. President Harry Truman felt growing distain for the scandal-ridden OSS, and Donovan's Washington enemies saw to it that none of his political maneuvers and private memos about the heroics of Missouri-born OSS agents changed the president's mind. On September 25, Donovan presided over OSS closing ceremonies, held in a skating rink. Each employee received a golden OSS lapel pin—provided he was willing to pay a dollar for it.[75]

The sudden end of the war with Japan caught the navy and everyone else unawares.

Sal Ciaccio, one of the Scouts and Raiders stranded in Kolkata since February, was finally shaken loose for duty in China in early August. Bound for a survey mission, his team was on the way to Fuzhou when Japan surrendered, and their plane landed at a Japanese-held airfield in China. It was an unnerving moment as the SACOs descended to the airstrip, but the Japanese treated them as honored guests, offering good food and respect.

Despite Miles's All SACO message, some eighteen hundred SACOs were scattered in small groups all over China. They slowly received orders for Chongqing and Shanghai, where they hoped it would be only a matter of days before they were heading home. But for most, it was a matter of months.

When Camp Six packed up to move to Zhangzhou headquarters in August, Storekeeper Clayton Mishler wondered what would become of all the locals who had come to rely on the camp doctor for treatment.

Like service members around the globe, he began adding up his points and dreaming of home. The U.S. armed forces had established a point system for returning personnel to the United States. Points were awarded according to time served, time overseas, time in combat, number of minor children, and other factors. But in September, Mishler received the disheartening news that as an essential storekeeper, the point system did not apply to him.

By October, twelve lucky men had been sent to Shanghai to await transport home. Those who remained moved to the Sea View Hotel on the island of Gulangyu and raised the U.S. flag as well as the "What the Hell?" pennant. Don Bell, the correspondent who had recuperated at Camp Six following his rescue from a plane crash, found out where the SACOs were and sent twenty-seven cases of beer to the hotel.

While on Gulangyu, Mishler's duties were light. He spent his free time exploring Xiamen with his houseboy Mickey, who had become his dear friend. They passed an internment facility for Japanese civilians, older couples who had lived in the city for years. The large, open buildings had no interior walls or furniture and were eerily quiet. Family groups squatted on straw mats around small clay firepots making tea and nodded silently in greeting as Mishler and Mickey walked by. At the abandoned garrison, Mishler helped blow up a battery of artillery guns the Japanese had left behind. One had a spine-chilling chart painted on the front with yardages and elevations for visible targets. Two of these targets were SACO coast watch stations, including the mountaintop pagoda that the Japanese had knocked down months earlier.

As autumn wore on, twelve SACOs received the coveted orders for Shanghai. The day after seeing them off, Mishler and three other men got word that they would remain stationed at Gulangyu "until further notice." The others were two pharmacists' mates and Mishler's beloved superior officer, Lieutenant Junior Grade Malcolm Lovell, whom he had served for most of his tour.

The weeks passed by. Thanksgiving came and went, and the group was getting testy. Then orders finally came for Lovell and the two pharmacists to proceed to Shanghai. Mishler began to wonder if he was to end up alone and forgotten in the Sea View Hotel. Christmas was coming, and he decided to take matters into his own hands. He typed up his own orders and coaxed Lovell to sign them. In a matter of weeks, the four "until further notice" men were in Shanghai.

THE CITY HAD BECOME the seat of China Theater Command and was bursting at the seams with military personnel from all over the world. Most of them were stuck in limbo waiting to be sent home. There were not enough planes and ships to handle everyone, and in Shanghai, the problem was compounded by the repatriation program for Japanese nationals. Americans resented having to wait in line while the people they had defeated took priority, but getting the Japanese home was in the interest of all parties.

For the men of SACO, it was a shock to be back in the world of salutes, spit-and-polish, and formal observances of rank. They had no official navy uniforms and had to scramble to get them or risk being targeted by the military police for wearing featureless khakis. Those who arrived in Shanghai in September were able to get local tailors to make them uniforms inexpensively, but by December, the tailors were swamped and prices were high.

SACOs were not the only ones uncomfortable with the rules. In the *Shanghai Stars and Stripes,* a newspaper written by and for enlisted men of all branches of the service, men began writing in with complaints about salutes, public inspection of their pocket buttons, and other details of military protocol. It seemed inappropriate treatment for adults who had volunteered to serve their country, finished the job, and were now trapped in military service until the machine could find a way to send them home. They especially resented having to salute in the streets thick with officers. An enlisted man might have to salute a dozen times per city block while packed shoulder to shoulder and risk bonking another pedestrian in the eye.

General Wedemeyer was sympathetic to these complaints. On November 16, he ordered that public saluting was no longer required except while on official business. He also ended reserved seating for officers in movie theaters.[76] Measures such as these paid off months later when angry protests among American servicemen trapped in foreign countries began all over the world. Shanghai demonstrations were few and orderly.

To placate the homesick Americans, the *Shanghai Stars and Stripes* sponsored an army–navy football game on December 1 with full China Theater Command support. The festivities began with a rickshaw race to the stadium gates. Roughly 1.5 million people turned out to watch nineteen crack drivers run a three-and-a-half-mile course with smiling American military women riding in the flower-draped cabs. All drivers received cash prizes, and the winner, who completed the course in just over eighteen minutes, got an extra bonus. His passenger was crowned Miss Rickshaw 1945 and Queen of the Army–Navy Game.

On the football field, three SACOs contributed to the navy's victory over the army before a packed stadium. Lieutenant Phil H. Bucklew, who had played for two seasons in the National Football League for the Cleveland Rams before joining the navy, coached the navy team. The twin brothers of SACO, Coxswains Keith E. Allen and Johnny G. Lough, were among the players. The day was chilly but sunny, and twenty thousand fans ate hotdogs courtesy of the Red Cross. The final score was twelve to nothing. The victory was especially sweet for the navy after losing to the army on Thanksgiving in the United States.

THE FOUR MEN FROM CAMP SIX missed the fun, arriving in Shanghai on December 15. Mishler had a nagging fear that someone would discover his self-written orders. He must have been alarmed when he was called before a navy board in Shanghai, but as it turned out, it was not a disciplinary action. They offered to promote him to ensign if he would stay in China another year. Although it would have more than doubled his salary, he said no. He was twenty-six and had been away from his wife for more than two years. It was time to go home.

Two weeks later, he was in San Francisco.

CHAPTER 20

Wrapping Up and Looking Back

BY THE TIME JAPAN SURRENDERED and the war was over, China Theater Commander General Albert Coady Wedemeyer so despised SACO and its connection with the dreaded Dai Li that he wanted it shut down within a week. Logistically, Rear Admiral Milton Miles could not have done so even if he had wanted to. Nevertheless, he, General Dai, and Generalissimo Chiang Kai-shek agreed that SACO had "fulfilled its mission and come to a conclusion on 4 September 1945."[77] On September 30, Naval Group China was dissolved, and Miles's rank reverted to captain.[78] It was still another six months before China and the United States formally dissolved the SACO Agreement, on March 1, 1946.[79]

But Dai Li still held hopes that Americans would continue to train his guerrillas at Happy Valley even if he had to hire them himself. Ensign Donald Leu had arrived in Chongqing in August and trained twelve hundred guerrillas before he got orders to return home in early 1946. Dai tried to get him to stay on, tempting him with a promotion, a generous salary, and a large house fully staffed with servants. At a callow twenty-three years old, Leu found the deal irresistible and dashed off a telegram to his wife in North Dakota. She, however, had no desire to spend a year on the other side of the world with a toddler in tow no matter what the benefits, and so Leu went back to the United States in early March.

The Leus' decision proved to be fortunate, because Dai would not have been able to make good on his promises. He died in a plane crash weeks after the ensign turned him down.

ON MARCH 17 AT 9:45 A.M., Dai Li and seven other passengers took off from the coastal city of Qingdao bound for Shanghai, about four hundred fifty miles to the south, in a plane with no radar. The weather was not promising, but Dai had the pilot load enough fuel so the destination could be changed to Nanjing or Chongqing en route if necessary. As the plane neared Shanghai, the pilot learned that the city was engulfed in heavy rain, so he headed for Nanjing, only to find himself flying smack into a thunderstorm. By radio, he announced first that he was turning back and then that he was coming into Nanjing after all. At 1:13 p.m., the pilot reported that he was beginning his descent. That was the last message.

Residents of Daishan, a village at the foot of Horse Saddle Mountain southwest of Nanjing, heard a plane that seemed to be flying too low. They saw it clip a tree, slam into the mountain, and erupt into a huge fireball.

A U.S. Navy reconnaissance plane found the wreck that night, followed soon by MBIS agents on the ground. There were no survivors. Investigators identified Dai Li's charred remains by shreds of long underwear, his gold front teeth, and the snubnose pistol Miles had given him the first day they met. Chiang Kai-shek wept for the loss of his staunchly loyal servant and friend of more than twenty-five years.

The aftermath of Dai's death proved an apt conclusion to his controversial, mystery-laden life. Admirers, friends, and enemies immediately began concocting stories of his untimely demise much more intriguing than a plane running into a thunderstorm and crashing. Some believed that a gun battle onboard between the spymaster and a Communist general had set the plane on fire. Others said Dai staged the crash and was not on the plane at all, but had escaped to America to elude his enemies. Many claimed that the aircraft had been sabotaged either by the Communists or the OSS.

In the eyes of World War II China scholar Maochun Yu, the sabotage theories are not that far-fetched. He cites two former OSS operatives who credited the agency with the crash. Edwin Putzell, William Donovan's executive officer and a member of his innermost circle, was at the OSS chief's side when he locked the agency doors in Washington for the last time.[80] Putzell said in a 1994 interview that the OSS played a role in Dai's death. OSS gadget master Stanley Lovell even described the device used: It was a bomb he had designed to explode in the air when the craft reached five thousand feet and that could be affixed to the tail of a plane from the outside.[81]

Yet witnesses said the plane did not catch fire until it hit the ground.[82]

Historians even disagree about why Dai was so intent on reaching Shanghai in the first place. One explanation is that he was hurrying to see his mistress, screen actress Hu Die, and wanted to find out whether her divorce was final so they could get married.[83] Another says he wanted to say good-bye to U.S. Navy Admiral Charles Cooke, who was supporting Dai's appointment to head a nascent Chinese Navy.[84] Neither of these explanations accounts for his willingness to fly to Nanjing or Chongqing instead. Miles claimed Dai was just characteristically impatient and wanted to get to Nanjing to tell the Generalissimo about a favor he had done for Admiral Cooke.[85]

In Washington, Milton Miles had fully recovered from multiple infections and self-medication and was working in the Office of Naval History when he received word of Dai's death. He made immediate plans to attend the funeral, only to be denied permission by General George Marshall, then President Truman's envoy to China. Marshall, in the midst of delicate negotiations with the Nationalists and Communists, feared that an official American presence at the funeral would alienate the Communists.

A year later, Miles was back in China as commander of the USS *Columbia*. As a private citizen in civilian clothes, he attended Dai Li's elaborate final burial outside Nanjing. He had a pair of winter plum trees planted at the tomb entrance. The trip back to Shanghai after the ceremony took three days as former SACO guerrilla units repeatedly stopped Miles's train to honor him.

In 1949, the Communists desecrated Dai's tomb and uprooted the trees after the Nationalists had fled to Taiwan. Pan Qiwu, the monk-turned-general who had worked with SACO when Dai was away, later planted two new winter plum trees on Miles's behalf outside a memorial to Dai Li near Taipei.

ALTHOUGH EVEN DEATH did not free Dai from the political quagmire swallowing SACO, most of the men of SACO were not even aware of the infighting. Thus they managed to achieve most of what Admiral Ernest King had hoped for. After more that a year of frustration and failed experiments, the weather net and coast watches came through for the Pacific Fleet and Army Air Force. SACO sabotage teams fulfilled their mission to harass the enemy, and the SACO guerrillas inflicted enough casualties to force the Japanese to take precautions against attacks. Miles gave SACO guerrilla columns credit for as many as seventy-one thousand casualties,[86] but his son Charles Miles compiled more modest numbers from his father's records. By Charles's reckoning, SACO and the Chinese guerrilla columns they supported killed 26,717 Japanese and puppet troops, wounded 8,702, and captured 346. They sunk 35 enemy steamers, blew up 158 bridges, and destroyed 66 locomotives.[87]

Five American SACOs were killed while serving, but only one from enemy fire. A pharmacist's mate was killed in a plane while treating an injured passenger as the aircraft was attacked over Burma. Two radiomen died accidentally when a bomb went off by mistake. One man was killed in a rifle range accident in Kolkata, and one died in a truck accident on Stilwell Road in Burma. The numbers of Japanese versus Americans killed are ridiculously lopsided for two reasons. First, relatively few American SACOs served in the line of fire. Second, guerrillas by definition did not go into action unless they had a decided advantage over the enemy, either in numbers or location.

AMERICAN SACOs WERE DISHEARTENED to discover that the end of the war with Japan only meant the beginning of another for the Chinese. The United States sent fifty thousand marines to northeast China to prevent Communist troops from moving in as the Japanese withdrew. U.S. Ambassador Patrick Hurley and General George Marshall each made futile attempts to broker some kind of coalition between the Nationalist Chinese government and the Communists. But none of these measures could prevent a showdown twenty years in the making.

By July 1946, full-scale civil war had broken out. Although Chiang started out with more soldiers and equipment, Mao and the Communists patiently built their war machine and political support while waiting for the overextended Nationalists to crumble. By 1948, the Communists began pushing south. On October 1, 1949, Mao declared the People's Republic of China in its new capital, Beijing, and on December 10, Chiang Kai-shek and two million supporters retreated to Taiwan, new seat of the Republic of China.

Thus began a stalemate between two Chinas that continues as of 2012.

CHINA HAD SEEPED INTO THE VERY BONES of men like Clayton Mishler, Roger Moore, and John Ryder Horton. At a stage in life when all the world was fresh, they had bonded to an utterly exotic land and people that few Americans had ever seen.

Although Mishler witnessed his share of tragedy and violence, he viewed China through the lens of a poet. He found a magical place where gentle duckmen led files of fowl to the rice paddies each morning to feed and then scooped up the eggs they laid before guiding them back into the city for the night.

As a photographer, Moore looked at the country through a literal lens. He was drawn to the cheerful, courageous working people who were undaunted by poverty and the relentless struggle of daily life. He spent his idle months after the war in the streets of Shanghai capturing their images, from a dockworker on a smoke break to a pretty girl selling knitting needles. Galleries in Shanghai, Hong Kong, and the National Museum of the Pacific War in Fredericksburg, Texas, exhibited the photographs in 2009 and 2010.

Horton found the Chinese—their penchant for making empty promises, their poker-faced corruption, and their stubbornness—maddening. But as soon as he left China, all he had been through became a lost treasure—the half-starved men who risked everything for one good crack at the enemy, the wonderful taste of pork, and the bond with his men united by terror and success.

The singular experience in China intensified the fast and deep connections men commonly forge while sharing the horrors and boredom of war. But while these military-born friendships normally give way to time, space, and responsibility like summer love affairs, SACOs have miraculously hung together. In 1955, the veterans of the Rice Paddy Navy first reunited on Cape Cod in Massachusetts for a weekend of *gambei* toasts and stories. They have continued to meet annually in cities from coast to coast to toast their "perpetual skipper," Milton "Mary" Miles, and hoist the "What the Hell?" pennant. Seventeen veterans attended the 2011 reunion with members of their extended families who are now forging their own friendships while perpetuating the story of SACO.

Milton Miles was the star attraction at the first few gatherings when navy duties allowed him to attend. After SACO, he recovered his health and went on to serve as Director of Pan-American Affairs for the navy and later as Commandant of the 15th Naval District based in Balboa, Panama. He retired from the navy as a Vice Admiral in 1958. When he turned sixty, Chiang Kai-shek sent him a scroll that read, "Two men in the same boat help each other." Liu Shih-feng, Miles's cook dating back to the Fairy Cave days, came to the United States to comfort Miles and cook up his favorite dishes during his last illness. Miles died of cancer in Bethesda Naval Hospital on March 25, 1961, just shy of his sixty-first birthday.

IN THE UNITED STATES, the Sino–American Cooperative Organization is an obscure slice of history largely known only to scholars, a smattering of history buffs, and the families of those who served in it. But in the People's Republic of China, the government has exercised a victor's prerogative to write its own version of history. Every child knows about SACO as a prison where Americans teamed up with the Military Bureau of Information Statistics to torture and murder enemies of the Guomindang.

The story took root thanks to an historical novel entitled *Red Crag,* published in China in 1961. The book describes in detail a heinous "SACO Prison" run by the Guomindang and American interrogation experts in the hills outside Chongqing. Written by Luo Guanbin and Yang Yiyan, actual survivors of a mass prison killing in 1949—four years after the end of the war in the Pacific—on the former grounds of Happy Valley, its pages are full of sinister Americans presiding over unspeakable atrocities committed against brave Communist revolutionaries. The Chinese heroes remain faithful to their cause and to their comrades in the face of inhuman suffering. *Red Crag,* a runaway bestseller read by millions of Chinese of all ages, inspired intense hostility toward Americans and patriotic fervor.

At the novel's climax, taking place on November 27, 1949, the Guomindang shoots hundreds of political prisoners and sets fire to the buildings in which the bodies lay as the Red Army closes in on Chongqing. A handful of prisoners escape.

A real-life survivor of this event, Fu Boyong, recounted his experience to Hugh Deane, an American journalist and East Asia scholar. The prisoners were rounded up and taken to cells in the lower level of Bai mansion, which SACO had once used as a guesthouse.[88] Soldiers splattered the cells with machine gun fire until the prisoners' screams and defiant strains of the "Internationale" ceased, then systematically shot each victim in the head. Some thirty people survived the slaughter. Fourteen escaped through an opening in the prison complex wall while the others were gunned down in their desperate dash across a courtyard.[89]

The story of the massacre was published in the *Shanghai News* in 1950. The article, part of a Chinese government campaign to incite anti-American zeal as the Korean War was heating up, emphasized the roles of SACO-trained and -armed police. It characterized SACO headquarters as a Nationalist Chinese–American facility whose primary business was the detention and brutal interrogation of Chinese political prisoners.[90]

This was precisely the outcome Davies, Gauss, Stilwell, Wedemeyer, and others had dreaded when they tried to shut down Camp Nine, Dai Li's American-supplied and -staffed FBI-style police academy next door to Happy Valley. They had warned that Dai Li's MBIS agents could potentially use the interrogation techniques taught at the school against Chiang Kai-shek's political enemies.[91] Even though the massacre occurred more than three years after Dai Li had died and the last American SACO had gone home, the remnants of the school provided fodder for the Communist propaganda machine to pin it on SACO.

The site of the massacre was retroactively named SACO Prison. A member of the Communist underground held there in 1948 never knew it by that name. To him, it was the Moral Education Institute.[92]

After the publication of *Red Crag*, Communist Party authorities capitalized on its emotion-charged portrayal of evil Americans in a manner far worse than the U.S. State Department's worst nightmares. In 1963, the PRC converted Happy Valley to a museum called "SACO: Crimes of America and Chiang." The Party recreated torture chambers, prison cells, and a detention hellhole called the Refuse Pit based on descriptions in the novel.

A sadist's dream toolkit of implements supposedly made in the United States was spread out on a rough-hewn wooden table. A huge photo of a pit filled with dead bodies wearing handcuffs stamped "Springfield, Massachusetts" served as evidence that Americans had taken part in the 1949 massacre. In Milton Miles's former house, the walls were covered with signs and photos depicting Miles as a crazed, reactionary naval officer unleashed on the innocent Chinese people, a precursor to the lunatic Colonel Walter Kurtz in the film *Apocalypse Now*.

The museum drew millions of visitors eager to pay respects to the *Red Crag* martyrs, not unlike Sherlock Holmes fans flocking to 221B Baker Street in London. But at the Chongqing museum, fiction had blended inseparably with history. School field trips brought busloads of children who shuddered in the torture chamber and watched teary-eyed as the red handkerchiefs they dropped over the tomb of the martyrs drifted down. Xujun Eberlein, born and raised in Chongqing and now residing in the United States, recalls making an emotional pilgrimage to the museum each year on November 27, her heart seething with hatred of Americans.

China's accusations thrust daggers into the hearts of SACO veterans. In the pages of their newsletter, they protested the demonization of their Perpetual Skipper and highlighted the holes in the Communist-constructed story. They insisted that SACO and the MBIS had maintained scrupulous separation, and that SACO's activities focused on fighting the Japanese.[93]

By the late 1980s, the Communist Party of China's official story began to unravel. Former SACO museum staffer Deng Youping wrote a scholarly article that listed by date of death the prisoners killed there. No deaths were recorded in the years 1943, 1944, or 1945. Fewer than twenty people were killed at the site prior to 1943, but hundreds after 1945. This article was not widely circulated. To get it past the censors, it fell short of claiming that the U.S. Navy was in China to fight the Japanese.[94]

By 2002, the museum's name was changed to the Gele Mountain Revolution Memorial Museum, and its atmosphere was transformed to that of a theme park, complete with a monumental sculpture in Red Crag Soul Square. The old anti-American message was still there, but it took a back seat to glorification of the martyrs.

Seven years later, the museum was having growing pains. SACO was depicted within a single exhibit both as an American-Chinese partnership fighting Japan and as an agency for the persecution of progressive Chinese. A museum employee said the anti-American sign just had not been changed yet. In an interview with Eberlein in 2009, long-time museum director Li Hua said that there was no connection between SACO and the prison. He blamed the museum's former anti-American claims on an historical "mix-up."[95]

DONALD LEU'S WIFE ANNE finally made it to Chongqing in 1997 on a tour of China with her husband, more than fifty years after she had declined to pack up and move there. Donald, a retired college professor and the father of six, had always yearned to return. If he visited the museum on the old site of Happy Valley, it did not dampen the experience, one of the most treasured of his charmed life. In the city, he met an elderly man who had trained at Happy Valley. Leu did not remember the vanished young face amid a thousand. But the old gentleman remembered Leu and wept at the sight of him.

John Ryder Horton also made a moving pilgrimage to China in 1986 with six other SACOs. Chinese authorities kept foreign tourists on a short leash at that time, but the group managed permission to visit the old site of Camp One, where Horton had been commander. The people of the surrounding farms, most too young to have any recollection of the war, gathered for a look at the Americans. As the party boarded the bus to leave, one elderly woman came forward, her face animated with laughter and streaked with tears, testament to forty-year-old memories. Horton's postwar career began with a master's degree in international relations, followed by thirty years in the Central Intelligence Agency. He retired to a tree farm in Maryland, where he wrote three spy thrillers and his war memoir, *Ninety-Day Wonder*.

The most prolific post-SACO writer was William Sanford LaSor, the chaplain who had toured the SACO camps of central China on horseback. He joined Fuller Theological Seminary in 1949 and stayed thirty years as a professor of the Old Testament. Holding six degrees in subjects ranging from chemistry to Oriental languages, he wrote seventeen books about the Bible, ancient biblical languages, and the Dead Sea Scrolls.

The other SACO chaplain, Msgr. Philip Shannon, remained a navy chaplain until 1959 at stations around the globe. After his navy service, he was the pastor of several Catholic parishes in New York City until his death in 1989.

He let loose once a year, removing his clerical collar to join "his boys" at SACO conventions.

Dr. Victor Goorchenko, the White Russian physician who performed the primitive, emergency appendectomy on Earl Randolph in the early days of SACO, was born in China of Russian parents. He served Camp One informally for the rest of the war while working with the United Nations Relief Association and was affectionately known as "Dr. Goo." After the war, he moved to California, raised a family, and became an eye surgeon.

Phil Bucklew, the victorious football coach in the Shanghai army–navy game, had joined SACO after receiving two Navy Crosses for his part in the Normandy Invasion as a member of the Scouts and Raiders. After the war, he coached football at Columbia University while completing his Ph.D. and then returned to active service in the navy. Known to military historians as the "Father of Naval Special Warfare," he was a founder of the Navy SEALs and commander of SEAL Team One as well as two underwater demolition units.

Although China's beauty and heart enchanted Clayton Mishler, as the war ended, he ached to get back to his new wife and get on with the business of adult life. He corresponded with his old houseboy Mickey until his last three letters were returned in the 1960s. After thirty-two years as an executive for the U.S. Veterans Administration hospital system, Mishler shared the enchantment he had discovered with his wife, traveling all over Asia and Europe. He had just completed the manuscript for his memoir, *Sampan Sailor,* when he died in 1992.

Roger Moore, Miles's photographer, was among the youngest SACOs, only nineteen when he arrived at Happy Valley in spring 1945. After the war, he put down his camera and took up a slide rule. For the next forty years, he engineered highway bridges and founded his own bridge contracting firm. Retiring to Florida, he launched an encore career as a photographer, photography teacher, and illustrator of children's books.

ON OCTOBER 10, 2011, Richard Rutan, Roger Moore, and nine other octogenarian SACO veterans sat in the open air on a lovely, flag-snapping day in Taipei. As guests of the Republic of China's Military Intelligence Bureau, they and their families had prime seats in the reviewing stand in front of the regal

Presidential Office Building to watch the pageantry marking the centennial of the founding of the republic. The ROC Marine Corps frogmen, clad only in camouflage shorts and white shoes, performed a precision martial arts drill punctuated by unison shouts. The Republic of China's answer to the Navy SEALs, their lineage could be traced to men like Matthew Komorowski-Kaye and Phil Bucklew, who brought unique skills and moxie to China nearly seventy years earlier.

Rutan felt like a prince throughout his visit as people showered him and his friends with gifts, friendship, and lavish hospitality, from luxury hotel suites to elaborate banquets. Military Intelligence Bureau staffers served as guides, and no detail was overlooked. ROC officials, in deference to the advanced age of their guests, retained a physician and a nurse to accompany the SACOs throughout their ten-day stay. The guides honored Moore's special request to visit a Buddhist temple, taking him on a private tour revealing its architecture and the most intimate details of spiritual practice. He even visited a special station where young singles meditate on finding a soulmate.

Although none of their hosts was old enough to remember World War II, they inherited the memory of SACO. The American veterans remain the Republic of China's tenuous connection to past happier relations with the United States. These men had shared the Nationalists' golden triumph over Japan in 1945 but were gone before the republic's own spiral of defeat in the civil war and retreat to Taiwan.

At the end of the centennial visit, the MIB guides, institutional heirs to Dai Li, walked with their American friends to the airport security gate. They paused for a round of hugs, warm wishes, and tears, a final farewell to the men who had stood by their country at its darkest hour and its last victory.

Acknowledgements

Thanks to Spencer Morrow for encouraging me to start this book and to finish it, for reading and editing my toughest chapters, and for love and support through it all.

Thanks to my editor Kelli Christiansen for seeing a book in this story, pushing me gently, and finding the perfect words when mine fell flat.

Thanks to Beth Mahar for helpful suggestions mixed with outrageous flattery when I needed it.

Thanks to Garry Emmons for untangling my first attempt to write the article that became this book.

Thanks to SACO veterans Frank Bellotti, Sal Ciaccio, Roger Moore, Guy Purvis, Frank Reynnet, and Richard Rutan, who shared their memories and photos, and special thanks to Richard for decades of editing the *SACO News*.

Thanks to Professor Maochun Yu of the U.S. Naval Academy for sharing his expertise and to Evelyn Cherpak of the Naval War College Library.

Thanks to Guy Aceto, Don Kochi, and Frank Arre for helping me gather photos, and Beth and Philip Moore for the generous loan of Edward J. Moore's albums.

Selected Bibliography

BOOKS

Aldrich, Richard James. *Intelligence and the War Against Japan: Britain, America, and the Politics of Secret Service.* Cambridge, United Kingdom: Cambridge University Press, 2000.

Asprey, Robert B. *War in the Shadows: The Guerrilla History.* New York: Doubleday, 1975.

Bagby, Wesley Marvin. *The Eagle-Dragon Alliance: America's Relations with China in World War II.* Cranbury, New Jersey: Associated University Presses, 1992.

Bartholomew-Feis, Dixee. *The OSS and Ho Chi Minh: Unexpected Allies in the War Against Japan.* Lawrence, Kansas: University of Kansas Press, 2006.

Byrd, Martha. *Chennault: Giving Wings to the Tiger.* Tuscaloosa, Alabama: University of Alabama Press, 1987.

Camp, Richard. *Leatherneck Legends.* Minneapolis, Minnesota: Zenith Press, an imprint of Quayside Publishing Group, 2006.

Cammann, Schyler. *The Land of the Camel—Tents and Temples of Inner Mongolia.* New York: The Ronald Press Company, 1951.

Chennault, Claire Lee; Robert Hotz, ed. *Way of a Fighter: The Memoirs of Claire Lee Chennault.* New York: G. P. Putnam's Sons, 1949.

Christensen, Erleen. *In War and Famine: Missionaries in China's Honan Province in the 1940s.* Montreal, Quebec, Canada: McGill-Queen's University Press, 2005.

Cornebise, Alfred Emile. *The Shanghai Stars and Stripes: Witness to the Transition to Peace, 1945–1946.* Jefferson, North Carolina: McFarland & Company, 2010.

Davies, John Paton. *Dragon by the Tail: American, British, Japanese, and Russian Encounters with China and One Another.* New York: Norton and Company, 2nd edition, 1980.

De Vosjoli, P. L. Thyraud. *Lamia.* Boston: Little Brown, 1970.

Deane, Hugh. *Good Deeds & Gunboats: Two Centuries of American–Chinese Encounters.* San Francisco: China Books & Periodicals, 1990.

Fairbank, John King. *China: A New History.* Cambridge, Massachusetts: Belknap Press of Harvard University Press, 1992.

Fairbank, John K., ed. "Republican China 1912–1949, Part 1." From *The Cambridge History of China Vol. 12. Cambridge Histories Online.* Cambridge University Press (1983), accessed September 9, 2011. histories.cambridge.org

Fairbank, John K., and Albert Feuerwerker, eds. "Republican China 1912–1949, Part 2." From *The Cambridge History of China Vol. 13. Cambridge Histories Online.* Cambridge University Press (1986), accessed September 11, 2011. histories.cambridge.org

Fenby, Jonathan. *Chiang Kai-shek: China's Generalissimo and the Nation He Lost.* New York: Carrol & Graf, 2004.

Fluckey, Eugene B. *Thunder Below! The USS Barb Revolutionizes Submarine Warfare in World War II.* Champaign, Illinois: University of Illinois Press, 1992.

Harvey, Robert C. *Meanwhile ...: A Biography of Milton Caniff.* Seattle, Washington: Fantagraphis Books, 2007.

Horton, John Ryder. *Ninety-Day Wonder: Flight to Guerrilla War.* Bloomington, Indiana: iUniverse, 2000. First edition published by Ballantine, New York, 1994.

Hsieh, Chiao-min and Jean Kan Hsieh. *Race the Rising Sun: A Chinese University's Exodus During the Second World War.* Lanham, Maryland: Hamilton Books, 2009.

Kreis, John F., ed. *Piercing the Fog: Intelligence and Army Air Force Operations in World War II.* Washington, D.C.: Air Force History and Museums Program, Bolling Air Force Base, 1996.

Kurlansky, Mark. *Salt: A World History.* New York: Walk and Company, 2002.

Lampe, David, and Gary Sheffield. *The Last Ditch: Britain's Secret Resistance and the Nazi Invasion Plan.* London: Greenhill Books, 2007.

Lee, Bradford. *Britain and the Sino–Japanese War, 1937–1939: A Study in the Dilemmas of the British Decline.* Palo Alto, California: Stanford University Press, 1973.

McCallum, Jack Edward. *Military Medicine: From Ancient Times to the 21st Century.* Santa Barbara, California: ABC-CLIO, Inc., 2008.

Miles, Milton. *A Different Kind of War.* New York: Doubleday, 1967.

Miles, Milton. *The Navy Launched a Dragon.* Unpublished manuscript, Naval War College Library, Newport, Rhode Island.

Mishler, Clayton. *Sampan Sailor.* Dulles, Virginia: Potomac Books, 1994. Originally published by Brassey's.

Morison, Samuel Eliot. *A History of United States Naval Operations in World War II: Volume 13, The Liberation of the Philippines—Luzon, Mindanao, the Visayas, 1944–1945.* Boston: Little, Brown, 1959.

Patti, Archimedes L. A. *Why Vietnam? Prelude to America's Albatross.* Berkeley, California: University of California Press, 1982.

Powers, Dennis M. *Tales of the Seven Seas: The Escapades of Captain Dynamite Johnny O'Brien.* Plymouth, United Kingdom: Taylor Trade Publishing, 2010.

Reynolds, Bruce. *Thailand's Secret War: The Free Thai OSS, and SOE During World War II.* Cambridge, United Kingdom: Cambridge University Press.

Smith, Richard Harris. *OSS: The Secret History of America's First Central Intelligence Agency.* Guilford, Connecticut: Globe Pequot Press, 2005. First edition published by the University of California Press, Berkeley, 1972.

Stratton, Roy Olin. *SACO: The Rice Paddy Navy.* Pleasantville, New York: C. S. Palmer Publishing Company, 1950.

Taylor, Jay. *The Generalissimo: Chiang Kai-shek and the Struggle for Modern China.* Cambridge, Massachusetts: Belknap Press of Harvard University Press, 2009.

Tolley, Kemp. *Yangtze Patrol: The U.S. Navy in China.* Annapolis, Maryland: Naval Institute Press, 2000.

Wakeman, Frederic. *Spymaster: Dai Li and the Chinese Secret Service.* Berkeley, California: University of California Press, 2003.

Walker, William O. *Drug Control Policy: Essays in Historical and Comparative Perspective.* University Park, Pennsylvania: Pennsylvania State University Press, 1992.

Waller, Douglas. *Wild Bill Donovan: The Spymaster Who Created the OSS and Modern American Espionage.* New York: Free Press, 2011.

Winborn, Byron R. *Wen Bon: A Naval Air Intelligence Officer Behind Japanese Lines in WWII.* Denton, Texas: University of North Texas Press, 1994.

Wojniak, Edward J. *Atomic Apostle: Thomas M. Megan, S.V.D.* Techny, Illinois: Divine Word Publications, 1957.

Yu, Maochun. *The Dragon's War: Allied Operations and the Fate of China, 1937–1947.* Annapolis, Maryland: Naval Institute Press, 2006.

Yu, Maochun. *The OSS in China: Prelude to Cold War.* New Haven, Connecticut: Yale University Press, 1997.

Zedric, Lance Q. and Michael F. Dilley. *Elite Warriors: 300 Years of America's Best Fighting Troops.* Ventura, California: Pathfinder Publishing, 1996.

ARTICLES, WHITE PAPERS, REPORTS, DOCUMENTS

_____. "A Twentieth Century Battle with Pirates in China." *The New York Times,* September 3, 1911.

_____. "Chinese Guerrillas Found Set to Fight." *The New York Times,* August 10, 1957.

_____. "Milton Miles, 60, Admiral, Is Dead." *The New York Times,* March 26, 1961.

_____. "Mystery Veils General Tai's Fate; China's Police Chief in Air Crash." *The New York Times,* March 25, 1946.

Antony, Robert. "Piracy in Early Modern China." *IIAS Newsletter,* March 2005, p. 7.

Associated Press. "Book Tells Bataan, Shipwreck Survivor's Struggles." *The New Mexican,* February 19, 2000, B2.

Associated Press. "Exhibit Hints U.S. Sanctioned Torture." *Rocky Mountain News,* December 1, 1990.

Barton, Charles. "The Rice Paddy Navy." *The Retired Officer,* January 1989. Reprinted in *SACO News,* No. 18 (May 1999): 20–24.

Bell, Don. "Air Notes From China: PB4Y-2 of VPB 119 Shot Down Near Amoy 22 March." Prepared with introductory notes by the U.S. Naval Air Force Unit Headquarters, 14th Air Force, May 1945. Downloaded from http://www.cnac.org/emilscott/beliel01.htm February 9, 2012.

Bergin, Bob. "China's Spymaster and War Lord Tai Li Proved OSS Nemesis." *The O.S.S. Society Newsletter,* Winter 2008, p. 10.

Boxer, C.R. "Piracy in the South China Sea." *History Today,* December 1980, pp. 40–44.

Chiang Kai-shek. "Captive Chiang Almost Wept As He Saw His Wife." Chiang's diary excerpts. *The New York Times,* April 24, 1937.

Colgrove, Earl. "Earl Colgrove Recalls Dr. Victor A. Goorchenko." *SACO News,* No. 5 (February 1991): 21.

Colgrove, Earl. "U.S. Navy Combat Photo Unit in China." *SACO News,* No. 4 (May 1990): 11–12.

Corell, John T. "The Decision That Launched the *Enola Gay.*" *Air Force Magazine,* April 1994, p. 30.

Dizikes, Peter. "Wind, War, and Weathermen." *MIT News,* June 7, 2011. Massachusetts Institute of Technology News Service, accessed January 18, 2012. http://web.mit.edu/newsoffice/2011/timeline-forecasting-0607.html.

Dobbins, Charles G. "China's Mystery Man." *Colliers,* February 16, 1946, p. 19.

Eberlein, Xujan. "Another Kind of American History in Chongqing," five-part blog series posted Jan. 31–Feb. 4, 2011. *The Atlantic.* The Atlantic Monthly Group, accessed July 23, 2011. http://www.theatlantic.com.

Furman, Bess. "U.S. 'Cloak and Dagger' Exploits and Secret Blows in China Bared." *The New York Times,* September 14, 1945.

Graham, Steve, Claire Parkinson, and Mous Chahine. "Weather Forecasting Throughout the Ages." *NASA Earth Observatory.* EOS Project Science Office, NASA Goddard Space Flight Center, accessed January 18, 2012. http://earthobservatory.nasa.gov.

Greer, William L. and James C. Bartholomew. "Psychological Aspects of Mine Warfare." Naval Studies Group, Center for Naval Analysis, Alexandria, Virginia. Professional Paper 365, October 1982.

Gutch, Betty. "Letters to Betty from Her Husband Charley Gutch, Lt. JG, While in India & China in WWII." *SACO News,* No. 37 (December 2009): 61–65.

Johnson, Cecil David. "Memories of Naval Service as Reserve Officer." *SACO News,* No. 37 (December 2009): 17–19.

Komorowski-Kaye, Matthew. "With the U.S. Navy Scouts & Raiders: The SACO Assignment." *SACO News,* February 2007: 74–78.

Leu, Del. "My Father and SACO." *Del's Journey.* Del Leu, accessed May 14, 2011. http://www.delsjourney.com/saco/saco.htm.

Miles, Charles. "Celebration of the Life of Billy Miles." *SACO News,* No. 14 (November 1996): 18–21. Reprinted from the program for the funeral of Wilma Sinton Jerman Miles.

Miles, Charles. "Happy Valley." *SACO News,* No. 39 (November 2010): 20–24.

Miles, Milton. Letter to Chiang Kai-Shek, September 6, 1945. Reprinted in *SACO News*, No. 38 (May 2010): 70–71.

Miles, Milton. "Mission Accomplished—SACO Closes Book of Secrecy." Memo to All Hands September 24, 1945. Reprinted in *SACO News*, No. 38 (May 2010): 72.

Miles, Milton. "U.S. Naval Group, China." *U.S. Naval Institute Proceedings*, Vol. 72 No. 7/521 (July 1946): 920–931.

Miles, Milton and Dai Li. "Commendation," to all members of SACO, September 27, 1945. Reproduced in *SACO News*, May 2008: 16.

Reynolds, J. Lacy. "China Agents: The Duties of Naval Group China Were Right out of Terry-and-the-Pirates. Their Accomplishments Were Spectacular." *Shipmate*, April 1946. Reprinted in *SACO News*, No. 36 (June 2009): 23–31.

Ringle, Ken. "Appreciation: The Woman Who Went Where Life Led Her." *Washington Post*, July 3, 1996.

Ritter, Ben. "Ben Ritter Recalls Voyage to China." *SACO News*, No. 18 (May 1999): 30.

Rutan, Richard. "A Different Lone Journey to the Unknown in a Different Kind of War." *SACO News*, No. 35 (October 2008): 24–27.

Rutan, Richard, ed. "Father Phil Dies." *SACO News*, No. 3 (September 1989): 1.

Rutan, Richard. "From the Editor's Desk." *SACO News*, No. 38 (May 2010): 5.

Rutan, Richard, ed. "Remembering SACO Chaplains." *SACO News*, No. 34 (May 2008): 26. Reprinted from an article for the U.S. Naval Training correspondence course *The History of the Chaplain Corps*.

Rutan, Richard, ed. "Sino–American Special Technical Cooperation Agreement." *SACO News*, No. 9 (July 1993): 9–19. Reproduction of a copy provided by Republic of China Army Major General Fan Chi-yao, Military Intelligence Bureau, April 16, 1993.

Rutan, Richard, ed. "Taps and Farewell." *SACO News*, No. 5 (February 1991): 12–13. Obituaries of William Sanford LaSor and Victor Goorchenko.

Rutan, Richard. "The Twins of SACO." *SACO News*, No. 33 (October 2007): 53–54.

Sager, William. "The Day the Head Blew Up." *SACO News*, No. 36 (June 2009): 64.

Sager, William. "Marines in China, World War II." *Marine Corps Gazette, Professional Journal of U.S. Marines.* Marine Corps Association, accessed December 12, 2011. http://www.mca-marines.org/gazette.

Schaller, Michael. "SACO! The United States Navy's Secret War in China." *Pacific Historical Review*, Vol. 44, No. 4 (November 1975): 527–553.

Shadduck, Nobel. "Calcutta to Kunming Sept.–Oct. 1945, Convoy over Ledo-Stilwell Road." *SACO News*, No. 12 (October 1995): 35–49.

Sheffer, William. "Irvin H. Sheffer." *SACO News*, No. 36 (June 2009): 17–19.

Tate, S. Shepherd. "The Rice Paddy Navy and the China I Knew." *Experience*, published by Senior Lawyers Division of the American Bar Association, Spring 2003, pp. 30–33.

Thomas, Martin. "Silent Partners: SOE's French Indo-China Section, 1943–1945." *Modern Asian Studies*, Vol. 34, No. 4 (2000): 943–976.

United States Census. Milton E. Robbins, Jerome, Arizona, 1900; Milton E. Rabins and May Robins, San Bernardino, California, 1910; Maebelle Miles, King, Washington, 1920. Accessed November 3, 1911, via familysearch.org.

United States Navy. "Press Release: Now It Can Be Told: American Naval Group and Chinese Guerillas Obtained Valuable Data While Operating Among Japanese Force in China." September 13, 1945. Reproduced in *SACO News*, No. 33 (October 2007): 47–52.

Wu, Tien-Wei. "Chiang Kai-shek's March Twentieth Coup d'Etat of March 26." *The Journal of Asian Studies*, Vol. 27, No. 3 (May 1968): 585–602.

Xiang, Ah. "Zhongshang Warship Incident." *Republican China*. Ah Xiang, accessed September 10, 2011. www.republicanchina.org.

Yu, Maochun. "In God We Trusted, in China We Busted: The Commando Group of the Special Operations Executive." *Intelligence and National Security*, Vol. 16, No. 4 (Winter 2001): 37–60.

Yu, Shen. "SACO Re-Examined: Sino–American Intelligence Cooperation During World War II." *Intelligence and National Security*, Vol. 16, No. 4 (Winter 2001): 149–174.

WEBSITES

"Naval Group China Muster Roll and Report of Change Punch Cards, 1942–1945." *National Archives*. U.S. National Archives and Records Administration. Database of personnel monthly muster roll, searchable by name and location. http://aad.archives.gov/aad.

Naval History & Heritage Command. "Biographies in Naval History: Vice Admiral Milton E. Miles, Vice Admiral Willis A. Lee, Fleet Admiral Ernest J. King." http://www.history.navy.mil/index.html.

SACO: Sino American Cooperative Organization, U.S. Naval Group China Veterans. The most complete SACO roster, camp locations and descriptions, history of SACO, history of the veterans group, bibliography. www.saconavy.com.

Stone & Stone Second World War Books War Diary. Day-by-day list of events from September 1, 1939, through September 2, 1945. http://books.stonebooks.com/wardiary.

Notes

1. Yu, Maochun. *The Dragon's War*, p. 69.
2. Miles, Milton. *The Navy Launched a Dragon,* p. 8.
3. Miles, Milton. *A Different Kind of War,* p. 16.
4. Miles, Milton. *The Navy Launched a Dragon*, p. 3.
5. Letter from McHugh to Knox, August 1, 1942. "Secret and Personal," in The James McHugh Papers. Quoted in Maochun Yu, *The Dragon's War,* p. 72.
6. Yu, Maochun. *The Dragon's War,* p. 85.
7. Fairbank, John K. *China: A New History,* p. 222.
8. Interview with the author, March 29, 2010.
9. Wakeman, Frederic. *Spymaster,* p. 365.
10. Interview with the author, November 3, 2006.
11. See Chapter Two.
12. Interview with the author, March 29, 2010.
13. Yu, Maochun. *The Dragon's War,* pp. 119–120.
14. See Chapter Five.
15. Miles, Milton. *A Different Kind of War,* p. 373.
16. Miles, Milton. *A Different Kind of War*, p. 436.
17. Dow, Arden, OSS Special Operations officer, China. Secret cable to Donovan, October 26, 1944. Quoted in Maochun Yu, *The OSS in China,* p. 174.
18. Miles, Milton. *A Different Kind of War,* p. 259.
19. See Chapter Two.
20. Yu, Maochun. *The OSS in China,* pp. 63–64.
21. Miles, Milton. *A Different Kind of War,* p. 262.
22. Miles, Milton. *A Different Kind of War,* p. 267.
23. American Merchant Marine at War, www.usmm.org, accessed April 24, 2012.
24. See Chapter Five.
25. Schaller, Michael. "SACO! The United States Navy's Secret War in China," p. 542.
26. Wakeman, Frederic. *Spymaster,* p. 339.
27. Waller, Douglas. *Wild Bill Donovan,* p. 205.
28. 41,475, based on a camp-by-camp tally by Charles Miles, son of Milton. From the SACO veterans' website, www.saco.org, accessed March 18, 2012.
29. Miles, Milton. *A Different Kind of War,* p. 153.
30. Miles, Milton. *A Different Kind of War,* p. 391.
31. See Chapter Fourteen.

32. Stratton, Roy. *SACO: The Rice Paddy Navy*, p. 103.

33. Miles, Milton. *A Different Kind of War*, p. 429.

34. Fluckey, Eugene. *Thunder Below!*, p. 273.

35. Quoted in *SACO: The Rice Paddy Navy* by Roy Olin Stratton, p. 63.

36. See Chapter Two.

37. *Air Notes from China*, Second Issue, U.S. Naval Unit Headquarters, 14th Air Force, May 1945.

38. See Chapter Ten.

39. Horton, John Ryder. *Ninety-Day Wonder*, p. 220. Quoting mission report filed by Milton Hull, December 1944. Horton was commander of Camp One.

40. Reminiscence of Chief Shipfitter Charles L. Kush, the author's father and "the Shipfitter from Chicago," with details from "China Agents" by Lieutenant Commander J. Lacey Reynolds, from *Shipmate* magazine, April 1946, reprinted in *SACO News*, June 2009. It is unknown whether Kush and the article refer to the same incident, but they are remarkably similar.

41. See Chapter Nine.

42. Naval Group China Muster Roll and Report of Change Punch Cards, 1942–1945, U.S. National Archives.

43. Kurlansky, Mark. *Salt: A World History*, pp. 72, 372–373.

44. See Chapter Thirteen.

45. See Chapter Twelve.

46. See Chapter Eight.

47. See Chapter Twelve.

48. Kreis, John F., ed. *Piercing the Fog: Intelligence and Army Air Force Operations in World War II*. Air Force History & Museums Program, Bolling Air Force Base, Washington, D.C., 1996. p. 329.

49. Miles, in his book, *A Different Kind of War*, p. 312, said six ships were sunk. William L. Greer and Commodore James Bartholomew concur in their 1982 white paper, "Psychological Aspects of Mine Warfare." However, the online World War II diary compiled by Stone & Stone World War Two Books lists only four ships by name. http://books.stonebooks.com/wardiary/19431026.

50. See Chapter Fourteen.

51. Miles, Milton. *A Different Kind of War*, p. 309.

52. Waller, Douglas. *Wild Bill Donovan*, p. 209.

53. Smith, Richard Harris. *OSS: The Secret History of America's First Central Intelligence Agency*, p. 243.

54. See Chapter Eight.

55. Miles, Milton. *A Different Kind of War*, p. 318.

56. Chennault, Claire Lee. *Way of a Fighter*, pp. 346–355.

57. De Vosjoli, P. L. Thyraud. *Lamia*, p. 86.

58. See Chapter Fourteen.

59. The hardships the members of the Brethren of the Green Circle suffered getting to Camp Eight were recounted in Chapter Ten.

60. Bartholomew-Feis, Dixee. *The OSS and Ho Chi Minh: Unexpected Allies in the War Against Japan,* p. 74.
61. De Vosjoli, P. L. Thyraud. *Lamia.* p. 89.
62. Miles, Milton. *A Different Kind of War,* p. 188.
63. De Vosjoli, P. L. Thyraud. *Lamia.* p. 97.
64. Bartholomew-Feis, Dixee. *The OSS and Ho Chi Minh: Unexpected Allies in the War Against Japan,* p. 84.
65. See Chapter Twelve.
66. Wakeman, Frederic. *Spymaster,* p. 387, Note 24.
67. Wojniak, Edward. *Atomic Apostle: Thomas M. Megan.* pp.170–71
68. *Ibid.*
69. Miles, Milton. *A Different Kind of War,* p. 492.
70. Corell, John T. "The Decision That Launched the *Enola Gay,*" p. 30. http://www.afa.org/media/enolagay/07-02.asp.
71. Miles, Milton. *A Different Kind of War,* p. 465.
72. See Chapter Fourteen.
73. Mishler, Clayton. *Sampan Sailor,* p. 175.
74. McCallum, Jack Edward. *Military Medicine from Ancient Times to the 21st Century,* p. 28.
75. Waller, Douglas. *Wild Bill Donovan,* from the prologue, pp. 1–6.
76. Cornebise, Alfred Emile. *The Shanghai Stars and Stripes,* p. 32.
77. "Commendation," from Milton Miles and Dai Li to all members of SACO, September 27, 1945. Reproduced in *SACO News,* Richard Rutan, ed., May 2008, p. 16.
78. Stratton, Roy. *SACO: The Rice Paddy Navy,* p. xii.
79. Wakeman, Frederic. p. 352.
80. Putzell, Edwin. Interview with Mary Jane Robinson, March 12, 2003. *Experiencing War: Stories from the Veterans History Project,* Library of Congress.
81. Yu, Maochun. *The OSS in China,* p. 256.
82. Wakeman, Frederic. *Spymaster,* p. 356.
83. Wakeman, Frederic. *Spymaster,* p. 355.
84. Yu, Maochun. *The OSS in China,* p. 256.
85. Miles, Milton. *A Different Kind of War,* p. 578.
86. Wakeman, Frederic. *Spymaster,* p. 294.
87. See www.saconavy.com. Charles Miles contributed histories of each camp, including statistics for casualties and material damage inflicted. These figures are the sums from those histories.
88. Eberlain, Xujun, citing a Chinese scholar, Deng Youpin, in Part 4 of her five-part blog, "Another Kind of American History," *The Atlantic.* The Atlantic Monthly Group, February 3, 2011, accessed July 23, 2011. http://www.theatlantic.com. The series, posted daily from January 31 through February 4, 2011, recounts her journey to discover the truth about the museum and the government's slow retraction of the original story. Growing up in Chongqing, she was deeply moved by the museum but grew skeptical about its accuracy after moving to the United States.

89. Deane, Hugh. *Good Deeds & Gunboats: Two Centuries of American-Chinese Encounters,* China Books & Periodicals, Inc., San Francisco, 1990. p. 125.

90. Wakeman, Frederic. *Spymaster,* p. 307.

91. See Chapter Nine.

92. Eberlein, Xujan. "Another Kind of American History, Part 3: Puzzle," *The Atlantic.* The Atlantic Monthly Group, February 2, 2011, accessed July 23, 2011. http://www.theatlantic.com.

93. *SACO News,* February 1991, p. 19; May 1999, p. 24.

94. Eberlein, Xujan. "Another Kind of American History," *The Atlantic.* The Atlantic Monthly Group, January 31–February 4, 2011, accessed July 23, 2011. http://www.theatlantic.com.

95. *Ibid.*

Index